VICTIMLESS CRIME?

Prostitution, Drugs, Homosexuality, Abortion

Robert F. Meier
Iowa State University

Gilbert Geis
University of California, Irvine

Roxbury Publishing Company
Los Angeles, California

Library of Congress Cataloging-in-PublicationData

Meier, Robert F. (Robert Frank), 1944-
Victimless crime?: prostitution, drugs, homosexuality, abortion/Robert
    F. Meier, Gilbert Geis.
    p. cm
    Includes bibliographical references and index.
    ISBN 0-935732-46-2
    1. Crimes without victims. 2. Crimes without victims—United
    States. 3. Law and ethics. I. Geis, Gilbert. II. Title.
HV6705.M45 1997   96-37333
364.973—dc21   CIP

VICTIMLESS CRIME? PROSTITUTION, DRUGS, HOMOSEXUALITY, ABORTION

Publisher and Editor: Claude Teweles
Copy Editor: Anton Diether
Production Editor: Dawn VanDercreek
Assistant Editors: Joyce Rappaport, Colleen O'Brien, and Heidi Edeskuty
Typesetting: Synergistic Data Systems
Cover Design: Marnie Deacon Kenney

Printed on acid-free paper in the United States of America. This book
meets the standards for recycling of the Environmental Protection
Agency.

ISBN 0-935732-46-2

Roxbury Publishing Company
P.O. Box 491044
Los Angeles, California 90049-9044
(213) 653-1068 • Fax (213) 653-4140
Email: roxbury@crl.com

The Roxbury Series in Crime, Justice, and Law

Series Coeditors:

Ronald L. Akers, *University of Florida*

Gary F. Jensen, *Vanderbilt University*

This new series features concisely and cogently written books on an array of important topics, including specific types of crime and central or emerging issues in criminology, justice, and law.

The books in this series are designed and written specifically for classroom use in criminology, sociology, deviance, delinquency, criminal justice, and related classes. The intent of the series is to provide both an introduction to the issues and the latest knowledge available—at a level accessible to undergraduate students.

For the Colonel, who is sadly AWOL, and Dolores
and in memory of Robley Elizabeth Geis.

Contents

Acknowledgments

We are grateful to a number of people who have helped us with advice and technical assistance. At Iowa State University, thanks are due to Leslie Daub for her keen organizational skills and unfailing managerial support, and to Jim Orr for his neverending computer assistance. Both of these great coworkers were important beyond measure. Although he may be surprised to read it here, I also greatly appreciate the help of Will Goudy, who has assisted in this project in a number of important ways, including his administrative encouragement. Jaima Anderson provided much needed and appreciated research assistance. Thanks are also due to Deb McKay and Ramona Wierson for their cheerful help on all kinds of matters that facilitate the academic enterprise, as well as to colleagues in the Sociology Department at Iowa State University.

At the University of California, Irvine, stalwart and highly competent assistance was provided by Carol Wyatt, who kept the word-processing logistics under control, and by Judy Omiya, who tried to keep scholarly life in order. Anybody engaged in writing would be privileged to work with people of such competence and helpfulness. Cindy Cooper and AnnaMaria C. Tejeda were intrepid research assistants. Thanks also are due to Joseph T. Wells, Dennis and Lori Suzucki, Steve Reynard, Jeff Walsh, Don Menaguale and Mary Josephine Dodge, as well as to colleagues in the Department of Criminology, Law and Society.

The following people read and commented on an earlier draft of the manuscript: Thomas J. Bernard of Pennsylvania State University, Scott Decker of the University of Missouri at St. Louis, Erich Goode of the State University of New York at Stony Brook, Leslie Kennedy of the University of Alberta, Jon'a Meyer of Rutgers University, Richard Tewksbury of the University of Louisville, and Richard A. Wright of the University of Scranton. We appreciate very much their careful comments and suggestions. We also wish to acknowledge the good work of Anton Diether in making the manuscript more literate, as well as the expert proof-reading of Joyce Rappaport and Colleen O'Brien.

Finally, we would like to thank Claude Teweles for his support, encouragement, and general mothering during the conception and writing of this book. Claude's tenacity was astonishing. It was also just what we needed.

Robert F. Meier
Gilbert Geis

1

Morality, Harm, and Criminal Law

This book is concerned with one broad area in which criminal law has grappled with the problem of reconciling ideas of justice, principles of harm, and state intervention into our private lives and practices. Our interest centers on four behaviors—prostitution, drug use, homosexuality, and abortion—about which American moral codes have historically dictated the imposition of penalties by the state. We have chosen these behaviors for several reasons.

First, they have traditionally been regarded as core issues in debates about victimless crimes and most readily come to citizens' minds when they consider such topics.

Second, there is a long course of scholarship and debate on the behaviors that offers some historical insight into how they have been regarded at different times. There are, of course, other behaviors which might reasonably be viewed by some people as more "important" matters that raise equally or more significant questions about the realm of victimless crimes. We have attempted to at least passingly tease from other possible behaviors (such as pornography, usury, and motorcycle helmet laws) substantive and interpretative material that supplements and complements our more extended focus on prostitution, drugs, homosexuality, and abortion.

Third, each behavior illustrates a different dimension of the relationship between law and effective social control. Abortion is presently legal everywhere in the United States, but the legal status of the fetus is debatable. Furthermore, there are such strong feelings about the legal status of abortion that no legal compromise seems to be possible. The use of some drugs is illegal, but aside from instances where others are harmed as a result of a person under the influence of a drug, it is not clear who is being injured by the consumption of such drugs. Prostitution is against the law in all states but one, but the law is not always invoked as a significant means of controlling this behavior. The law's true purpose apparently lies elsewhere, but this is not clear and may itself be controversial. Homosexual behavior is legal in most states; yet the law targets homosexuals, even though clear patterns of victimization either to homosexuals or others seem to be absent.

Those who favor criminalization of such behaviors insist most fundamentally that all societies need to enforce a common morality and that such behaviors fall inside the limits of what should be permitted by law. They further maintain that these behaviors inflict harm on those who engage in them, and that a decent society has the obligation to protect its less careful members from their own self-destructive impulses.

Those who oppose the inclusion of these behaviors within the boundaries of criminal law say that they do not represent a threat to the integrity of the society and that they should not be the business of the law. They often call attention to analogous kinds of acts that are regarded with indifference by criminal law. The use of outlawed narcotics, for instance, they consider to be no different and perhaps even less serious a personal and social problem than drinking alcoholic beverages or smoking cigarettes.

The trend has distinctly favored those who have campaigned for the removal of some of these offenses from the criminal law roster. Gambling, once forbidden, is now part of everyday life, with lottery tickets on sale in some states at many local grocery stores. Homosexuality has been buried away in the criminal law closet. And in a particularly dramatic development, the United States Supreme Court declared that abortion was legally permissible during the first trimester of pregnancy.

However, disputes over the proper legal response to these behaviors did not abruptly end with the removal of some of them from the statute books. The subject of abortion continues to arouse fierce passions in many people, and there exists a concerted, organized effort to reverse the Supreme Court's ruling. Homosexuality for some people remains a carnal sin that must not be implicitly sanctioned just because it is no longer defined as criminal. Many disputes today focus on the question of whether same-sex partners ought to be allowed to marry and enjoy the same legal advantages (such as tax and inheritance breaks) that marriage provides. After the Walt Disney Corporation extended health benefits to same-sex partners, delegates to the Southern Baptist Conference in June 1996, representing a membership of 16 million people, voted to "boycott Disney Company stores and theme parks if they continue this anti-Christian and anti-family trend" (Niebuhr, 1996: A10).

Controversy also abounds regarding the way the law should define narcotic use. Those favoring decriminalization believe that longstanding law enforcement efforts have proven to be a failure and only encourage the underground traffic in drugs by raising the risks and therefore the price. On the other side, those opposing decriminalization maintain that things would be even worse if the law was no longer able to at least nibble away at the edges of narcotics use and narcotics traffic.

Criminal law is a political product, and there are disagreements about most aspects of law, including which acts should be illegal, how severely violators should be punished, and which powers should be given to the police and under what circumstances should they be exercised.

The disagreements are acted out in political debates, arguments before courts and legislatures, and even conversations among neighbors. And because law is enacted within a political context, controversy about criminal law is virtually guaranteed. This is a book about some of those controversies.

We are aware that all laws are controversial, but we have become increasingly sensitive to the fact that there is a complex relationship between criminal law and the problems it addresses.

Consider two questions: What kinds of problems can the law solve? What kinds of problems can the law create? The questions themselves suggest that the law can do both, although most conceptions of law give little consideration to the fact that the law can sometimes make matters worse. Our starting point is the observation that law creates as well as solves problems and often requires other sources of social control to deal with them. The law is far from impotent, but it is limited. As we shall see, the most effective use of law requires a social consensus on which problems are deemed appropriate for legal intervention. In the absence of such agreement, the law is often ineffective.

Crimes Without Victims: Victims Without Crimes

The behaviors that we will address in some detail in this book—as well as some similar kinds of behavior—have come to be known in shorthand as "crimes without victims." The term first gained widespread attention in social science circles when it was used as the title of a monograph by Edwin Schur (1965). Graduating from Yale Law School, Schur earned a Ph.D. at the London School of Economics, where he wrote his dissertation on British drug policies. He subsequently taught sociology at Tufts University, then at New York University until his retirement in 1994. Schur wrote his monograph while on leave at the Center for the Study of Law and Society at the University of California, Berkeley. The draft was titled "Nonvictim Crimes," but Sheldon Messinger, a colleague of Schur's at Berkeley, thought that term was too awkward. The result was *Crimes Without Victims* (Schur, 1996).

Legal historians had earlier discussed somewhat parallel concepts, such as "public welfare offenses," which made criminal such activities as merchandising intoxicating liquors that the seller was unaware were alcoholic. (*Commonwealth v. Boynton*, 1861; Sayre, 1933) Sumptuary crimes, which forbade people of lesser social standing to wear more elegant kinds of clothing, were another kind of predecessor to the idea of "crimes without victims." (McManus, 1993) There are also offenses called "inchoate crimes," which tend to be vague catch-all statutes designed to give police the power to arrest persons whom they suspect of something untoward or whom they merely consider to be cluttering the landscape in an unappetizing way. Loitering was a quintessential inchoate crime; it was so vaguely defined that the Supreme Court, ruling on a Jacksonville, Florida ordinance, found it unconstitutional (*Papachristou v. City of Jacksonville*, 1972). Other such crimes are disorderly conduct and vagrancy, the definitions of which are often loose and differ from jurisdiction to jurisdiction.

For Schur, *crimes without victims* concern behaviors about which there is no complaining witness. The prostitute and the customer transact their business like any other merchant and customer; so do drug users and drug sellers. Homosexual couples mutually agree to do what they do, just as heterosexual couples do. When abortions were illegal, a female sought out a service that would satisfy her and unless there were dire complications, she would not complain to the authorities about what had happened to her.

But the concept of *crimes without victims* aroused early and strong opposition, primarily on the grounds that it failed to take into account the eddying kinds of harms surrounding different behaviors that could result from such crimes. Opponents argued that prostitutes rob and spread venereal diseases, narcotics make many users incapable of satisfactory social contributions, male homosexuals have a tendency to be promiscuous and (in more recent times) register a high rate of AIDS, a serious crisis which today drains public resources. The assumption was that outlawing these behaviors and arresting their perpetrators would alleviate some of the harm they were said to cause.

A recent attempt in the *Concise Dictionary of Sociology* to define the term *victimless crime* explains particularly well the semantic confusion that sometimes surrounds the term:

> An activity classified as a crime in the laws of a country which may therefore be prosecuted by the police or other public authorities, but which appears to have no victim in that there is no individual person who could bring a case for civil damages under civil laws.
>
> Unlike (say) a case of theft where the damage is to society as a whole, and to notions of morality, proper conduct, and so on. Examples might be drinking alcoholic beverages, reading Marxist literature, homosexuality, gambling, or drug-taking in societies where such activities are prohibited. . . . The concept is polemical, arguing in effect that certain crimes should not be prosecuted by the police, or should be decriminalized (Marshall, 1994:555-556).

This is a rather eccentric definition, but it offers a good basis for scrutinizing more closely some aspects of what commonly is and is not regarded as falling within the realm of crimes without victims, at least in the United States. Whether or not a victim can collect civil damages has never been seen as germane to the idea: its essence is that the offense is statutorily a crime. Also, although reading Marxist literature may be a victimless crime in some jurisdictions (most notably pre-Mandela South Africa, though it was not the reading but the possession of such material that was outlawed), it remains a protected constitutional right in the United States.

The second segment of the previous definition is quite on target: crimes without victims is a polemical concept and most commonly is invoked to persuade others that such offenses should not be outlawed, even if they are believed to be morally despicable. It is not unreasonable to suppose that Schur himself believed that decriminalization should probably be considered seriously in regard to the behaviors that he reviewed. In another writing, for instance, he favorably quotes Robert Lynd's (1939:183) observation that "research without an actively selected point of view becomes the ditty bag [a carryall used by sailors] of an idiot, filled with bits of pebbles, straws, feathers, and other random hoardings."

In an effort to level the polemical playing field, the following chapters will offer arguments that cut both ways and thereby balance the issue, so that the reader is better able to reach a personal conclusion on the facts and arguments that are presented here. We will also introduce a new term—*victims without crimes*—to include those behaviors that some people believe have been unreasonably eliminated from criminal law. Again, the focus here will be on behaviors in which there would be no complaining witness, such as in the cases of homosexuality and abortion. It might be argued that there is no true distinction between abortion and murder, because in both cases the object of the event no longer can enter a legal objection. For traditional homicides, however, the state assumes the role of complainant, usually on the assumption that survivors of the victim (unless, of course, they themselves are the perpetrators) demand redress. For abortion, the law assumes that the fetus is not a human and that the pregnant woman possesses the right to either eliminate it during the first trimester or to carry it to term.

The concept of *victims without crimes* inherently encompasses a broad reach to embrace acts that allegedly or in fact cause harm and create victims who would complain if they had a legal basis in criminal law. Many of the behaviors that would fit into a more expanded category fall under the heading of *white-collar crime*. The claim is often made that the corporations and industrialists of America are so powerful that by means of campaign contributions and other leverage they are able to inhibit the legislature from passing laws that might circumscribe some of their harmful behaviors. A corporation, for instance, is perfectly free to relocate a manufacturing plant (even out of the country), throwing thousands of people out of work so that it can secure cheaper labor elsewhere and thereby obtain a higher return for its stockholders.

Obviously then, neither harm nor Judeo-Christian moral precepts dictate totally what will or will not be included within criminal law. We continue to uphold by the use of criminal law countless such requirements imposed upon believers in the country's religious heritage. But we also pay little or no attention to some Biblical positions. Cursing at one's parents, for example, is a death penalty offense in the Bible, as it was in colonial times, though the penalty was never exacted. Adultery and fornication, now almost totally outside the scope of criminal law, are discussed today with gregarious exuberance on television talk shows. In early America, however, both were serious criminal offenses.

That there are remnants of these earlier statutory injunctions—ready to become manifest under certain circumstances—was demonstrated in 1996 by a wave of prosecution against those who impregnated unmarried Idaho teenage females. By invoking a long-dormant statute, the prosecuting attorney in one county justified his action by noting, "It's a sad thing for a child to only know his or her natural father as someone who had a good time with his mother in the back seat of a car." Typically, the boy and girl are given a three-year term of probation and required to attend parenting classes together, to complete high school, and to not use drugs, alcohol, or cigarettes. Civil rights advocates have objected that the law is enforced only against teenagers, which they insist is discriminatory (Brooke, 1996).

Opponents of the ideological position that calls for minimum interference with human choices believe that a civilized society has a right to enforce a "common morality." In a forceful argument for this position, Patrick Devlin (1965:13), then a British high court judge, maintained that social harm will result if we fail to secure adherence to a general standard of morality, and that such harm threatens a society's survival:

Societies disintegrate from within more frequently than they are broken up by external pressure. There is disintegration when no common morality is observed and history shows that the loosening of moral bonds is often the first stage of disintegration, so that society is justified in taking the same steps to preserve a moral code as it does to preserve its governmental and other institutions.

The same position found its way into the 1996 presidential race when Senator Robert Dole, defending his opposition to allowing abortions in the later months of pregnancy, raised this issue to the level of a more general commentary on contemporary American life: "As a society, we can't shake the feeling that our culture is in trouble and our values are under assault." Not surprisingly, Dole blamed the incumbent president for this unfortunate state of affairs (Nagourney, 1996).

Much better known, because it became the basis for the title of a novel by Ernest Hemingway, is the seventeenth-century dictum of John Donne (1624, No. 7):

No man is an island of itself; every man is a piece of the continent, a part of the main. . . . Any man's death diminishes me, because I am involved in mankind, and therefore never send to know for whom the bell tolls: It tolls for thee.

This position suggests that the injury or death of any of us, such as the narcotic addict or the prostitute, diminishes us all. Counter-arguments insist that nothing is all good or bad, that laws must represent a position that balances costs and outcomes.

History demonstrates that the use of criminal law to enforce moral positions on crimes without victims sometimes takes a cyclical form. Gambling was outlawed in colonial times except in some cases for gentleman who were allowed to place wagers on horse races. Criminal law took the moral position that to bet was to substitute human judgment for divine will. Nonetheless, public lotteries soon became common in the United States until the 1830s. Many universities, including Columbia, Harvard, and Yale, were financed in part by lotteries. But a moral upsurge and a large number of scandals led to the outlawing of gambling (Ezell, 1960).

The initial break with this criminalization tradition came in the state of Nevada in 1869 (Skolnick, 1978). Today, legal gambling is permitted in some form in every state except Utah and Hawaii. State lotteries began in 1964 in New Hampshire and now have spread to 36 additional states (Berry and Berry, 1990); voters typically prefer a lottery to a tax increase. Riverboat gambling, an old American tradition, has been revived, and gambling is now permitted on most Native American reservations, where it has often been said that it rips asunder traditional tribal values yet makes significant amounts of money for tribal coffers (Vizenor, 1992).

The Notion of Harm

The idea of *harm* is one of the key elements involved in an understanding of why certain behaviors are forbidden by criminal law and are subject to punishment by the state. The concept also plays a prominent role in arguments about whether certain kinds of behaviors are regarded as *victimless crimes* or whether they involve *victims without crimes*. Outlawed harms typically take the form of a loss of property which the owner has a legal right to possess, or they involve physical injury or death. There are also some offenses, most notably treason, where the damage is regarded as falling upon the state, which is said to represent the best interests of all—or, at least, most—of its citizens.

If the harm that results from a behavior injures the person who has committed the act, this is usually considered to be that person's own private problem and not the concern of criminal law. But arguments are made that private harm can have obvious public consequences. People who hurt themselves, even if they can personally bear the medical costs, tie up facilities that might be employed otherwise. Nonetheless, the law typically allows most "reasonable" risk-taking to remain beyond its concern.

Though criminal law, taken as a whole, can be regarded as protection against harm, it is neither consistent nor comprehensive in affording such protection. The harm need not be inflicted; it need only be seen as reasonably related to the act that is outlawed. Attempted rape may be charged, even though the overt act involved no more than light touching of a woman's shoulder (Chappell et al., 1971). Nor does criminal law usually attend to more subtle kinds of harm, most notably those that create psychological damage. Also, there may not be any harm at all created by some acts that are declared to be criminal, only the statistical probability that some harm might result. Driving under the influence of alcohol or drugs is a serious criminal offense, even though most drivers in such a condition navigate their way home uneventfully. The behavior is outlawed because, compared to other motorists, a higher percentage of intoxicated or drug-high drivers will not be in adequate control of their vehicles and may injure or kill other people. Also, such drivers who are arrested may serve as a warning to others to avoid driving when not in full control of their faculties.

Morality and Criminal Law

Criminal law draws its dictates from the moral preferences of those in a position to determine its content. Beliefs about morality interact with beliefs about harm in determining the roster of "victimless" offenses. Moral precepts that ruled early American colonial life were derived from Biblical roots, and many of them had found their way into English common law and hence into American criminal law. In fact, virtually every criminal statute in the Massachusetts Bay Colony appended a Biblical reference to indicate its irrefutable authority (Elliott, 1952:22). If behavior was not covered in the *Laws and Liberties of Massachusetts,* issued in 1648, it was declared that it should be dealt with according to biblical doctrine (McManus, 1993).

In early Maryland, for instance, the law called for penalties against a person who was a "common swearer, blasphemer, or curser." There are records of a number of prosecutions, including one against Captain Thomas Bradnox, who was charged with having uttered at least "100 oaths" (Semmes, 1936:162). It was only in 1969 that the 246-year-old Maryland law against blasphemy was finally declared unconstitutional in *West v. Campbell,* a case involving a man who had been charged with swearing at a police officer following his arrest. The judge noted that in England in 1656, a hole could be bored in the offender's tongue for the first offense of blasphemy. A second offense could result in burning the letter "B" on the culprit's forehead. Fear of blasphemy charges underlay the taboo nature of such English expressions as "bloody" (a corruption of "By Our Lady") and "zounds" (a corruption of "God's wounds").

Biblical justice was responsible for the hanging of a considerable number of colonial defendants for the crime of bestiality, that is, sexual intercourse with animals. Adultery, though consensual, was also a capital crime, but the letter of the law was almost invariably tempered with mercy. The only time the death penalty was used in New England occurred in 1644 in Massachusetts, when James Britton and Mary Latham were sent to the gallows (McManus, 1993). The Puritans adopted the Old Testament rule that adultery could be committed only with a married woman. The marital status of the male partner did not count. A married man could not be punished for sexual relations with a single woman, unless she was engaged to be married; nor could an unmarried woman be punished for relations with a married man. The underlying doctrine in this case involved the use of criminal law to seek to protect the male's bloodline (McManus, 1993).

Suicide and Attempted Suicide

Perhaps the most extraordinary intermingling of moral dictates and criminal law involved the outlawing of the "victimless" act of suicide in the United States and England. Attitudes in earlier civilizations toward suicide were contradictory. The Athenians prohibited it, showing their disapproval by cutting off the hand of the person who committed suicide and refusing to bury it with the body. In ancient Rome, the philosopher Seneca summarized what appears to have been the prevalent Stoic view regarding suicide with the observation, "As I choose the ship in which I will sail and the house I will inhabit, so I will choose the death by which I will leave life" (Lecky, 1904:220).

Those who committed suicide in medieval times could not be buried in hallowed ground but were instead interred at a crossroads with a stake driven through their body, a tactic designed to prevent the tainted soul from escaping (Radzinowicz, 1948-1953:I, 196-197). As Edmond Cahn (1959:236) has noted with both bemusement and sarcasm, there is no record of "whether this mode of burial did more to reduce the incidence of suicide than to disrupt vehicular traffic." Obviously, the suicide could not be punished personally, but the state confiscated the offender's property, an arrangement which gave rulers considerable incentive to keep the criminal prohibition in place.

The Bible contains no injunction against suicide. During the Council of Arles in 452 A.D., the Catholic Church adopted such a position, supporting it with the thesis that "whoever kills himself, thereby killing an innocent person, commits homicide." Suicide is seen in Christian doctrine as thwarting God's will, given that it is a divine prerogative to determine when life shall end. Later, when the law against suicide was removed from the statute books, there still remained a prohibition against "attempted suicide." This law has largely been employed to provide the state with the authority to take into custody persons whom its officials believe constitute a danger to themselves.

Physician-Assisted Suicide

The controversy surrounding the issue of criminal law's proper role in regard to some behaviors defined in moral terms is clearly demonstrated in the intense debate today about the question of doctor-assisted suicide and the broader issue of euthanasia. If sane people formally declare their desire to die, and if it can be shown that they are in pain—perhaps terminally ill—and there is little likelihood that their condition will improve, should they be allowed to enlist a doctor to assist them in leaving this life? If so, how far should such a "right" extend? If a physician is accorded the right to assist in suicide, why should that right be withheld from those close to the person, such as a husband or wife, if they are given the sufferer's written permission which is witnessed by a court official? On the other hand, is it not possible that a person, forced to live and given succor, might change his or her mind about suicide? If the person consents to die, is the act "victimless" and/or should it be a matter of criminal law concern? (For opposing viewpoints of two doctors see Angell, 1997, and Foley, 1997.)

Studies show that about 15 percent of American doctors annually receive one or more requests for help in suicide; they grant about one-quarter of such requests, despite the legal risks. In the past, most requests were from people with intractable pain from cancer and other diseases. Today, such pain can largely be controlled. What patients most fear now is loss of control and dignity and the dependence and financial burden often associated with the end state of a fatal illness (Back, Wallace, Starks, and Pearlman, 1966).

Two recent federal court decisions both struck down attempts by state legislatures to outlaw doctor-assisted suicide. The Ninth Circuit Appeals Court overturned by an 8-3 vote a Washington state statute against assisted suicide. Inferentially, this ruling also endorsed the terms of Oregon's Death with Dignity Act, which was passed after a referendum vote, then ruled unconstitutional by a federal district court on the grounds that it constituted discrimination against the terminally ill (*Lee v. Oregon*, 1995; see also Previn, 1996).

The Ninth Circuit decision outlined one of the tragedies that formed the basis of the lawsuit, that of a 69-year-old pediatrician who since 1988 had suffered from a cancer that had metastasized throughout her body. Chemotherapy and radiation had offered temporary relief, but she had been bedridden for the past three years and in constant pain. The court noted that she was mentally competent to determine that she preferred physician-assisted suicide to the condition she found herself in. The decision relied on the following reasoning:

> A competent terminally ill adult, having lived nearly the full measure of his life, has a strong liberty interest in choosing a dignified and humane death rather than being reduced at the end of his existence to a childlike state of helplessness, diapered, sedated, and incompetent. (*Compassion in Dying v. Washington*, 1996:812)

That court heard two hours of oral arguments during the second week of January 1997, and left little doubt that the justices would overturn the circuit court rulings and leave the issue to be debated and decided state by state. As a news reporter noted: "It was clear that the Justices were fascinated by the issue and deeply engaged by the arguments—but at the same time eager to keep the Court out of yet another momentous question of life and death" (Greenhouse, 1997:A1).

No one on the bench spoke in favor of the idea of physician-assisted suicide, while several justices raised strong objections to the practice. "You are asking us in effect to declare unconstitutional the law of all 50 states," said Justice Anthony Kennedy. Justice Sandra Day O'Connor maintained that deciding who would have the right to die and who would not "would result in a flow of cases through the court system for heaven knows how long." Justice David H. Souter appeared to be speaking for the large majority of his colleagues when he noted during the oral argument: "This is all fairly recent. Twenty years ago, we weren't even discussing the issue. Would it be better to leave it to the political process?" (*Washington v. Glucksberg*, 96-110, 1997; *Vacco v. Quill*, 95-1858, 1997)

Sauter's observation is, of course, a bit disingenuous. The Supreme Court itself is an integral part of the country's political process, as its decision on the right to abortion patently demonstrated.

The Dutch Experience. The situation in the Netherlands offers the most dramatic illustration of a political jurisdiction that has adopted a position on physician-assisted suicide that is much less restrictive than anything contemplated in the United States. Fears of a slippery slope decline once any door is opened for physician-assisted suicide also have been realized in the Netherlands. In a recently published study, Hendin (1996:44) claims that "The Netherlands has moved from assisted suicide to euthanasia, from euthanasia for people who are terminally ill to euthanasia for those who are chronically ill, from euthanasia for physical illness to euthanasia for psychological distress, and from voluntary euthanasia to involuntary (called 'termination of the patient without explicit request')."

A 1991 case in the Dutch city of Assen involved a healthy 50-year-old woman who asked her physician to help her die. One of her sons had committed suicide, another had died of cancer. She wanted to be with them. After an extended period of consultation, the doctor consented. He prescribed lethal pills and was at the woman's side when she died from taking them.

The doctor was tried on criminal charges because his patient was not terminally ill. Nor was she psychiatrically ill; only inconsolable. The doctor was acquitted by the trial court, the appellate court, and the country's Supreme Court (Hendin, 1996). Obviously, the country's law, as interpreted by its courts, now grants doctors the right to aid those who want to commit suicide for reasons that make sense to the person and to a doctor.

Usury

The practice of usury provides a further example of the manner in which Biblical morality was initially embalmed in criminal law, despite its consensual elements, but was subsequently removed from the statute books in the face of what proved to be the more compelling requirements of capitalist machinery. Usury refers to the lending of money at exorbitant rates of interest. John Noonan, Jr. describes the evolution of social and legal concern with usury from medieval to current times:

How can we appreciate the intensity of intellectual interest in usury in the sixteenth and seventeenth centuries, when its nature and extent were as lively an issue, and as voluminously discussed by reflective observers of commerce, as the nature and cure of business cycles are today? How much less can we grasp the spirit of a yet earlier age whose most perspicacious moralists describe usury as a great vice which corrupted cities and Church alike and held all men of property in bondage? Usury today is a dead issue, and except by plainly equivocal use of the term, or save in the mouths of a few inveterate haters of the present order, it is not likely to stir to life (Noonan, 1957:1).

Particularly significant in determining policies about usury were the ideas of Aristotle, the first major figure to oppose usury on theoretical grounds: "The term usury, which means the birth of money from money, is applied to the breeding of money because the offspring resembles the parent." Continuing, Aristotle wrote in *Politics* (Bk. I, Ch. 10): "Wherefore of all modes of making money this is the most unnatural."

Sanctions against usury were first leveled by church authorities against the clergy, based on the Biblical text of *Psalms* 15:5, which declared that a person who, among other things, "takes no interest on a loan" may dwell on God's sacred hill. The ban was extended from the clergy to laypersons by Pope Leo the Great, who wrote around 450 A.D., inveighing against the *turpe lucrum*, or the shameful gain, of usury. Finally, for the first time, the theological principle was translated into secular law when the capitularies of Charlemagne outlawed usury in the Holy Roman Empire in the ninth century, defining it as the financial act in which "more is asked than given."

Between 1050 and 1175, the elements of usury were more carefully stipulated. The term was extended to embrace credit sales, which today would have included the interest charged on the use of credit cards, as a criminal offense. Dante, the principal poet of the medieval church, in his *Divine Comedy* (Canto VII), relegated usurers to the outer edge of the seventh circle of Hell, calling them "the melancholy folk," their eyes "gushing forth their woe." Later, usury was seen as an offense against the words of Christ: "Lend freely, hoping to gain nothing thereby" (*Luke* 6:35). Professional usurers were excommunicated by the church and prosecuted in state courts.

John Calvin, the Protestant leader, was the first major theologian to have insisted on the "fertility of money." Calvin believed that moneylending should be judged by the Golden Rule: It would be sinful only if it injured one's neighbor; otherwise, it was desirable. Each person's conscience was to be the guide. Loans to poor people would clearly be wicked, whereas loans to the rich or to business people were no different from profit on a sale. "Biting usury," or usury that sucks the substance of another while the usurer runs no risk, and charges of interest above certain limits were both condemned by Calvin, whose ideas gradually found their way into criminal law.

It is striking to note how the legal denotation of what is considered to be criminal varies with the economic conditions and social conscience of the times. In the Middle Ages, the average annual interest rate was about 43-1/2 percent, a figure not much higher than that prevalent for small commercial businesses in the United States during the 1930s (Robinson and Nugent, 1935:248-265).

Today in the United States, there is neither a total ban on usury nor unrestricted freedom. Policies tend to show a crazy-quilt pattern. Most states impose some ceiling on interest rates, but on the theory that usury laws are designed to protect only small, individual borrowers, loans to corporations are usually exempted from legal limits. The early conceptions of the theological immorality and illegality of usury have obviously given way in our times to a very different point of view.

Bad Samaritans

Suicide and usury laws indicate that the tie between Biblical morality and criminal law can be readily broken if secular concerns come to dominate discourse, as they have most notably in recent developments in regard to major "crimes without victims." The "bad Samaritan" condition illustrates that criminal law sometimes pays no heed to certain matters of morality that most of us would regard as essential elements of a decent society. The situation also illustrates the occasional absence of consistency in arguments based on moral precepts that appear in discussions of acts regarded as *crimes without victims.*

"Bad Samaritanism" reflects the fact that American law does not require a person to aid another human being, even when this can be done easily and with no risk to the rescuer. For instance, a bystander has no legal obligation to intervene if a blind man walking without a cane is going to step off the edge of a cliff to his death (Geis, 1991).

American law traditionally takes the position that one need not be burdened with the responsibility of aiding another. The reigning legal principle was cold-bloodedly set forth by the Chief Justice of New Hampshire almost a century ago:

> Suppose A, standing close by a railroad, sees a two-year old babe on the track and a car approaching. He can easily rescue the child with entire safety to himself. And the instincts of humanity require him to do so. If he does not, he may perhaps justly be styled a ruthless savage and a moral monster, but he is not liable in damage for the child's injury or indictable under the statutes for its death. (*Buch v. Amory Manufacturing Co.*, 1898:809)

The legal doctrine goes a step further and indicates that a person compassionate or foolhardy enough to intervene becomes liable thereafter for the consequences; in the absence of such intervention, the person remains juridically unassailable. A few exceptions to this basic rule do exist. If the bystander has made an initial effort to assist, then that effort must be carried through. The bystander must also help those with whom there is a pre-existing relationship, such as a spouse or kin, as well as help those to whom there is owed a contractual duty.

This laissez-faire approach is based on the idea that a free citizen should have no personal obligation to keep the public order and uphold public well-being, though there have been a few statutory efforts to encourage such behavior. Vermont and Minnesota laws now insist that bystanders must intervene or face criminal penalties, Massachusetts has decreed that persons on the site must report crimes of violence, and Rhode Island's legislature enacted a law that declared that the authorities must be notified of crimes of sexual assault. These last two acts came in the wake of a 1993 episode in New Bedford, Massachusetts, in which a woman was raped by at least four men over the course of an hour, while bystanders failed to intervene or notify the authorities.

In contrast, virtually all European countries have provisions in their criminal codes that demand bystander intervention under reasonable circumstances, and prosecutions, particularly in France, are not uncommon. Doctors, for instance, may be criminally charged if they fail to stop at the scene of an accident to render aid. In 1979, the body of Jean Seberg, a prominent American actress, was found in a car on a Paris side street. It was presumed that she had died of an overdose of alcohol and pills. But since Seberg could not drive without her glasses (which were found in her apartment), it was believed that her body, when there might have remained a chance to save her life, had been transported to the site where it was discovered. Criminal charges were filed against those who had been in the apartment with her (Richards, 1981). In addition, a surgeon was criminally charged in France as a bad Samaritan when he refused to perform a caesarian section on the dead body of a woman eight months pregnant (Feldbrugge, 1965-1966).

Pornography

The debates over pornography involve well-etched positions. Many people maintain that pornography routinely depicts scenes of the male brutalization of women and thus encourages acts of rape and sadism directed against them. They also find pornography involving children (tagged "kiddie-porn") to be a particularly despicable form of sexual exploitation. On these grounds, they insist that the purveyance of pornography should be made a criminal act (MacKinnon, 1993).

Those on the other side, while they may be hard-pressed to say much good about the product, believe that the First Amendment of the U.S. Constitution protects unpopular forms of expression, including pornography (Hawkins and Zimring, 1988). They argue that not all pornography portrays women as victims: there is, for example, a thriving industry in pornography directed toward homosexual men. Others (Paglia, 1994) insist that pornography is tied to aggressive masculinity, a requisite trait in nature's plan for human reproduction. They maintain that feminists are engaged in a power struggle in which their constant portrayal of women as "victims" rather than as persons who must take control of their own fate does a disservice to their gender.

The debate over pornography also centers on the consequences of exposure to it and whether it possibly reflects social malaise rather than introduces it (Linz and Malamuth, 1993). Pornography is a common staple on Japanese television and an integral element in religious art in India, two countries with low rates of violence directed at women. It has also been pointed out that there is no shortage of violent content in "mainstream" literature, even for children. Nobody apparently wants to criminalize the sale of the classic stories of childhood, for example, though many are grim and gory. Diverse forms of homicide occupy a prominent position in classical literature. Theatergoers need only count the corpses in Shakespeare's *Hamlet* to appreciate the extent of violence in the theater.

As with other victimless crimes and crimes without victims, the fundamental question here is whether pornography and the depiction of violence produce harmful consequences for innocent people. Regardless of how this question is answered, a key issue remains: whether a free society should have to tolerate these activities, because they are part of a spectrum of constitutionally protected rights; that is, if they are harmful, is it harm that we should bear as part of the price of our guaranteed freedoms?

Motorcycle Helmets

Ideological dispute today also includes the riding of a motorcycle without a helmet, one of the relatively few victimless crimes that does not have a strong sexual component.

Studies show that of the 47,000 automobile fatalities in the United States every year, about 8 percent involve motorcycle drivers and 1 percent motorcycle passengers. The total number of such deaths has been declining, from 3,189 in 1975 to 2,394 in 1992, though the death rate of about 64 per 100,000 registered motorcycles has remained fairly constant. This rate compares with 15.7 per 100,000 for automobile drivers and their passengers. About half of the motorcycle deaths resulted from a crash with another vehicle, usually an automobile; in 42 percent of the cases, the motorcyclist had been drinking more than the legal minimum, a far higher percentage than is true for automobile fatalities. If helmets had been worn, it is estimated that about 30 percent of the deaths could have been prevented. Twenty-three states, as well as the District of Columbia and Puerto Rico now require that all motorcyclists wear helmets (Council on Scientific Affairs, 1994).

Opponents of these laws insist that the statutes penalize behavior that endangers only the persons engaged in it. They say that the choice should be that of the motorcyclists: if they elect not to wear a helmet, that is nobody else's business. They also challenge the validity of the statistical claims about the safety of helmets and note that "helmets, especially, full-face models, suppress the normal sensations of wind and speed and thus can give riders a false sense of invulnerability and can lead to excessive risk-taking and dangerous riding habits." Statistics that demonstrate a significant decrease in deaths of motorcyclists in the wake of laws that mandate helmets are rejected on the basis that the helmet requirement has cut dramatically into motorcycle riding and that this drop is responsible for the decline in the number of deaths. They also insist that the more important place for helmets is in automobiles, as car crashes inflict a higher percentage of head injuries than those resulting from motorcycle accidents (Teresi, 1995:15).

Responding to this position, the president of the Advocates for Highway and Auto Safety argued that motorcycle enthusiasts may delight in "feeling the wind in their hair" but that the rest of us "are feeling their hands in our pockets" because "bikers without helmets cost the rest of us big money" (Stone and Davis, 1995). Or, as Laurence Tribe (1988:1372), a leading constitutional authority, has put the matter: "In a society unwilling to abandon bleeding bodies on the highway, the motorcyclist or driver who endangers himself plainly imposes costs on others."

Another part of the argument about motorcycle helmets is that all human existence is filled with risks and that we cannot handcuff every exercise of freedom in an attempt to eliminate or reduce risks. After all, nobody would seriously suggest that we cut down the awful toll of highway deaths by banning automobiles, or even by putting mechanical governors on them that would restrict their speed to 45 miles an hour or less, though the savings in life and limb would be impressive.

In places where helmet wearing is mandatory for motorcyclists, the general supporting rationale is that the inconvenience to the rider is hardly so burdensome as to constitute an intolerable deprivation of personal liberty. It is noted that there has been an almost universal acceptance of the requirement to fasten seat belts. As one eminent legal scholar argued, "Any new law at all is some restriction on liberty, but not all restrictions are threats to it" (Woozley, 1983).

During the 1960s and early 1970s, a number of state courts heard motorcycle helmet law challenges. A New York court ruled that "to hold that a citizen may be required to protect his health alone would be an enlargement of the police power beyond traditional limits" (*People v. Carmichael*, 1967). State courts in Michigan (*American Motorcycle Association v. Davids*, 1968) and Illinois (*People v. Fries*, 1969) ruled that it was unconstitutional to demand under threat of criminal penalty that motorcyclists wear helmets. Shortly following these decisions, appeals and new cases occupied the courts, and many of the earlier decisions were reversed (see, for example, *People v. Kohrig*, 1986), including the *Carmichael* case. Finally in 1989, a federal circuit court put a likely end to anti-helmet claims by ruling that a Florida statute mandating helmets violates no right to privacy nor any privilege of a kind that the appellants labeled "the right to be left alone" (*Picou v. Gillum*, 1989).

What Should Be Against the Law?

Determining the problems that law should solve and those that it should avoid is a difficult task, but there have been suggested standards against which the appropriateness of law has been measured. Many believe that official action may legitimately be taken against a behavior if some substantial harm to others can be demonstrated to result from it. John Stuart Mill said in a classic statement (1859/1892:6):

> The sole end for which mankind are warranted, individually or collectively, in interfering with the liberty of action of any of their number, is self-protection. . . .
> The only purpose for which power can rightfully be exercised over any member of a civilized community, against his will, is to prevent harm to others. His own good, either physical or moral, is not a warrant.

The Mill statement, however, is not definitive enough when an attempt is made to use it as a guide to public policy. The terms "self-protection" and "to prevent harm to others" allow so many interpretations that honest people may disagree on the same issue when confronted by the same set of facts. Mill does not tell us how serious the harm has to be and how directly it can be tied to the given act before the act can be reasonably banned. Would the harm be sufficient enough, for example, if it could be shown that homosexuality is producing a decline in the population that leads to inadequate numbers for economic growth and satisfactory military defense?

Nor is there any uniform agreement regarding Mill's views about official action to protect individuals from, as it were, themselves. There are those who insist that the state has the right or obligation to interfere in a situation where an individual is likely to be "exploited," such as in the case of twelve-year-old children who take factory jobs because their families sorely need funds. The difficulty of relying on Mill's guidelines to advocate or oppose public policy is illustrated by three recent articles, each of which argued that Mill would have adopted a different position regarding the law and pornography (Dyzenhaus, 1992; Skipper, 1993; Vernon, 1996).

It is against a background of such considerations that we will examine prostitution, narcotics, homosexuality, and abortion in subsequent chapters. One useful approach to determine what should be the proper attitude of criminal law toward such actions was offered by Herbert Packer (1968), then a law professor at Stanford University. The conditions that Packer believed should be present before criminal sanctions are invoked against conduct include: (1) the conduct must be regarded by most people as socially threatening and must not be approved by any significant segment of society; (2) the conduct can be dealt with through evenhanded and non-discriminatory law enforcement; (3) controlling the conduct through the criminal process will not expose that process to severe qualitative or quantitative strain; and (4) no reasonable alternatives to the criminal sanction exist for dealing with the behavior. These criteria are not, of course, the last word on the subject. There are those who would take issue with them, but they can be useful for drawing out some of the concerns that we face in determining what ought to be done—and not done—about the forms of behavior that we will consider in the following chapters.

The issues that these activities raise, both individually and as a group, speak directly to some of the core aspects of the kind of society that we now have and the one that we seek to construct. It is the aim of this book to provide information and insights that will contribute meaningfully to that ongoing debate.

References

American Motorcycle Association v. Davids. 1968. 11 Mich. App. 351.

Angell, Marcia. 1977. "The Supreme Court and Physician-Assisted Suicide—the Ultimate Right." *New England Journal of Medicine* 336:50-53.

Back, Anthony L., Jeffrey I. Wallace, Helene E. Starks and Robert A. Pearlman 1996. "Physician-Assisted Suicide and Euthanasia in Washington State: Patient Requests and Physician Responses." *Journal of the American Medical Association* 275:919-925.

Berry, Francis S., and William D. Berry. 1990. "State Lottery Adaptation as Policy Innovation: An Event History Analysis." *American Political Science Review* 84:395-415.

Bopp, James J., and Richard E. Coleson. 1995. "The Constitutional Case Against Permitting Physician-Assisted Suicide for Competent Adults with 'Terminal Conditions' " *Issues in Law and Medicine* 11:239-268.

Brooke, James. 1996. "Idaho County Finds Ways to Chastise Pregnant Teens: They Go To Court." *New York Times,* October 28:A26.

Buch v. Amory Manufacturing Co. 1898. 44 Atl. 809 (N.H.)

Cahn, Edmond. 1959. *The Moral Decision.* Bloomington: Indiana University Press.

Chappell, Duncan, Gilbert Geis, Stephen Schafer, and Larry Siegel. 1971. "Forcible Rape: A Comparative Study of Offenses Known to the Police in Boston and Los Angeles." Pp. 169-190 in James M. Henslin, ed., *Studies in the Sociology of Sex.* New York: Appleton-Century-Crofts.

Commonwealth v. Boynton. 1861. 84 Mass. (2 Allen) 160.

Compassion in Dying v. Washington. 1996. 79 F.3d 790 (9th. Cir.).

Council on Scientific Affairs. 1994. "Helmets and Preventing Motorcycle- and Bicycle-Related Injuries." *Journal of the American Medical Association* 272:1535-1538.

Devlin, Patrick. 1965. *The Enforcement of Morals.* London: Oxford University Press.

Donne, John. 1624. *Devotions Upon Emergent Conditions and Several Steps in My Sickness.* London: Augustine Matthewes.

Dyzenhaus, David. 1992. "John Stuart Mill and the Harm of Pornography." *Ethics* 102:534-551.

Elliott, Mabel A. 1952. *Crime in Modern Society.* New York: Harper.

Ezell, John. 1960. *Fortune's Merry Wheel: The Lottery in America.* Cambridge: Harvard University Press.

Feldbrugge, Ferdinand J. M. 1965-1966. "Good and Bad Samaritans: A Comparative Study of Criminal Law Provisions Concerning Failureto Rescue." *American Journal of Comparative Law* 14:630-667.

Foley, Kathleen M. 1997. "Competent Care for the Elderly Instead of Physician-Assisted Suicide." *New England Journal of Medicine* 336:54-55.

Geis, Gilbert. 1991. "Sanctioning the Selfish: The Operation of Portugal's New 'Bad Samaritan' Statute." *International Review of Victimology* 1:297-313.

Greenhouse, Linda. 1997. "High Court Hears Two Cases Involving Assisted Suicide." *New York Times,* January 9:A1,A10.

Hawkins, Gordon, and Franklin E. Zimring. 1988. *Pornography in a Free Society.* New York: Cambridge University Press.

Hendin, Herbert. 1996. *Seduced by Death Doctors, Patients, and the Dutch Cure: A Study of Euthanasia and Suicide in the Netherlands.* New York: Norton.

Lecky, William E. H. 1904. *History of European Morals from Augustus to Charlemagne.* 3rd ed. New York: Appleton.

Lee v. Oregon. 1995. 891 F. Supp. 1429.

Linz, Daniel, and Neil Malamuth. 1993. *Pornography.* Newbury Park, CA: Sage.

Lynd, Robert S. 1939. *Knowledge for What?: The Place of Social Science in American Culture.* Princeton: Princeton University Press.

MacKinnon, Catharine A. 1993. *Only Words.* Cambridge: Harvard University Press.

Marshall, Gordon, ed. 1994. *The Concise Dictionary of Sociology.* New York: Oxford University Press.

McManus, Edgar J. 1993. *Law and Liberty in Early New England: Criminal Justice and Due Process, 1620-1692.* Amherst: University of Massachusetts Press.

Mill, John Stuart. [1859]/1892. *On Liberty.* London: Longmans, Green.

Nagourney, Adam. 1996. "Heatedly, Dole and Clinton Escalate a Split on Abortion." *New York Times,* May 24:A1, A8.

Niebuhr, Gustav. 1996. "Baptists Censure Disney on Gay-Spouse Benefits." *New York Times,* June 13:A10.

Noonan, John T., Jr. 1957. *The Scholastic Analysis of Usury.* Cambridge: Harvard University Press.

Packer, Herbert L. 1968. *The Limits of the Criminal Sanction.* Stanford: Stanford University Press.

Paglia, Camille. 1994. *Vamps & Tramps.* New York: Vintage Books.

Papachristou v. City of Jacksonville. 1972. 405 U.S. 156.

People v. Carmichael. 1967. 279 N.Y.S. 272 (New York).

People v. Fries. 1969. 250 N.E.2d 149 (Illinois).

People v. Kohrig. 1986. 498 N.E. 2d 1158 (Illinois).

Picou v. Gillum. 1989. 874 F.2d 1519 (11th Cir.), cert. den., 493 U.S. 920.

Previn, Matthew P. 1996. "Assisted Suicide and Religion: Conflicting Conceptions of the Sanctity of Human Life." *Georgetown Law Journal* 84:589-616.

Quill, Timothy E. 1996. *A Midwife Through the Dying Process.* Baltimore: Johns Hopkins University Press.

Quill v. Vacco. 1996. 80 F.3d 716 (2d Cir.).

Radzinowicz, Leon. 1948-1953. *A History of English Criminal Law.* London: Macmillan.

Reitman, James S. 1995. "The Debate on Assisted Suicide: Redefining Morally Appropriate Care for People with Intractable Suffering." *Issues in Law and Medicine* 11:299-329.

Richards, David. 1981. *Played Out: The Jean Seberg Story.* New York: Random House.

Robinson, Louis N., and Rolf Nugent. 1935. *Regulation of the Small Loan Business.* New York: Russell Sage.

Sayre, Francis B. 1933. "Public Welfare Offenses." *Columbia Law Review* 33:55-88.

Schur, Edwin H. 1965. *Crimes Without Victims: Deviant Behavior and Public Policy.* Englewood Cliffs, NJ: Prentice-Hall.

Schur, Edwin H. 1996. Telephone Interview (June 6).

Semmes, Raphael. 1936. *Crime and Punishment in Early Maryland.* Baltimore: Johns Hopkins University Press.

Skipper, Robert. 1993. "Mill and Pornography." *Ethics* 103:726-730.

Skolnick, Jerome H. 1978. *House of Cards: The Legalization and Control of Casino Gambling.* Boston: Little, Brown.

Stone, Judith Lee, and Don Davis. 1995. "Bikers Without Helmets Cost Us Big Money." [Letter to the Editor], *New York Times,* June 24:14.

Stone, T. Howard, and William J. Winslade. 1995. "Physician-Assisted Suicide and Euthanasia in the United States." *Journal of Legal Medicine* 16:481-507.

Teresi, Dick. 1995. "The Case for No Helmets." *New York Times,* June 15:15.

Tribe, Laurence H. 1988. *American Constitutional Law.* 2nd ed. Mineola, NY: Foundation Press.

Vernon, Richard. 1996. "John Stuart Mill and Pornography: Beyond the Harm Principle." *Ethics* 106:621-632.

Vizenor, Gerald. 1992. "Gambling on Sovereignty." *American Indian Quarterly* 16:411-413.

West v. Campbell. 1969. Case No. 2814 (Criminal), Circuit Court, Carroll County, Maryland (May 1).

Woozley, Anthony D. 1983. "A Duty to Rescue: Some Thoughts on Criminal Liability." *Virginia Law Review* 69:1273-1300.

2

Prostitution

There are any number of definitions of prostitution. It has been defined as any sexual exchange in which the reward for the prostitute is neither sexual nor affectional (James, 1977), and also as the performance of acts of nonmarital sex as a vocation (Polsky, 1967). A more elaborate definition was proposed by Paul Gebhard (1969:24): "A female prostitute is a person who for immediate cash payment will engage in sexual activity with any person (usually male), known or unknown to her, who meets her minimal requirements as to age, sobriety, cleanliness, race, and health."

It has been argued that sexual intercourse between a married couple, particularly in the days before the feminist impact on contemporary attitudes and behavior, was much like prostitution. According to this argument, a woman typically refused sexual favors to a man until she was engaged or was married to him and assured of his financial support. Thus, sexual access was being exchanged for financial security, as if it were a commodity to be bartered. Such a stance stimulates debate but fails to acknowledge the very real difference between the commercial enterprise of prostitution and other social arrangements that are governed by far more complex conditions and rules.

Prostitutes, of course, are found in any gender. But both historically and currently the spotlight tends to be on female prostitutes for two reasons: they far outnumber their male counterparts and unlike male prostitutes, they are regarded as exemplars of gender subordination and exploitation, a matter which highlights important political and ideological issues. In any case, the clients of both male and female prostitutes are overwhelmingly male. For these reasons, we will concentrate on women and girl prostitutes (for representative studies of male prostitution see Cates and Markley, 1992; Reiss, 1961; van der Poel, 1992).

The Biblical Heritage

The dominant view of prostitution among Americans, one that is reflected in the laws which condemn its practice, has its roots in biblical tradition. The Old Testament contains many warnings against the pagan harlot, whose wantonness was seen as threatening the Hebrew theocracy. It cautioned against the prostitute, saying that "her house is the way to hell, descending to the chambers of death" (*Proverbs* 7:27). Jewish fathers were forbidden to turn their daughters into prostitutes (*Leviticus* 19:29), and the daughters of Israel were forbidden to practice prostitution (*Deuteronomy* 23:17).

Early Christian writers were more inclined to regard prostitutes as a necessary, even vital, evil. Saint Augustine believed that although what the prostitute did was morally wrong, even worse evils would arise if she did not provide an outlet for male lust. Augustine declared that the prohibition of prostitution would threaten a society's existence: "Suppress prostitution, and capricious lusts will overthrow society" (Augustine, 386/1844-1864:984). Saint Thomas Aquinas (1273/1947:II.1222), the medieval theologian who with Saint Augustine represents "by far the most important source of western sexual ethics" (Primoratz, 1993:167), reiterated this position. The prostitute, Aquinas wrote in *Summa Theologica*, "is like the filth in the sea or the sewers in the palace. Take away the sewer and you will fill the palace with pollution and likewise with the filth in the sea. Take away prostitutes from the world and you will fill it with sodomy" (Aquinas, 2a2ae, q. 10, art. 4). This attitude, more tolerant than that of the Old Testament, finds part of its roots in the story of Christ and Mary Magdalene. Magdalene, according to tradition, was a prostitute who was forgiven her errant ways by Jesus and who anointed his feet in penance (*Luke* 7:36-50; cf. Rushing, 1994).

Criminal Law and Prostitution

On the roster of victimless crimes, only the laws against prostitution have resisted change in the United States during recent decades. Gambling, once outlawed throughout the country with the exception of Nevada, now flourishes under the protection of the law. There are state-run lotteries and gambling casinos throughout the country. Slot machines are found on many Indian reservations, sometimes bringing riches to once-impoverished tribes and changing dramatically their traditional way of life and values. Abortion, once a tawdry, cheapening, and dangerous experience that was always under threat of criminal prosecution, is now permitted during the initial period of pregnancy by mandate of the United States Supreme Court. Marijuana laws, formerly enforced with draconian fierceness, have largely disappeared for those who use the drug in recreational quantities, though sanctions against such "heavier" drugs as heroin and cocaine remain severe.

Homosexuality, previously outlawed in all American states, is now regarded with indifference by criminal law in virtually every jurisdiction, and most state legislatures have been debating the possibility of sanctioning homosexual marriages. The Supreme Court in Hawaii is expected to uphold its legislature's approval of such marriages when it issues a decision in 1997 on a case challenging the law. Many business enterprises, including the Disney corporation, now allow same-sex partners to be covered by the medical insurance of a corporate employee.

Explaining the Law's Intransigence

Why have these different kinds of victimless crimes had such diverse histories? And why has prostitution remained steadfastly beyond the legal pale?

For one thing, prostitution continues to be illegal because it largely involves dispossessed and politically weak persons. There will be no prominent authors like Simone de Beavoir, nor any sports celebrities or famous Hollywood actresses as there were on the issue of abortion, who will announce that they once had been a practicing whore. Nor will there be any middle-class and upper-class parents, such as those in the debate over marijuana who lobbied for decriminalization because of anxiety over their pot-smoking children being arrested and burdened with a criminal record. Nor will there be any respectable citizens, such as those who spoke up on the issue of gambling because they were inconvenienced and worried when they placed an illegal bet on a number or a sports event. For another thing, neither marijuana nor gambling have any overlay of sexuality. Americans are often prudish when it comes to taking public positions on controversial sexual issues such as prostitution. Consider, for instance, the almost universal presence of and casual attitude toward topless and nude beaches in most European countries, which are virtually absent in the United States.

Finally, there will be no parades of artists and successful people fighting for the legalization of prostitution as they did for gay rights. Prostitutes may proclaim that their way of life is a choice and not a sickness, as gays have done, and they may even try to mount the equivalent of Gay Lib public consciousness raising. But American lawmakers, at least at this time, remain unimpressed. In their view, prostitutes lack political power and probably rarely vote. When those in control of the business of prostitution contribute to political campaigns, their aim is not to legalize the activity but to protect themselves from law enforcement efforts. Prostitutes themselves have little or no political clout.

Consequently, although the law has bent dramatically in regard to other kinds of victimless crimes, it has been unyielding over prostitution. Sex for pay continues to be interdicted, its practitioners— most notably those who receive the pay and not those who provide it—continue to be harassed, arrested, convicted, fined, tested for venereal infections and HIV, and sometimes sentenced to brief jail terms.

Prostitution and Sexual Liberation

For a time, it seemed that prostitution would devolve into a non-issue like homosexuality as far as the law was concerned, though for very different reasons. The introduction of birth control pills, feminist efforts for equality in all spheres, and the pronounced loosening of sexual taboos have combined to create considerably greater opportunities for consensual sexual activity prior to and outside of marriage. Prostitution, it was thus presumed, would be priced out of existence because of the declining necessity to resort to pay-for-sex.

At least three major factors worked against such a development. First and undoubtedly foremost, the appearance of AIDS, a lethal immune system disorder, has checked dramatically the growing number of casual sexual encounters.

Second, prostitution continues to survive because it offers a commodity that cannot be readily found in other sexual arenas. That commodity involves the marketplace exchange of money for the unemotional provision of sexual gratification with no strings attached. Today, women, particularly those who are well-educated and informed, demand sexual satisfaction from a partner as their right—a demand that some men may not always be willing (or able) to satisfy (McCormick, 1994). Some males who try to stereotype women claim that prostitutes do not need to be wooed, flattered, or entertained, either romantically or sexually. Prostitutes will not complain the next morning that they were callously used or that their personal integrity was abused. As an example of customer satisfaction, one study indicates that almost half of the streetwalkers' clients in a New Jersey city were repeat clients, engaging in sex with a prostitute more than once a month (Freund, Leonard, and Lee, 1989). Though prostitutes do not provide romance or love, these males further contend, neither will they make any claim to continue a relationship nor interpret their sexual conduct as anything beyond a mere business transaction.

This point was emphasized in the pioneering study of male sexual behavior by Alfred Kinsey and his colleagues. "At all social levels men go to prostitutes because it is simpler to secure a sexual partner commercially than it is to secure a sexual partner by courting a girl." Kinsey et al. also observed that intercourse with a prostitute is likely to be a good deal cheaper than intercourse resulting from courtship, which could involve (in Kinsey's oddly detailed inventory) "flowers, candy, 'coke dates,' dinner engagements, parties, evening entertainments, moving pictures, theaters, night clubs, dances, picnics, weekend house parties, car rides, longer trips, and all sorts of other expensive entertainment" before the male "might or might not be able to obtain the intercourse he wanted" (Kinsey, Pomeroy, and Martin, 1948:608). Sexual etiquette has changed considerably since Kinsey's time, but the underlying accuracy of his chauvinistic position, however outdated, is probably true for at least some portion of sexual interactions.

Third, prostitutes offer a service that is not otherwise readily available to persons who find themselves beyond the pale of sexual appeal. Those too old, unattractive, or shy, or those who are unable to easily find a consenting sexual partner can turn to prostitutes as a simple solution to their problem. Prostitutes will also perform certain sexual acts (e.g., fellatio) that might be unavailable to some males in normal relationships. For the right price, all this can be accomplished in less than fifteen minutes.

Arrest Statistics for Prostitution

From 1970 to 1983, prostitution was the fastest growing individual arrest category in the national crime report, rising 143 percent during that period. The peak was in 1983 when 125,600 persons were arrested for what the Federal Bureau of Investigation labels "prostitution and commercialized vice." But by 1994, that figure had dipped to 98,190, which was 15.8 percent lower than ten years earlier. Only four other offenses showed sharper decade drop-off rates than prostitution: gambling (which had largely been legalized), driving under the influence (probably the result of tougher enforcement), drunkenness, and vagrancy. The falloff was especially true of women, where the decrease in the number of arrests in the past decade has been 36 percent, while that for men has risen 7.5 percent. Males, most probably customers, now make up 39 percent of the total number of persons arrested on prostitution offenses. Ten years ago, that figure was 30 percent. Arrests of blacks for prostitution have shown a downswing of 8 percent over the past ten years. In 1970, blacks made up 64 percent of all persons arrested for prostitution; today whites, at 62 percent, constitute the largest racial category (Prostitution Arrest Trends, 1995). These figures should be interpreted with caution, however, because prostitution arrest figures can be easily manipulated by urban police who can "generate" prostitution crimes—and arrests—through aggressive enforcement.

The Cast in the Performance of Prostitution

Prostitution involves people and institutions that play a number of different roles in the enterprise. At the core of the business of prostitution are the men and women who provide direct sexual stimulation to others in return for money. Within this group, there is a considerable distinction between streetwalkers at the bottom of the heap, prostitutes who work in massage parlors, and call girls (including outcall and escort services), who are considered the elite of the business (Bryant and Palmer, 1975). Debra Satz (1995:68) provides a vignette of members of the latter group:

> Many call girls drift into prostitution after "run of the mill promiscuity," led neither by material want nor lack of alternatives. Some are young college graduates, who upon graduation earn money by prostitution, while searching for other jobs. Call girls can earn between $30,000 and $100,000 annually. These women have control over the entire amount they earn as well as an unusual degree of independence, far greater than in most other forms of work. They can also decide who they wish to have sex with and when they wish to do so. There is little resemblance between their lives and that of the streetwalker.

From interviews with working prostitutes, Wardell Pomeroy (1965:184) documented that 40 percent of these women remained in the business because of "the interesting people they meet." One call girl told him: "I have an eighth grade education and nearly every day I meet doctors, lawyers, bankers, and actors who I never would meet if I wasn't in the life." Her point was brought home in scandalous fashion when a $200-a-night call girl told a tabloid newspaper in 1996 about her assignations with 48-year-old Dick Morris, a top advisor to President Clinton and the major proponent of the administration's focus on "family values." Morris encouraged the call girl to eavesdrop on his telephone conversations with Clinton. After Morris resigned his position under pressure, it was disclosed that, although married, he had maintained a long-term relationship with a woman he had met through a Dallas escort service, had fathered a child by her, and was supporting her while she completed a university degree (Gooding, 1996; see also Morris, 1997).

In addition to the prostitutes themselves, there are others who derive income from some part of the prostitution network. Best known are pimps, who almost invariably associate only with female prostitutes. They promote the prostitute's work and take most of her earnings. Pimps, who often run a stable of prostitutes, typically offer protection, romance, and security (Milner and Milner, 1973). Then there are the cab drivers, bellhops, hotel desk men and elevator operators, the bartenders, and others whose jobs put them in a position to attract customers for a prostitute in return for a percentage of the woman's earnings (Reichert and Frey, 1985). Those who rent premises which they know are used for the purposes of prostitution also depend on the business for at least a portion of their livelihood. Finally, there are the customers of prostitutes—the "johns"—who form another set of major players.

Patterns of Legal Response

There have been a number of ways in which different countries have sought to respond to prostitution. The Soviet Union before its breakup demanded that prostitutes abandon their business for a more legitimate pursuit. In 1923, the Soviets began to send prostitutes to so-called prophylactorums, where they were given educational and trade training. The Soviets claimed that there was no prostitution in their society and noted that no employable person could go without a job for more than four months without being charged with "parasitism." Prostitution became a part-time avocation, with some women— the "foreign currency girls"—catering exclusively to tourists. Because women who were caught as prostitutes were charged with parasitism, it is impossible to determine how many arrests were in actual fact for prostitution. Nonetheless, fear of tough punishments and rehabilitation efforts undoubtedly kept the rate of such offenses relatively low (Zeldes, 1981). More than 40,000 prostitutes had been registered in St. Petersburg alone before World War I. That figure dropped dramatically during times of full employment, then began to rise significantly when the state economic system broke down after the collapse of the communist regime (Quigley, 1992).

In the United States, Nevada allows house prostitution under controlled circumstances in all but its three most populated counties; in other states where it is illegal, tough enforcement or informal tactics, such as rousting streetwalkers, are employed. In Great Britain, prostitution is permitted, but prostitutes may not solicit on the streets to procure sexual assignations. In many European countries, prostitution is legal, though there may be some attempts to restrict its practice for the benefit of residents who are offended by its presence (see the various reports in Davis, 1993). We will examine some of these responses to prostitution before evaluating the arguments over its proper legal status.

Urban Enforcement: Los Angeles

Like most metropolitan areas, Los Angeles has pockets of prostitution that cater to a particular clientele. The area around Disneyland is notorious for streetwalkers who make contacts with visiting foreigners. In some Los Angeles ghetto areas, prostitutes provide sex services for men who come to the United States to work, often illegally, but are unable to bring their wives or girlfriends from their own country. In addition, Los Angeles is believed to have the second highest rate of male homosexual prostitution in the country, trailing only behind San Francisco.

As the center of the motion picture industry, Hollywood provides a natural venue for prostitution and for the scandals that can accompanying it. Two such episodes that recently made national headlines illustrate revealing components of the practice of prostitution. One involved a brief sexual encounter between a hooker and a British film star cruising in his sports car, the other a young woman who ran a call girl service for motion picture and business moguls.

The BMW Caper

Hugh Grant, a 34-year-old British actor, who had achieved critical acclaim for his role in the film "Four Weddings and a Funeral," was suddenly propelled into a different kind of limelight. He was apprehended by police at 1:30 a.m. while parked in his open-top BMW on a Hollywood residential street, engaging in oral sex with a 23-year-old prostitute. The prostitute, an unmarried mother of three children with the working name of Divine Marie Brown, alleged that she had talked Grant into wearing a condom, but that he did so only after reluctantly agreeing to pay her $60 for oral sex. Had he agreed to pay another $40, Brown said, they could have gone to a hotel room and avoided arrest (Ehrlich, 1995). Following his arrest, Grant expressed the anticipated regret, calling his behavior "a dumb thing."

For Brown, the result was exclusive interviews and instant celebrity. She was hired to do a lingerie advertisement for Brazilian television, in which she warned wives and girlfriends that if they did not purchase racy undergarments, their men might end up seeking out someone like her ("Divine Brown's Unpromising Career," 1995).

In court, both Brown and Grant were charged with lewd conduct and pleaded no contest. Brown was fined $1,350 and sentenced to jail for 180 days for having violated a probation order on a similar charge in 1993. Grant was given a $1,180 fine and a sentence of two years' probation.

William Buckley, a prominent columnist on the right side of the political spectrum, drew a general lesson from the Grant-Brown episode that goes straight to the heart of the complicated effort to distinguish prostitution from other kinds of sexual behavior in the eyes of criminal law. Writing under the title of "Thou Shalt Not. . . .What?", Buckley (1995:71) noted, "Fornication is okay in a hotel, in front of a movie camera, but not in a car, certainly not in a car in Los Angeles."

The Hollywood Madam

Heidi Fleiss was in her late twenties when she was arrested for operating a call girl service. At the time, her pediatrician father had reacted flippantly, "I guess I didn't do such a good job on Heidi after all" (Koltnow, 1996). Later, he would be convicted of conspiring to hide profits from his daughter's call girl ring. Fleiss had dropped out of school when she was sixteen and established a liaison with a playboy-financier who gave her a Rolls-Royce for her twenty-first birthday. In her early twenties, Fleiss interned in the world of prostitution by working for Madame Alex (Elizabeth Adams), Hollywood's reigning call girl entrepreneur until her death in 1995. In 1990, backed by television director and pornography filmmaker Ivan Nagy, 24-year-old Fleiss opened her own business. She now refers to her call girl operation as nothing more than a sensible adjunct to many other Hollywood enterprises. One telling anecdote was how she was paid $40,000 a night by a customer to do little more than play Scheherazade, the Sultan's wife in *Arabian Nights*.

On her income tax return, Fleiss reported that her earnings were generated by "personal counseling." SONY officials paid her thousands of dollars for one such counseling session for executives of an overseas branch; SONY's tax report listed the outlay as a "development deal" (Shah, 1993). Government officials estimate that Fleiss earned several hundred thousand dollars during a period in which she reported income of only $33,000 on her tax return.

At Fleiss' trial, business executive Manuel Santos testified that he sent his private jet to pick up some of Fleiss' call girls. One of them alleged that she flew to Paris, Athens, and Las Vegas to have sex with clients, and that she gave 40 percent of what she earned to Fleiss (Boyer, 1995:B4). Fleiss was sentenced to three years in prison and a $1,000 fine after a jury found her guilty of three counts of pandering. She was also convicted in federal court of eight counts of conspiracy, income tax evasion, and laundering money.

In January, 1997, Fleiss received a 37-month prison sentence for the federal crimes. She also was fined $400, ordered to participate in a substance-abuse program and to perform 300 hours of community service.

Earlier, the California District Court of Appeal had thrown out the previous state verdict and ordered a new trial on the grounds that jury members had been confused about their decision: They had opted for guilt on the pandering charge because they believed that it would result in a lesser sentence than a narcotics conviction, not understanding that pandering carried an automatic three-year term of imprisonment. The appellate court decision further determined that jury members had "traded" votes on the different charges in order to avoid a deadlock, an impermissible procedure (Hubler, 1996). The state case is due to be retried in mid-1997.

For some, Fleiss' situation aroused passions that have remained persistently prominent in the feminist debate over prostitution. In an op-ed piece, attorneys Gloria Allred and Lisa Bloom (1994:B7) asked rhetorically: "Why is it immoral to be paid for an act that is perfectly legal if done for free?" They proceeded to offer an answer to their own question:

> The lines that our society has drawn in the name of morality have become absurd. A woman may agree to sexual acts with men she doesn't love as long as she does not directly charge them for sex. She may legally pose nude for money, genitalia displayed for photographers. She may dance nude, as provocatively as the customer likes, for money. She may engage in sexual acts for money with men she does not know or like in erotic films, magazines or before a live audience. She may sell her voice for "phone sex" with strange men. She may give a naked man an erotic massage. She may marry a man she does not love and have sex in return for his financial

support for the rest of her married life. Yet the sale of direct sexual acts remains illegal.

For some, the logic of the foregoing statement leaves something to be desired. They insist that Allred and Bloom's argument would not be best resolved by adding prostitution to the list of those behaviors now exempt from legal consequences, but rather by criminalizing most of the other specified acts, such as posing nude for money, acting in erotic films, and engaging in "phone sex." This, however, could be construed as being in violation of constitutional rights.

Licensed Brothels: Nevada

Prostitution is legally permissible in 14 of Nevada's 17 counties (though only 11 actually have it), providing the most unusual legal arrangement for prostitution in America. In the early 1990s, there were 37 licensed brothels in the state. In Las Vegas of Clark County, one of the exceptions, many illegal prostitutes operate clandestinely but are careful not to interfere with local residents, tourists, or casino customers who have other things than paid-for-sex on their minds. At the same time, these women are readily but discretely accessible for those who want to include them in their vacation package (Frey, Reichert, and Russell, 1981).

Prostitutes working in the legal Nevada brothels are usually fingerprinted and required to carry identity cards. County laws also generally require that they undergo weekly medical examinations, and they are usually prohibited from leaving their brothels or mingling with other community residents. State law requires that houses of prostitution cannot be located on a principal business street or within 400 yards of a schoolhouse or church, nor can they disturb the peace of a residential neighborhood. Typically, prostitutes work in a complex of trailers on sites that are euphemistically called "ranches" (Reynolds, 1986).

Information about Nevada prostitution became public in 1988, when a group intent on selling shares in the state's largest licensed brothel, the Mustang Ranch, filed a prospectus with the Securities and Exchange Commission in order to seek investors and raise $18 million to buy the Ranch. Open seven days a week, the Ranch had grossed $5.4 million in the 1987-1988 fiscal year, of which $917,000 was reported to be profit. The prospectus noted that women worked for the Ranch as independent contractors and set their own prices. They turned over half of their receipts to the company and paid $10 a day for room and board. In the end, the stock solicitation failed and the Mustang Ranch, behind in payment of its federal taxes, declared bankruptcy in 1990.

Nevada prostitution briefly returned to public attention in 1996, when a 54-year-old woman who had worked in one of the brothels announced that she planned to run for Congress. Her campaign slogan read, "Vote for Jessi or she'll tell your wife" (Siebert, 1996:1A).

As Americans, it would seem that we are not sure whether we loathe prostitution or are intrigued by it—or both. Consider, for instance, the great success enjoyed by actresses who portray prostitutes in films—from the first Oscar in 1928 given for best actress to Janet Gaynor for "Street Angel" to Jane Fonda's Oscar for "Klute." In 1996, three of the five nominees for Academy Awards had portrayed hookers: Elizabeth Shue in "Leaving Las Vegas," Sharon Stone in "Casino," and Mira Sorvina in "Mighty Aphrodite." Interpreting this phenomenon, film critic Molly Haskell (1974) believed that it represented what she called "hooker chic."

Kerb Crawling in Great Britain

One of the most significant developments regarding the law of prostitution in the Anglo-American world was spurred in Great Britain by the 1957 report of the Committee on Homosexual Offences and Prostitution, known as the Wolfenden Report after the committee chair (Great Britain, 1957). Two committee recommendations received almost immediate parliamentary approval—that public solicitation by prostitutes be dealt with more severely and that those living on the earnings of prostitutes be criminally punished. The Wolfenden Committee, however, did not favor any change in the British policy that prostitution itself should not constitute a criminal offense. On this point, it observed:

> [W]e are not attempting to abolish prostitution or to make prostitution in itself illegal. We do not think that the law ought to try to do so; nor do we think that if it tried it could by itself succeed. What the law can and should do is to ensure that the streets of London and our big provincial cities should be freed from what is

offensive or injurious and made tolerable for the ordinary citizen who lives in them or passes through them. (Great Britain, 1957:95)

Committee members granted that there might be something to the view that "the mere presence of prostitutes carrying on their trade was no more, and no less, a matter for police intervention than the presence of street photographers or toysellers" (Great Britain, 1957:128). But they were not taken with the argument sufficiently to endorse it. On the question of whether to punish the customers of prostitutes, committee members rendered what many regard as a rather chauvinistic conclusion: The purpose of the state, it was noted, is to legislate against "those activities which offend against public order and decency or expose the ordinary citizen to what is offensive and injurious." The committee further stated, "The simple fact is that prostitutes do parade themselves more habitually and openly than their prospective customers" (Great Britain, 1957:87).

The committee also reviewed an increasingly prevalent form of solicitation, called "kerb crawling." Kerb crawlers are motorists who drive slowly, overtake women pedestrians, and stop beside them with the intention of inviting them into their automobile. The committee granted that such behavior might offend women who are mistaken for prostitutes, but it concluded that the difficulties of legal proof are so burdensome that it does not appear worthwhile to make such behavior a criminal offense.

The Wolfenden recommendations were in large measure translated into law by enactment in 1959 of the Street Offences Act. Parliament attempted to overcome the danger of the inadvertent harassment of respectable women and to encourage the novice prostitute to mend her ways by requiring two warnings before a woman could be arrested for soliciting in public. The result was a rapid increase in the mobility of prostitutes from one site or city to another, but no particular decline in their activity. Also, having exempted kerb crawlers from punishment, Parliament watched the increased use of automobiles as roving whorehouses. Taxi drivers and others were chauffeuring prostitutes and soliciting business from likely male pedestrians. Despite the Wolfenden Report's provisions, certain areas of London began to be unofficially sanctioned for on-the-street solicitation by prostitutes. Police interference occurred only when the boundaries of the areas were transgressed.

Almost forty years after the Wolfenden recommendations had been translated into law, large numbers of British prostitutes continue to be arrested for street soliciting. In 1990, there were proceedings against 10,470 persons, with an estimated one warning for every two arrests. This represents a very sizeable increase over the two decades since 1970, an increase said to represent in part shifts in police operations and in considerable part an actual rise in the number of women engaging in street prostitution. Almost 90 percent of the women arrested are fined about $60. In short, although the Street Offences Act may immunize call girls and others who practice less visible forms of prostitution, it has provided no relief from prosecution for streetwalkers (Edwards, 1993).

The inadequacy of these efforts to secure a significant reduction in street prostitution is portrayed by Roger Matthews in his description of what went on in Finsbury Park, an area in the north of London:

> The most visible presence of prostitutes, often congregating in groups, as well as the problem of kerb-crawling began by the earlier eighties to seriously affect the daily lives of all those living and working in the area—particularly of women. For some, even the simple business of walking along the street, waiting for a bus, or going shopping was a hazardous experience. Noise, harassment, frequent obscenities, the specter of prostitutes and their clients haggling or arguing on the street—erupting occasionally into overt violence—became a common feature of everyday life (Matthews, 1986:5).

The local residents orchestrated efforts to improve the area, involving the police and a host of other agencies. In particular, barriers were placed on many of the roads, despite the fear of merchants that this would harm business. Within two years, Finsbury Park became a relatively tranquil residential area, but there are doubts that anything was accomplished beyond moving the street solicitors to other parts of the city and country. (Lowman, 1992)

The most recent campaign against prostitution in London has focused upon sexually explicit advertising cards placed in telephone booths in the central city by prostitutes. The presence of the cards is said to discourage some people from using the booths and to encourage schoolchildren to collect and trade them. From 10 to 100 cards can usually be found in any one booth. In eight weeks the phone company removed 1.1 million of these advertisements. An ordinance now allows the police to issue a cease and desist order to advertisers. If the practice continues, phone service to the advertised number can be cut off. Skeptics presume that prostitutes will develop other tactics to attract customers.

"They don't call it the world's oldest profession for nothing," said one (Ibrahim, 1996:4).

Feminism and Prostitution

The women's movement that flourished for a time in the early years of the twentieth century took a strong position against prostitution (Musheno and Seeley, 1986). Jane Addams, a social worker and one of the movement's leaders, maintained that curtailing prostitution, particularly in public places, would considerably reduce any allure that might attract perspective recruits to the business. Her reasoning is similar to the argument today that the attractive lifestyle of drug dealers in the slums—their expensive automobiles, elegant clothes, and desirable female companions—encourages youngsters there to emulate them. Addams put her case this way:

> Were the streets kept clear, many young girls would be spared familiar knowledge that such a method of earning money is open to them. . . . The legal suppression [of prostitution] would not only protect girls but would enormously minimize the risks and temptation for boys (Addams, 1912:48-49).

The more recent revival of the feminist movement, part of the social revolution that swept America in the 1960s, initially placed prostitution at the head of its agenda of the major criminal behaviors that needed to be addressed. But feminist attention to prostitution largely evaporated soon after because of an inability to convince streetwalkers and other women "in the life" that they ought to give up what they were doing and adopt a safer, more respectable, and more dignified lifestyle. As one prostitute put it, "A woman has the right to sell her sexual services just as much as she has a right to sell her brains to a law firm" (Jenness, 1990:405). Another said, "Radical feminism . . . sees all pros [prostitutes] as exploited sex slaves. I think this has left people confused, especially other feminists and the political left" (Overs, 1994:119).

After a while, the women's movement switched its criminal justice focus to rape (and later also to child and spousal abuse), though every once in a while issues regarding prostitution resurface, only to be abandoned because they produce an acrimonious internal splintering within feminist circles. The feminist debate on prostitution pits two conflicting interpretations against each other. The question is whether prostitution is an ugly and intolerable consequence of the power of men over women and the sexual exploitation of women, or a commercial enterprise like so many others that is engaged in by a seller who possesses a commodity that has a market value.

These questions have been difficult and divisive for American feminists (Reanda, 1991:202), and the schism within the women's movement on prostitution is said to be deep (Jolin, 1994:69). One arm of the feminist movement repudiates the idea that women freely choose prostitution, that prostitution is a valid job, and that it can be carried on in a humane manner. Prostitution, opponents of this position insist, is based on male domination, the treatment of women as commodities, and enforced sexual access and sexual abuse. It is said to violate women's dignity and to represent a crime against women by men (Romenesko and Miller, 1989; Weitzer, 1991).

Women who take this position regard prostitution as the product of a patriarchal society in which females are defined from an early age as sex objects. Child sexual abuse, incest, and similar female victimizations are said to lie at the core of one's entry into prostitution (Freeman, 1989-1990). This position equates prostitution with slavery and points out that few words can evoke such contempt and loathing as the word "whore" or its equivalent in any language (Reanda, 1991:203). Often quoted is Simone de Beauvoir's (1953:569) observation in *The Second Sex* that "prostitution sums up all the forms of feminine slavery at once." This viewpoint has also been expressed by Laurie Shrage (1989:349):

> Because of the cultural context in which prostitution operates, it epitomizes and perpetuates pernicious patriarchal beliefs and values and, therefore, is both damaging to the women who sell sex and, as an organized social practice, to all women in our society.

A milder version of Shrage's position is offered by Debra Satz who believes that prostitution is wrong "insofar as the sale of women's sexual labor reinforces basic patterns of sex discrimination." Satz (1995) writes, "I argue that contemporary prostitution contributes to, and also introduces, the perception of women as socially inferior to men." Satz's position, of course, raises questions about any social occurrence in which members of one gender do something that cannot be done, or at least not done as well, by members of the other gender. Athletic events, such as track meets, almost invariably show the men outshining the women. Should such events be eliminated because they make women appear to be inferior?

On the other side are feminists who believe that the problem is that their sisters-in-arms focus only on what they see as male sexual domination of women and that they fail to campaign for policies that would allow prostitutes and potential prostitutes to choose a more redeeming way of life. Laura Reanda (1991:203) has berated some women—"antiporn feminists and other moralists"—for not attending to the financial impoverishment of working and underclass women. "Eliminate this mammoth motivating force and much prostitution would disappear," she maintains. Those left doing "sex work" (the emerging term of preference among feminists for prostitution) would be "on the game" because they liked it; in this regard, "true sexual determination (a basic feminist demand) should include a woman's right to sell sex—if she wants to." Another woman close to the world of prostitution had made the same point: "Antiporn feminists have patronizingly told strippers and prostitutes that we should raise our consciousness and develop self-esteem (by working as toilet cleaners and factory hands). No thanks, sisters" (Roberts, 1994:45). The viewpoint being criticized has been called the "brainwash theory" which, according to Gayle Rubin, "explains erotic diversity by assuming that some sexual acts are so disgusting that no one would willingly perform them. Therefore, the reasoning goes, anyone who does so must have been forced or fooled" (Rubin, 1984:306). Others go to the furthest extreme, like Camilia Paglia (1994:58-59) who insists that the prostitute is the "ultimate liberated woman, who lives on the edge and whose sexuality belongs to no one."

Legalizing Prostitution: Yeas and Nays

Some people believe that prostitution ought to be made legal, with no regulation whatsoever regarding how it is carried on, except for already existing laws about public decency (e.g., sex in public places) and similar matters. Others believe that it should be decriminalized but that practitioners ought to be licensed and subject to periodic tests to determine if they are free of venereal infections and AIDS. Still others maintain that for reasons of morality or for the betterment of the position of women in general, prostitution should remain outside the sanction of the law. Among these, there are some who believe that enforcement ought to be tougher and others who insist that the true failure resides in the unwillingness of the police to be aggressive in their pursuit of customers who buy sex from prostitutes. Along the continuum of these viewpoints, there exist additional positions and further refinements. In this section, we will look more closely at some of the major considerations that bear on the debate about the proper legal attitude toward the practice of prostitution.

Prostitution, Venereal Disease, and AIDS

For a long period of time, until the arrival of the death-dealing AIDS virus, considerable discussion centered about other diseases that prostitutes might transmit, most notably syphilis and gonorrhea. Given so high a level of intercourse for many prostitutes with so diverse a clientele, it was regarded as inevitable that many of them would sooner or later contract a venereal infection and pass the illness on to other customers who, in turn, would pass it on to other females with whom they had sexual contact—girl friends, wives, etc.

That such a chain of events occurred and continues to occur can hardly be doubted. The issue concerns the rate at which it occurs under different arrangements for prostitution. Today, with the threat of AIDS, prostitutes by and large are particularly insistent about the use of condoms in any kind of sexual act: their livelihood (not to mention their lives) depends on their caution about contracting disabling diseases, and their sexual work is neither spontaneous nor romantic but simply business (Freund, Lee, and Leonard, 1989). On the other hand, those prostitutes who use drugs, particularly crack cocaine, have often been reported to neglect taking precautions to avoid being infected with the HIV virus, the precursor of AIDS.

Paul Gebhard (1969), a member of the Kinsey team, maintained almost thirty years ago that only 4 percent of the prostitutes he interviewed were addicted to "hard" drugs (e.g., heroin) and another 5 percent had experimented with them without becoming addicted. Users of amphetamines and marijuana were found to be more frequent.

Since Gebhard's time, however, there has been a dramatic rise in the use of illicit drugs, especially crack cocaine (Goldstein, Ouellet, and Fendrich, 1992), and prostitutes are reported to contract AIDS more through intravenous drug use than from customers. In a study of 72 prostitutes, David Bellis (1990) found that those who used drugs did little to protect themselves or their customers from AIDS by relying on sterile needles or requiring the use of condoms. "Yeah, I'm concerned [about AIDS]," one woman said, "until I stick the needle in. When I'm hurting, dope's the only thing on my mind" (Bellis, 1990:30).

In a sophisticated study of the 350 licensed prostitutes in Nevada, where condom usage was made mandatory by law in 1988, Campbell (1991) found that not one prostitute had ever tested HIV positive in the mandatory monthly procedure, though 13 applicants for brothel positions had done so. Campbell contrasts the Nevada rate with that in a number of other cities, including Colorado Springs (3.8 percent HIV positive); Los Angeles (3.7 percent), San Francisco (9.9 percent); New Jersey statewide (57 percent), and Miami (26.6 percent). Following up on Campbell's work, Albert and her colleagues (1995) noted that by the end of 1993, after 20,000 tests, there still had not been a single positive HIV result for a licensed Nevada prostitute. The same study reported that its review of 353 acts of sexual intercourse over nine days by Nevada prostitutes found no condom breakage, though there was slipping in about one out of twenty-five usages during intercourse and about the same rate during withdrawal (Albert, Warner, Hatcher, and Trussell, 1995; Remez, 1996).

For prostitutes, the greatest danger of AIDS has been found to occur not from their work but from their sexual relations with high-risk non-paying customers with whom they have formed a romantic attachment and with whom they do not insist on the use of condoms (Campbell, 1991). As an Australian prostitute noted, "I can't use a condom with my boyfriend. What'll he think—that I'm gonna charge him next?" (Waddell, 1996:81). Margo St. James (1987:84), the leader of COYOTE (Call Off Your Old Tired Ethics), a group of "working women" that lobbies for the decriminalization of prostitution, commented, "Condoms are used more for privacy than for disease and pregnancy control because that's the way prostitutes separate their work from their play." Streetwalking prostitutes also often will not carry condoms on their person for fear that the police will use them as evidence that they are plying their trade (Campbell, 1991).

Other Impacts of Prostitution

Alfred Kinsey and his associates, in their monumental study of human sexual behavior, expressed surprise at the amount of attention concentrated on prostitution when it is measured by the importance that it shows numerically as a sexual outlet:

> The world's literature contains hundred of volumes whose authors have attempted to assay the social significance of prostitution. For an activity which contributes no more than this does to the sexual outlet of the male population, it is amazing that it should have been given such widespread consideration. Some of the attention undoubtedly has been inspired by erotic interest; but a major part of the interest has centered around the question of the social significance of prostitution. The extent of the attention which the subject still receives in this country today is all out of proportion to its significance in the lives of most males (Kinsey et al., 1948:605).

The Kinsey quotation is itself rather puzzling, seeming to imply that the extent rather than the nature of behavior should be the criterion by which its importance may be reasonably measured. More people are killed by a variety of means—including traffic accidents—and many more die of avoidable lethal conditions, such as inadequate medical care, than are murdered each year in the United States. Nonetheless, murder is considered, and reasonably so, to be a very important issue. The reason that prostitution compels interest and concern, despite its relative unimportance in any numerical sense, is that it challenges values, raises basic moral questions, and involves the lives of human beings like the rest of us who may (or may not) be injured by whatever view the law takes about their behavior.

Nevertheless, the extent to which men frequent prostitutes is not great and there is some evidence that it is declining. In an extensive national probability survey of adult sexual behavior, it was reported that only about 16 percent of men ever paid for sex (Michael et al., 1994: 63), and that the proportion of men whose first sexual intercourse was with a prostitute declined from 7 percent of those who came of age in the 1950s to 1.5 percent of the men who came of age in the late 1980s and early 1990s (Michael et al., 1994: 95).

Prostitutes, Pimps, and the Public

To adjudicate arguments regarding the proper status under law that prostitution should have, it is necessary to look at the various impacts that the behavior has in terms of at least four major groups: the prostitutes themselves, their customers, their pimps, and the larger society.

The Prostitute

Research studies regarding prostitution indicate that in contemporary times it is almost totally an occupation entered into voluntarily. Prostitution offers a considerable range of vocational advantages, including flexible work hours, contact with diverse kinds of people, a heightened sense of activity, and the opportunity to make substantial sums of money and pay no taxes. Such consequences do not accrue to all prostitutes, nor perhaps even to very many. For those women whose involvement is the most tawdry, prostitution can be a dirty and dangerous enterprise. There can be beatings, loveless copulations, and little financial reward (Miller, 1993). The loss of self-esteem that seems to result from the practice of prostitution is, of course, a function of broader social attitudes, which themselves are at least partly a function of the legal sanctions raised against such behavior. It seems likely, at any rate, that removing the legal ban against prostitution would not harm the self-esteem of its practitioners and might help them to realize that they are employed in an acceptable occupation.

The harms that come to the individual prostitute from her work seem to be neither so extreme nor so totally unavoidable that laws should be enacted to protect her by outlawing her behavior. If society prefers women to follow what it regards as more admirable kinds of pursuits, it could provide such outlets and make them more accessible in order to counteract whatever appeal prostitution offers.

Unfortunately, no large-scale studies exist concerning the outcomes of the lives of prostitutes. This enormous gap in important knowledge was observed more than half a century ago by Walter Reckless in a pioneering study of vice in Chicago. "What happens to girls who have once practiced prostitution?" asked Reckless (1933:57). "No investigations so far made offer information upon which to base a positive statement."

An examination of the records of 1,022 prostitutes working in Colorado Springs between 1970 and 1988 showed that 53 were "evanescent," that is, they only rarely and only for a brief period practiced prostitution, whereas 12 percent hustled for a short term, usually a few weeks or months, and 35 percent for a longer time, usually four to five years. Extrapolating their figures, the authors calculated that there were 84,000 prostitutes at work in the United States, though they recognized that Colorado Springs, where the prostitutes largely have contact with servicemen stationed there, cannot be regarded as a particularly representative venue for prostitution. In addition, many of the women may have continued their trade in other places, unknown to the researchers (Potterat, Woodhouse, Muth, and Muth, 1990).

Part of the barrier limiting more comprehensive longitudinal studies of prostitutes has stemmed from the fact that these women were particularly difficult to locate years later, because when they married they took their husbands' family name. This is not as common today, but prostitutes often use aliases instead of their actual names. In addition, of course, former prostitutes in other roles would not be too willing to have an interviewer show up at their front door, questionnaire in hand. So we remain uninformed about a matter of great significance that could be resolved by diligent, tactful research. Winick and Kinsie (1971) reported a notably high suicide rate among prostitutes, with 75 percent of a sample of call girls said to have attempted to kill themselves. They also claimed that 15 percent of all persons who attempt suicide and are brought to public hospitals are prostitutes. This claim needs further substantiation but, if accurate, it suggests a high degree of alienation and unhappiness. Many fictional portraits depict prostitutes as golden-hearted damsels, who, because of their innumerable contacts with men and a learned ability to cater to male desires, ultimately marry well above their original social position and settle down comfortably in suburbia. Others see them ending up prematurely as neglected corpses, lying anonymously on city morgue tables and buried in paupers' graves. The collection of accurate information on such an issue would be enormously helpful if we are to make more informed public policy decisions about how to deal with prostitution.

It seems likely, though uncertain, that no longer defining prostitution as a crime would lead to an increase in the number of its practitioners, unless it is true that the law is so peripheral that it has no impact on the participation in prostitution. Some would take the position that a possible increase in sex workers is nobody's business but that of the workers themselves. After all, they might declare, writing cigarette advertisements hardly seems more ennobling than catering sexually for profit to a lonely, perhaps crippled customer.

Customers

In a society characterized by sexual inhibitions, it could be argued that the abatement of prostitution by whatever means would encourage chastity and sexual abstinence among those who now consort with prostitutes for the purposes of sexual outlet. America is not, however, such a society. The assumption has to be that the absence of prostitutes for sexual activity would lead men deprived of them to other means of releasing strong, compelling sexual energies. Such outlets could be masturbation, more intense courtship or seduction patterns, sex by force, or behavior patterns that psychiatrists label as inhibitions and sublimations, commonly involving the transfer of sexual energies into nonsexual pursuits, such as the drive for power or acts of aggression.

The possibility exists that the availability of sexual liaisons with prostitutes discourages marriage, which some men may find more demanding than impersonal sexual contact. But American society does not seem to be that strongly dedicated to the encouragement of marriage, and a considerable percentage of prostitutes' customers—both male and female prostitutes—are married men.

Much discussion has centered around the possibility that the absence of prostitution would lead men to seek sexual satisfaction by force. Acts of forcible rape and prostitution may indeed share some characteristics. Both are illicit, both can involve brutality beyond the sex itself, and both seem to require the humiliation of the female. In neither behavior is the woman viewed as a person requiring sexual satisfaction nor is she likely to achieve such satisfaction. In neither are demands for sophisticated sexual performance placed upon the male. Indeed, studies of rape report that to a very large degree the offender is impotent during the commission of the crime (Burgess and Holstrom, 1974).

The research of Eugene Kanin (1957; Kanin and Parcell, 1977; Kirkpatrick and Kanin, 1957) on the incidence of forced intercourse in dating situations on a college campus is particularly informative. The value of Kanin's work abides in the fact that he queried students during two widely separated times—first in 1957 and then in 1977. He found that the number of cases in which sexual force was employed by college males during a date had increased dramatically. Kanin believed that this was because at the time of the initial study, college men were much more were willing to grant their dates the moral right to say no. Following the sexual revolution, a new generation of college men more frequently assumed that their dates were sexually experienced and that their reluctance was a personal rejection. In that sense, they regarded their own aggression, despite strong signals to the contrary, as reasonable.

Information concerning the relationship between prostitution—legal or otherwise—and crimes of sexual violence is inconclusive, perhaps necessarily so, given the number of confounding variables involved. Societies probably encourage or discourage both rape and prostitution as a consequence of commitments to certain attitudes and values. It is likely that these commitments, rather than legal codes, significantly influence the rates for both behaviors.

The results of the only research study that has looked at the issue of rape and prostitution, conducted in Australia in the late 1960s, presented methodological difficulties that serve as warning signs for cautious interpretations. Between the early 1950s and the middle 1960s, the rape rate had risen steadily in the Australian state of Queensland. The increase was particularly precipitous after 1961, characterized by a sharp rise in the number of gang rapes, or "pack" rapes as they are known in Australia.

The legal position on prostitution had shifted during this period. Brothels were tolerated by Queensland police until the end of 1958. Thereafter, they were closed. Rape rates jumped 149 percent following the closing of the brothels, although other personal offenses committed by men rose only 49 percent. The Australian researcher expressed concern over his interpretation of these figures: "This, of course, does not of itself prove that the increase in the number of convictions for rape and attempted rape was caused by the closing of the brothels, but it does show clearly that there was a remarkable increase in the conviction rate for these two crimes after this closing" (Barber, 1969).

The researcher suggests that persons who perpetrate forcible rape share to a considerable extent the socioeconomic traits of those who most often visit prostitutes. It was this group, he argues, that was most severely affected by the closing of the brothels and whose members turned to rape when denied such a sexual outlet. Interviews with the rapists to verify or disprove this assumption would seem to be essential before the interpretation could be regarded as anything more than a very tentative finding. Another possible explanation for this rise in rape is that it was part of the increased enforcement efforts in the area of sexual crimes that included the closing of brothels. Pending further research, we would be inclined to endorse the brief summary statement on the matter by Kinsey and his colleagues:

> There is constant rumor of an increase in the frequency of forced intercourse or outright rape among the girls of a community where prostitution has been suppressed. We have no adequate data to prove the truth or falsity of such reports (Kinsey et al., 1948:607).

Today, commentators would be puzzled by Kinsey's artificial distinction between "forced intercourse" and "outright rape." And of course, today's verbal etiquette dictates that females beyond a certain age—say 16 or 18—are no longer "girls." But almost 50 years after it was first published, Kinsey's conclusion remains the best that can be said on the subject.

Customers of prostitutes—the johns—have been the recent focus in San Francisco of a unique training approach that seeks to reduce their recourse to sex-for-pay. In 1995, 6,000 persons were arrested for prostitution in San Francisco, about one-fourth of them customers. Instead of being convicted of the misdemeanor violation of soliciting a prostitute and paying a fine or doing community service, the men were offered the option of taking a class to learn about the health and social implications of the sex trade. Those who took the class did not have their criminal offense placed on record. Few prostitutes, though they are also eligible for the training, exercised that right. As one told a district attorney, "Honey, being in that class for six hours is money."

The men were exposed to a compelling slide show illustrating various visual close-up effects of sexually transmitted diseases, and they heard lectures from, among others, a health care worker who quit prostitution seven years ago. She talked of the danger, disease, degradation, and sometimes death that follows in the wake of prostitution. "How can anyone say it is a victimless crime?" she asked scornfully. One man, interviewed after his exposure to the class, summarized what he had learned: "Going to a prostitute is cheaper financially, but not emotionally. I'm going to be working on finding a real girl-friend" (Ybarra, 1996).

Pimps

The belief that prostitutes represent the innocent victims of males often forms part of the arsenal of arguments raised against the abandonment of attempts to use the law to control or at least to ameliorate certain aspects of the practice of prostitution. Public attitudes toward prostitutes seem to have become increasingly tolerant, although those toward pimps remain relentlessly hostile.

There appears to be general agreement among researchers that the relationship between the pimp and the prostitute usually represents a mutual exchange in which both parties provide and secure things important to them. To the outsider, however, the prostitute clearly seems to be giving a good deal more than she gets. At the same time, there also exist pimp-prostitute relationships, especially those involving underaged girls, where the acts of prostitution are coerced and the females are treated as chattels. For such situations, Neal Katyal (1993) has recently urged that authorities should apply the Thirteenth Amendment that prohibits slavery in order to punish the pimps and others who force women into prostitution.

A common psychiatric explanation of the pimp-prostitute relationship is that the pimp serves symbolically as a debased person to the prostitute, someone even lower than herself, who lives parasitically on her earnings. Others, less taken by symbolic interpretations of such matters, suggest that prostitutes—like all of us—prefer to be loved and to love, and that the pimp is the only person with whom they can form such an relationship. That the pimp lives on the work of women, often several women, is by definition his condition.

Pimps seem to be less common as their social and emotional functions decrease in a more sexually free society in which women demonstrate increasing independence. It could well be that pimping tends to be encouraged by stringent laws against prostitution. Some argue that to the extent that an adult female chooses of her own volition to affiliate with a pimp, the liaison could be regarded as like any other formed freely by two persons who have reached the age of consent. Others disagree, contending that some women need to be protected from the unpleasant and dangerous consequences of actions that they may believe are voluntary but that are actually the product of their inferior status and, in some cases, the consequence of earlier sexual abuse within their own families or elsewhere.

Impact of Prostitution on Society

Illegal prostitution exists in large measure as a function of the efforts of our society and its citizens to regulate sexual behavior, so that in a sense the crime of prostitution is created by attempts to prohibit it. That paradox can perhaps be best understood by imagining a society in which sexual relationships are readily obtainable by all who seek them, in whatever form. Such a society is not likely to exist any more than is one in which all persons can secure whatever it is that they desire. Prostitution then serves to provide something that is not otherwise available, as Kingsley Davis has indicated:

> In short, the attempt to control sexual expression, to tie it to social requirements, especially the attempt to tie it to the durable relation of marriage and the rearing of children, or to attach men to a celibate order, or to base sexual expression on love, creates the opportunity for prostitution. It is analogous to the black market, which is the illegal but inevitable response to an attempt to control the economy. The craving for sexual variety, for perverse gratification, for novel and provocative surroundings, for ready and cheap release, for intercourse free from entangling cares and civilized pretense—all can be demanded from the woman whose interest lies solely in the price. The sole limitation on the man's satisfactions is

in this instance, not morality or convention, but his ability to pay (Davis, 1966:360).

The impact of legal or illegal prostitution on the moral fiber of the nation under any of the diverse kinds of arrangements suggested is one of those questions that we cannot pretend to have adequate answers for. We can only observe that moral fibers contain a large number of strands, and that the encouragement of hypocrisy by outlawing a trade that is nonetheless covertly allowed to continue may be just as, or more, damaging to a social system than the tolerance of lawful prostitution. So too, encouragement of a philosophy of live-and-let-live may or may not be a contribution to democratic vitality.

Among the major reasons for supporting legalized prostitution is that if it were legal and licensed, it could be more readily controlled and, for that matter, taxed. Prostitutes, like barbers, attorneys, bus drivers, or doctors, could be licensed after required training sessions to keep up with the latest understanding of the basic aspects of their work, and there could be penalties imposed for violation of certain regulations.

On the other side is the argument that uncontrolled prostitution would result in a heavy increase in public annoyance on the streets and residential disturbances in neighborhoods in which prostitutes ply their trade. The issue of the limits that should be imposed on public behavior poses knotty questions. People are allowed to beg from passersby, even though it may frighten some and annoy many. But they are not allowed to walk about unclothed on public thoroughfares, presumably because this would offend some and outrage others. If their work were to be made legal, should prostitutes nonetheless be prevented from approaching potential customers, as in England, or from publicly advertising their wares in less than subtle ways? Similar questions arise in regard to houses where prostitutes carry out assignations. If efforts are made to ban them from certain neighborhoods, it is a safe prediction that they will end up among the poor and powerless, a situation that hardly seems just. The resolution of this issue, like that of begging and other public nuisances, seems far from simple.

That prostitution encourages derivative kinds of criminal activity can hardly be denied by its defenders, though they may point out by analogy that allowing kissing does not necessarily encourage illegitimate births. One might suggest that crimes derived from prostitution, such as theft from a customer, should be prosecuted vigorously, and that the halfhearted tactics now employed for dealing with prostitution should yield to a more intensive effort to ensure that prostitutes stick to their basic business.

A clearer directive to law enforcement on how to deal with prostitution might contribute to more effective use of personnel and particularly to the elimination of some unsavory police practices. In a novel about the Los Angeles Police Department, written by a former sergeant on that force, there is a detailed and accurate depiction of a roundup of prostitutes, carried out more in the nature of a police recreational exercise than anything else. The women are dumped into a paddy wagon, driven about the city, then deposited far from the places where they had been "arrested." According to the police officers, this was done because there was no chance of gaining a court conviction against the women, and this procedure was the best alternative they could think of (Wambaugh, 1970).

Conclusion

A number of arguments opposed to outlawing prostitution were offered recently by an Englishwoman who told how as a youth she had been coerced into sexual behavior by a policeman who threatened to arrest her for "living off the earnings of prostitution." Her only crime was that, as a runaway, she had been supplied with food by prostitutes. She offered the following arguments that she believed supported decriminalization of prostitution:

1. The laws breed corruption.

2. The laws turn the government into the trades' biggest pimp through fines which the women have to go out and earn.

3. The laws institutionalize and reinforce the whore stigma, which encourages rape and violence against prostitutes and also against other women thought to behave like hustlers.

4. The laws are a denial of a prostitute's basic civil and human rights. They make it illegal for women to work

together for safety's sake (two or more women constitute a brothel), effectively forcing women into the streets, where they must work alone and at great personal risk.

5. Much of the taxpayers' money is wasted on prosecuting and imprisoning prostitutes. This would be better spent on improving women's lives, providing housing, health care, child care, and education (Roberts, 1994).

A compilation of arguments for and against decriminalized prostitution has been set out in a document issued by the United Nations (1959) that based its information on prostitution worldwide. Though the roster is now almost forty years old, the issues it raises remain as essential to the debate today as they did at the time.

The following are the major arguments offered in the UN report for defining prostitution as a criminal offense:

1. It is the responsibility of the government to regulate public morals in the interest of the public good; hence, to make prostitution a punishable offense.

2. The abolition of the legal ban against prostitution will merely replace controlled prostitution by clandestine prostitution.

3. It would be difficult to enforce regulatory provisions against prostitution, when prostitution itself is not considered a punishable offense.

4. Women and girls on the borderline will be encouraged to take up prostitution by the mere fact that it is legal.

5. The absence of laws against prostitution will be interpreted by the public as the government's support of commercialized vice as a "necessary evil," thereby admitting its inability to control it.

A similar list, with slightly different emphases, is offered by John Decker (1979:20). Those favoring the continuing criminalization of prostitution, Decker observes, rely on one or all of the following points:

1. Protection of the conventional morality.

2. Humanistic concerns for the prostitute, the prostitute's family, her children, and her customers.

3. Prevention of incidental crime.

4. Control of the criminal culture surrounding prostitution.

5. Protection of juveniles who might be attracted to the occupation.

6. Abatement of a public nuisance.

7. Prevention of venereal disease.

Elliott M. Abramson (1978-1979:371) focuses his attention on the second point above and stresses the need for society to use whatever force it can muster to lift the prostitute out of a degrading and self-defeating gutter of life. To concede the inevitably of prostitution, he argues, is a misguided and defeatist position: "Is it any more 'unreasonably' intrusive to seek to protect people from the self-inflicted torments and privations of a life of prostitution than it is to try to protect them from perversely ingesting adulterated food which could make them seriously ill or kill them?" He thinks that psychotherapy, medical attention, job training, educational experiences, and child support are some of the services that ought to be provided to prostitutes—and mandated for them by law, if necessary—to move them from " 'the life' to life" (Abramson, 1978-1979:374).

Finally, there is the strong feminist position of Susan Brownmiller (1975:392) who believes that practicing and tolerating prostitution reinforces in men a vicious attitude about the nature of women and produces attitudes that lead to rape:

> [M]y horror at the idea of legalized prostitution is not that it institutionalizes the concept that it is a man's mandatory right, if not his divine right, to gain access to the female body, and that sex is a female service that should not be denied the civilized male. Perpetuation of the concept that the "powerful male impulse" must be satisfied with immediacy by a cooperating class of woman, set aside . . . and licensed for the purpose, is part and parcel of the mass psychology of rape.

The following represent counterarguments offered by the United Nations in support of the position that prostitution should be removed from the concerns of criminal law:

1. Outlawing prostitution represents an unwarranted invasion into the private lives of persons participating in a voluntary activity.

2. Between prostitution and other sexual relations outside of marriage, there is only a difference of degree; hence, it is too arbitrary to penalize only those who meet the arbitrary criteria for crime that defines only one form of the same kind of behavior.

3. Experience teaches us that prostitution cannot be eliminated by mere legal enactments, and that making prostitution a crime often encourages clandestine operations and control by underworld organizations. As long as the demand for prostitution exists, there will always be a corresponding supply of persons to cater to that demand.

4. Illegal prostitution often leads to police behavior that is in itself detrimental to the common good.

5. Declaring prostitution against the law creates among those engaged in it an antagonistic attitude that hampers their chances of abandoning it for employment that society may regard as more desirable.

That there may be a greater number of arguments on one side or the other is of no importance in resolving the debate. For one thing, those seeking change are typically more vocal than those interested in keeping things as they are. It is the power of any given argument or set of arguments that must prevail. There may be ten items on one side of the issue and only one on the other, but that one can prove decisive for an informed decision. For its part, the United Nations group was more persuaded by the arguments against declaring prostitution a criminal offense than those favoring criminalization (see also Rio, 1991). It recommended an array of educative and retraining programs for prostitutes and for those who seem likely prospects for prostitution.

We believe that there will continue to be some state concern with prostitution, in the manner that the state concerns itself with other trades. The issues surrounding prostitution are likely to continue to be examined, debated, and regularized. One alternative to legal repression is to offer reasonable opportunities for prostitutes to pursue other callings and reasonable methods of persuasion to convince prostitutes and those contemplating prostitution that their self-interest lies in such other callings. Perhaps Geoffrey Simons' (1972:96) observation offers a key ground rule for adjudicating the controversy about the legal status of prostitution in the United States: "In a society which values liberty, social phenomena are, like individuals, innocent until proven guilty."

References

Abramson, Elliott M. 1978-1979. "A Note on Prostitution: Victims Without Crime—Or There's No Crime but the Victim is Ideology." *Duquesne Law Review* 17:355-379.

Addams, Jane. 1912. *A New Conscience and an Ancient Evil.* New York: Macmillan.

Albert, Alexa E., David L. Warner, Robert A. Hatcher, and James Trussell. 1995. "Condom Use Among Female Commercial Sex Workers in Nevada's Legal Brothels." *American Journal of Public Health* 85:1514-1520.

Allred, Gloria, and Lisa Bloom. 1994. "Perspective on Prostitution: Prosecution or Persecution?" *Los Angeles Times,* December 6:B7.

Aquinas, Thomas. 1273/1947. *Summa Theologica.* New York: Benziger Brothers.

Augustine of Hippo. 386/1844-1864. "De Ordine." Pp. 977-1020 in Jacques-Paul Migne, ed., *Patrologiae Cursus Completus, Series Latina.* Paris: P. Geuther.

Barber, R. N. 1969. "Prostitution and the Increasing Number of Convictions for Rape in Queensland." *Australian and New Zealand Journal of Criminology* 2:169-174.

Bellis, David J. 1990. "Fear of AIDS and Risk Reduction among Heroin-Addicted Female Street Prostitutes: Personal Interviews with 72 Southern California Subjects." *Journal of Alcohol and Drug Education* 35:26-37.

Boyer, Edward J. 1995. "Official Business: Former Clients Testify as Heidi Fleiss Trial Begins." *Los Angeles Times,* June 30:B4.

Brownmiller, Susan. 1975. *Against Our Will: Men, Women and Rape.* New York: Simon and Schuster.

Bryant, Clifford D., and C. Eddie Palmer. 1975. "Massage Parlor and 'Hand Whores': Some Sociological Observations." *Journal of Sex Research* 11:227-241.

Buckley, William. 1995. "Thou Shalt Not...What?" *National Review,* July 31:71.

Burgess, Ann W., and Lynda Lytle Holstrom. 1974. *Rape: Victims of Crisis.* Bowie, MD: Brady.

Campbell, Carole A. 1991. "Prostitution, AIDS, and Preventive Health Behavior." *Social Science and Medicine* 32:1367-1378.

Cates, Jim A., and Jeffrey Markley. 1992. "Demographic, Clinical, and Personality Variables Associated with Male Prostitution by Choice." *Adolescence* 27:695-714.

Davis, Kingsley. 1966. "Sexual Behavior." Pp. 354-372 in Robert K. Merton and Robert Nisbet, eds., *Contemporary Social Problems,* 2nd ed. New York: Harcourt, Brace, and World.

Davis, Nanette, ed. 1993. *Prostitution: An International Handbook of Trends, Problems, and Policies.* Westport, CT: Greenwood.

de Beauvoir, Simone. 1953. *The Second Sex.* Howard M. Parshley, trans. New York: Knopf.

Decker, John F. 1979. *Prostitution: Regulation and Control.* Littleton, CO: Fred B. Rothman.

"Divine Brown's Unpromising Career." 1995. *Tampa Tribune,* August 12:14.

Edwards, Susan S. M. 1993. "England and Wales." Pp. 108-128 in Nanette J. Davis, ed., *Prostitution: An International Handbook on Trends, Problems, and Policies.* Westport, CT: Greenwood.

Ehrlich, Dan. 1995. "Take It for Granted, She Walks Out On Hugh." *Daily News* (New York), July 3:3.

Freeman, Jody. 1989-1990. "The Feminist Debate Over Prostitution Reform: Prostitutes' Rights Groups, Radical Feminists, and the Impossibility of Consent." *Berkeley Women's Law Journal* 5:75-109.

Freund, Matthew, Nancy Lee and Terri L. Leonard 1989. "Sexual Behavior of Prostitutes with Their Clients in Camden, New Jersey." *Journal of Sex Research* 28:579-591.

Frey, James H., Loren R. Reichert, and Kenneth Y. Russell. 1981. "Prostitution, Business and Police: The Maintenance of an Illegal Economy." *Police Journal* 54:239-249.

Gebhard, Paul H. 1969. "Misconceptions about Female Prostitutes." *Medical Aspects of Human Sexuality* 8 (March):24, 28-30.

Goldstein, Paul J., Lawrence J. Ouellet, and Michael Fendrich. 1992. "From Bang Brides to Skeezers: A Historical Perspective on Sex-for-Drugs Behavior." *Journal of Psychoactive Drugs* 24:349-361.

Gooding, Richard. 1996. "Clinton Aide Kept Mistress 15 Years." *Star*, September 17:5-8,38,45.

Great Britain. 1957. Committee on Homosexual Offences and Prostitution, *Report* (Command 247). London: Her Majesty's Stationery Office.

Haskell, Molly. 1974. *From Reverence to Rape: The Treatment of Women in the Movies.* New York: Holt, Rinehart, and Winston.

Hubler, Shawn. 1996. "Court Overturns Fleiss' Conviction, Orders New Trial." *Los Angeles Times*, May 30:A1, A24.

Ibrahim, Youssef M. 1996. "In Kiosks of London, Card Games Get Dirty." *New York Times*, August 17:4.

James, Jennifer. 1977. "Prostitutes and Prostitution." Pp. 368-428 in Edward Sagarin and Fred Montanino eds., *Deviants: Voluntary Actors in a Hostile World.* Morristown, NJ: General Learning Press.

Jenness, Valerie. 1990. "From Sex as Sin to Sex as Work." *Social Problems,* 37:403-420.

Jolin, Annette. 1994. "On the Backs of Working Prostitutes: Feminist Theory and Prostitution Policy." *Crime and Delinquency* 40:69-83.

Kanin, Eugene J. 1957. "Male Aggression in Dating Courtship Relations." *American Journal of Sociology* 63:197-204.

Kanin, Eugene J., and Stanley R. Parcell. 1977. "Sexual Aggression: A Second Look at the Offended Female." *Archives of Sexual Behavior* 6:67-76.

Katyal, Neal K. 1993. "Men Who Own Women: A Thirteenth Amendment Critique of Forced Prostitution." *Yale Law Journal* 103:791-826.

Kinsey, Alfred, Wardell B. Pomeroy, and Clyde E. Martin. 1948. *Sexual Behavior in the Human Male.* Philadelphia: Saunders.

Kirkpatrick, Clifford, and Eugene J. Kanin. 1957. "Male Sex Aggression on a University Campus." *American Sociological Review* 63:197-204.

Koltnow, Barry. 1996. "A Woman Scorned." *Orange County* (CA) *Register,* February 20:Accent 1-2.

Lowman, John. 1992. "Street Prostitution Control: Some Canadian Reflections on the Finsbury Park Experiment." *British Journal of Criminology* 32:1-17.

Maslin, Janet. 1996. "Hollywood Woman of Affairs." *New York Times*, February 9:B3.

Matthews, Roger. 1986. "Policing Prostitution: A Multi-Agency Approach." Middlesex Polytechnic, Centre for Criminology, Paper no 1.

McCormick, Naomi B. 1994. *Sexual Salvation: Affirming Women's Sexual Rights and Pleasures.* Westport, CT: Praeger.

Michael, Robert T., John Gagnon, Edward O. Laumann and Gina Kolata. 1994. *Sex in America: A Definitive Survey.* Boston: Little, Brown.

Miller, Jody. 1993. "Your Life Is on the Line Every Night You're on the Streets: Victimization and Resistance Among Street Prostitutes." *Humanities and Society* 17:422-446.

Milner, Christina, and Richard Milner. 1973. *Black Players: The Secret World of Black Pimps.* Boston: Little, Brown.

Morris, Dick. 1997. *Behind the Oval Office.* New York: Random House.

Musheno, Michael, and Kathryn Seeley. 1986. "Prostitution, Policy and the Women's Movement: Historical Analysis of Feminist Thought and Organization." *Contemporary Crises* 10:237-255.

Overs, Cheryl. 1994. "Sex Work, HIV and the State." *Feminist Review* 48:110-121.

Paglia, Camille. 1994. *Vamps & Tramps.* New York: Vintage Books.

Polsky, Ned. 1967. *Hustlers, Beats and Others.* Chicago: Aldine.

Pomeroy, Wardell B. 1965. "Some Aspects of Prostitution." *Journal of Sex Research* 1:177-187.

Potterat, John J., Donald E. Woodhouse, John B. Muth, and Stephen Q. Muth. 1990. "Estimating the Prevalence and Career Longevity of Prostitute Women." *Journal of Sex Research* 27:233-243.

Primoratz, Igor. 1993. "What's Wrong with Prostitution?" *Philosophy* 68:159-182.

"Prostitution Arrest Trends." 1995. Pp. 283-286 in *Crime in the United States 1994: Uniform Crime Reports for the United States.* Washington, DC: Federal Bureau of Investigation, United States Department of Justice.

Quigley, John. 1992. "The Dilemma of Prostitution Law Reform: Lessons from the Soviet Russia Experiment." *American Criminal Law Review,* 29:1197-1234.

Reanda, Laura. 1991. "Prostitution as a Human Rights Question: Problems and Prospects of United Nations Action." *Human Rights Quarterly* 13:202-228.

Reckless, Walter C. 1933. *Vice in Chicago.* Chicago: University of Chicago Press.

Reichert, Loren D., and James H. Frey. 1985. "The Organization of Bell Desk Prostitution." *Sociology and Social Research* 69:516-526.

Reiss, Albert J. 1961. "The Social Integration of Peers and Queers." *Social Problems* 9:102-120.

Remez, Lisa. 1996. "Nevada's Licensed Sex Workers Achieve Minimal Condom Breakage Rates." *Family Planning Perspectives* 28:35.

Reynolds, Helen. 1986. *The Economics of Prostitution.* Springfield, IL: Thomas.

Rio, Linda M. 1991. "Psychological and Sociological Research and the Decriminalization or Legalization of Prostitution." *Archives of Sexual Behavior* 20:205-218.

Roberts, Nickie. 1994. "The Game's Up." *New Statesman & Society* 7(July 16):44-45.

Romenesko, Kim, and Eleanor M. Miller. 1989. "The Second Step in Double Jeopardy: Appropriating the Labor of Female Street Hustlers." *Crime and Delinquency* 35:109-135.

Rubin, Gayle. 1984. "Thinking Sex: Notes for a Radical Theory of the Politics of Sexuality" Pp. 267-319 in Carole S. Vance, ed., *Pleasures and Danger: Exploring Female Sexuality.* Boston: Routledge and Kegan Paul.

Rushing, Sandra M. 1994. *The Magdalene Legacy: Exploring the Wounded Icon of Sexuality.* Westport, CT: Berin & Garvey.

Satz, Debra. 1995. "Markets in Women's Sexual Labor." *Ethics* 106:63-85.

Shah, Diane K. 1993. "The Hardest Working Girl in Show Business." *Esquire* 120 (November):66-73.

Shrage, Laurie. 1989. "Should Feminists Oppose Prostitution?" *Ethics* 99:347-361.

Siebert, Mark. 1996. "From House of Prostitution to the Halls of Congress?" *Des Moines Register,* April 2:1A, 2A.

Simons, Geoffrey L. 1972. *Pornography Without Prejudice: A Reply to Objections.* London: Abelard-Schuman.

St. James, Margo. 1987. "The Reclamation of Whores." Pp. 81-87 in Laurie Bell ed., *Good Girls/Bad Girls: Sex Trade Workers and Feminists Face to Face.* Toronto: The Women's Press.

Thomas, Kevin. 1996. "Dark Side of Hollywood Glitz in 'Madam.' " *Los Angeles Times,* February 9:F10, F12.

United Nations. 1959. *Study on Traffic in Persons and Prostitution .* New York: United Nations.

van der Poel, Sari. 1992. "Male Prostitution: A Neglected Phenomenon." *Crime, Law and Social Change* 18:259-275.

Waddell, Charles. 1996. "HIV and the Social World of Female Commercial Sex Workers." *Medical Anthropological Quarterly,* 10:75-82.

Wambaugh, Joseph. 1970. *The New Centurions.* New York: Dell.

Weinraub, Bernard. 1996. "Play a Hooker and Hook an Oscar." *New York Times,* February 20:B1-B2.

Weitzer, Ronald. 1991. "Prostitutes' Rights in the United States: The Failure of a Movement." *Sociological Quarterly* 32:23-41.

Winick, Charles, and Paul M. Kinsie. 1971. *The Lively Commerce: Prostitution in the United States.* Chicago: Quadrangle.

Ybarra, Michael J. 1996. "A Graphic Lesson for Patrons in Fight Against Prostitution." *New York Times,* May 11: 12.

Zeldes, Ilya. 1981. *The Problem of Crime in the USSR.* Springfield, IL: Thomas.

3

Drugs

In October 1995, inmates disrupted normal prison routine in more than a dozen federal institutions. The level of violence was low, however, and the inmates were more interested in making a political statement than fomenting a riot or breaking out. At issue were the different penalties for persons convicted of possession of powder and crack cocaine. Federal law imposes a five-year mandatory minimum prison sentence for selling only five grams of crack cocaine, but it takes 500 grams of powder cocaine to justify the exact same sentence. As almost 90 percent of federal crack defendants are black, some black leaders, including the Rev. Jesse Jackson, were prompted to label this penalty disparity as "racist."

Weeks earlier, a federal sentencing commission had recommended that the penalties for possession of these two drugs be the same, and that the penalty for crack cocaine be lowered to match that for powder cocaine. In a decision announced immediately prior to the prison uprisings, President Clinton rejected the sentencing commission's recommendation. The rioting started within days of his decision.

The disruptions were only the tip of the iceberg. Throughout the country, community, law enforcement, and political leaders had been questioning the current policy on drugs. Newspaper editorials, television commentaries, network news specials—one of them made by venerated former news anchor Walter Cronkite—examined the national drug policy and found it to be wanting. Opinion spanned the political continuum, with liberals protesting over vio-

lations of individual privacy and conservatives complaining that
the policy was simply ineffective.

Few issues have been more controversial than drugs, partly because many Americans are ambivalent about their usage. On the
one hand, most Americans engage in drug taking on a daily basis,
some several times a day. Most of these substances are legal, such
as headache and cold remedies; others are illegal, such as marijuana
and cocaine. Some of the legal substances are regulated by law, such
as alcohol and tobacco, but are easily obtained by adults. On the
other hand, most people have a fear of drugs. Many people believe
them to be artificial and unnatural. Others dislike the effects of many
of these drugs, including the health hazards associated with alcohol
and tobacco, as well as the link between alcohol and violence. Furthermore, some of the drugs cause an unwanted condition of physical dependency, or addiction. If all this weren't enough, drug taking
is seen by some as immoral behavior that reflects the character, or
lack thereof, of the users.

So, drugs are both good and bad, depending on which drugs,
who is taking them, the conditions under which they are taken, and
a host of other more personal reasons. We want it both ways, which,
of course, is the essence of ambivalence.

Since the 1800s, the United States has asked legal authorities not
only to resolve this ambivalence but to solve the problem of drug
taking. Legislatures have employed a policy of legal repression to
control, prevent, and restrict the manufacture, sale, and use of certain drugs. American policy is at odds with that in many other countries, and observers are now wondering whether our present
approach is not only inappropriate but whether it can ever work.
To understand the dimensions of this policy, we need to understand
the scope of drug "problem," how this problem is conceived or
defined, and what alternatives are available to address it. We will
begin here with a seemingly simple question: What is a drug?

What is a Drug?

To say that drug taking is an everyday experience for many
Americans fails to give meaning and scope to the importance of
drugs in the United States. The word "drug" is used in a number of
different contexts and the meaning often changes with the speaker.
To some, drugs are substances that cause addiction; to others, they

are healing chemicals when prescribed by a medical specialist; to others, they are recreational substances to be used only in social situations; to others, they are sources of high income and substantial prestige; and to still others, they are nothing more than perfectly legal foods, such as coffee, cola drinks, and cigarettes. Who is right? They all are.

Erich Goode (1993:37) says that a drug is anything we *call* a drug. This simple statement reflects the current confusion regarding drugs. What is a drug? A chemical? Something that alters one's mood, alters one's body, or creates a habit? Drugs are not just chemicals; everything is made up of chemicals. Drugs may alter one's moods, but there are plenty of things that alter our moods that are not commonly perceived as drugs, such as the effect a woman wearing a perfume has on some men, or the way a man walking in a certain way affects some women. In the same respect, drugs may alter one's body, but then so does a disease, fatty foods, or a bullet in the heart, for that matter. Some drugs can be habit-forming, but so can everything from a popular television show to a particular breakfast cereal to a favorite chair. Likewise, some drugs can be addicting, but not everything that is addicting is a drug; a husband and wife in a codependent relationship can be just as addicted to each other. The properties that are said to belong to drugs clearly belong to countless other things, some of which are more emotional than chemical. Consequently, the overall confusion regarding the nature of drugs and the meaning of the word "addiction" makes the very notion of "drugs" a broad subject impregnated with many different meanings.

So, Goode reasons, drugs are simply things we call drugs. The important question is why some things are called drugs while others are not. We commonly consider heroin a drug but often fail to give that same label to nicotine, even though both produce physical dependency with prolonged use. We usually consider marijuana to be a drug but do not always apply the same label to cola soft drinks, even though both are used recreationally and share a number of common properties. In some respects, the definition of "drug" is not nearly as important as its connotation. The social connotation of a term refers to how it is used in society, thus its context and meaning beyond the word's formal definition. The term "drug" contains two morally opposing connotations, each of which relates to how the drug is used: (1) a substance used in medicine, under controlled circumstances, to help people with a medical problem; or (2) a substance used illegally, under clandestine circumstances, with the effect of harm either to the user and/or to others. The former connotation refers to a "normal" circumstance, the latter implies deviant drug use.

These connotations—one socially approved, the other disapproved—can be used for the very same drug, depending on the circumstances. Opiates are "good" if used under medically approved circumstances to help relieve pain in a patient. However, they are "bad" if used illegally outside a medical context and/or for physical self-gratification. To make matters even more confusing, the same individual can use drugs legally at one time and illegally at another. The medical profession has a high number of addicts compared to other professions. Medical professionals can administer a legal drug appropriately at one time, such as to a patient, and administer that same legal drug inappropriately at another time, such as to themselves to get high.

The connotations for some drugs are so powerful that they are considered deviant regardless of the medical context. Heroin, for example, is an extremely powerful painkiller that has not been approved for medical use in the United States despite that it is more effective than morphine, its medical cousin.

Contemporary concern over drugs is widespread and has often reached the level of public hysteria. The present "War on Drugs" has failed to take into account two points having to do with the overall context in which drug taking is found. First, public concern over drugs is extremely faddish. For instance, some drugs are considered to be "in" at certain times; at other times they are "out." That is, public concern about drugs focuses for a short time on a particular drug and then moves on to another, independent of any characteristic of the drug or the result of the public attention. In the 1960s, marijuana was of great concern. In the 1970s, there was much national discussion about methaqualone or "Quaaludes" and "Angel Dust." Heroin is always in vogue in drug discussions, but it appeared to be an epidemic in the 1970s. Through the mid-1980s, cocaine and heroin were the most talked about drugs. In the 1990s, it is crack cocaine, though there is some evidence that heroin is again surfacing as a drug of choice among many users. In each instance, the law has been perceived as not only the preferred method of intervention but the most effective as well—as long as, that is, the penalties are high enough.

Second, drug-taking behavior in general is so much a part of the behavioral patterns of people in the United States that it is inconceivable that all segments of the American public will abstain from all drug use. Legal drug use is so common that it is virtually unrecognized as drug use at all. Many people do not consider coffee, cigarettes, or soft drinks as drugs or substances containing drugs.

Drug taking is learned initially by most persons in the context of using legally available drugs. Taking such drugs is the first time most of us experience the association between chemical substances and desired end-results, such as reducing headaches, increasing bowel regularity, suppressing appetite, clearing stuffed noses, or keeping us awake at night. This connection is crucial because some of the desired end results involve certain moods that can be produced only by certain drugs, some of which are illegal.

Most of our concern with drugs has been focused on relatively few substances, most of which are against the law to use. These substances, including marijuana, heroin, cocaine, and methamphetamines, share two important characteristics: (1) we have defined them as a "problem," and (2) we believe the law is the best means to solve this problem. Both of these characteristics have been questioned, especially in recent years, and one source of that doubt is the role of all drugs in our daily lives and the ways in which illegal drugs are used.

Patterns of Drug Use

Many Americans wake up in the morning with one drug on their mind: coffee (in effect, caffeine). At work, they may feel the need for a mid-morning drug (aspirin) as pressures build, then another drug (alcohol) at lunch. A mid-afternoon break may involve a cigarette (nicotine) and a cola (more caffeine). Then cocktails (alcohol) before supper, with wine (more alcohol) perhaps during the meal. Then an after-dinner drink, followed by another cigarette (how many drugs is that for the day?). At bedtime, some people need pills to stay awake, others want pills to sleep. At different times during the day, we might have consumed a prescription medicine for an illness or taken some over-the-counter cold remedy to relieve congestion. The next day, the cycle starts all over again.

Drugs are connected to several features of American life (especially television commercials) that promote their use. First, as previously suggested, there is a close connection in the minds of most people between drugs and physical well-being. For example, we come to learn that various physical discomforts can be alleviated with drugs. So if you have a headache, take aspirin. Upset stomach? Take Alka-Seltzer. Menstrual cramps? Athletes foot? Pains of any kind? The solution to all these problems is the same: drugs.

Second, the use of a drug like alcohol is often associated with certain social and life events and just as often dissociated with any discussion of drugs, particularly among lay people. Even the oft-used phrase "drugs and alcohol" suggests that alcohol is not a drug. Yet alcohol is a widely recognized drug, one that is frequently used in the United States. Although most people do not drink heavily, some people consume large amounts of alcohol with considerable regularity—as clearly evidenced by countless Alcoholics Anonymous meetings across the country. For many, though certainly not everyone, drinking is closely associated with particular social or religious occasions. The following are among those occasions that commonly require alcohol consumption:

Birthdays

New Year's Eve celebration

Parties

Celebrating a job or promotion

Getting fired or demoted

Birth of a baby

Wake or funeral

Sporting events

Dates

Religious ceremonies

Graduations

Weddings

Meals

Hospitalization

Recovery

Meetings with friends

"Night-caps"

Saturday nights

There are as many occasions for drinking as there are for greeting cards. And of course, some people don't need any occasion at all to drink.

Third, drug taking is also closely associated with the attainment of desired moods or psychological well-being. If we happen to have a mood that we do not like, we can alter it with drugs. Sometimes, we can generate a new mood (e.g., euphoria) or alter an existing one (e.g., depression) with the same drug. It is the mood-altering property of some drugs that has both attracted and repelled many potential users, thus adding to the ambivalence many people experience about drugs. An example of this ambivalence is reflected in a *Time* magazine cover story a few years before cocaine grabbed national headlines. The cover illustrated a martini glass filled with white powder with the caption, "Cocaine: A Drug with Status—and Menace." In the story, cocaine was described as "no more harmful than equally moderate doses of alcohol and marijuana, and infinitely less so than heroin" (Baum, 1996:142).

In these ways, drugs are seen by many as being very versatile as well as functional. Yet, regardless of specific pharmacological properties, some of the drugs that help create physical and mental well-being and contribute to the meaning of social and religious events are illegal. They are either closely regulated by law, to be dispensed only by a physician and pharmacist, or they are illegal under all circumstances. Yet, patterns of the use of illegal drugs do not differ in many respects from the use of legal drugs. In fact, there are many similarities between the consumption patterns we see with alcohol and those associated with such illegal drugs as marijuana, heroin, and cocaine.

Illegal Drug Use: Marijuana

Marijuana is the most widely used illicit drug in the United States, based on the percentage of the population that is known to use the drug. The manufacture, sale, and use of marijuana is a crime in the United States, although some jurisdictions have reduced the penalty for possession of a small amount of marijuana to a misdemeanor. At the other extreme, some states have historically had very severe penalties associated with the possession of marijuana, including life imprisonment. Some other countries, such as the Netherlands, make marijuana illegal but tolerate its sale.

Marijuana use patterns in the United States show that it is confined mainly to persons in their twenties and younger (Goode, 1993). Much of this use is irregular, and there are many people who have tried the drug once and not repeated the experience. Experimentation and continued use among people over 35 is rare but not unheard of. Marijuana use is found in all social classes, but it may be higher in the lower class than in other socioeconomic groups. This situation may reflect differences in the choice of drugs by social class. At the present time, about a quarter of the total American population has used marijuana at least once.

In 1972, the National Commission on Marijuana and Drug Abuse reported from surveys in the United States that an estimated 24 million people had tried marijuana. Of this number, 8,300,000 generally used it less than once a week, and there were about 500,000 "heavy" users, those who used it more than once a day (National Commission on Marijuana and Drug Abuse, 1972).

There is continued concern over the use of marijuana among younger people, especially adolescents. The National Institute of Drug Abuse (NIDA) sponsors an annual survey of roughly 50,000 high school students about their self-reported drug use. These surveys—often referred to as the "Monitoring the Future Study"—report that although marijuana use has declined, a sizable proportion of high school students indicated they had used the drug at least once. In the late 1970s, more than 60 percent of all high school seniors reported they had ever used marijuana, but by 1994, the figure was less than one-third. Smaller proportions of ever having used were reported by older respondents. One of the reasons for this overall reduction in marijuana usage is that high school seniors have been more likely in recent years to perceive greater risk—physical, medical, or legal—in smoking marijuana than during the years of peak usage.

The most recent survey, however, has reported an increase both in the prevalence and daily use of marijuana (Johnston et al., 1995). The survey indicated that about one in 20 (5 percent) high school seniors reported daily use of marijuana. The reasons for this increase, according to the investigators, parallel those for the declines in use from recent years: changes in the degree of social disapproval for drug use.

> Teens from a decade ago knew more about drugs because there were more people around them who were users, and they could observe the effects of drug use first hand, or, in the case of public figures, through the media. They were also hearing more about drugs from the news and public service announcements. . . . Also, parents of a decade ago may have been more likely than today's parents to talk to their children about drugs, because more of today's parents actually used drugs when they were teens and may feel hypocritical telling their own teens not to use. (Johnston et al., 1995:6)

It is not, in other words, changes in the legal penalties that account for fluctuations in use among young people but changes in non-legal or social control approaches, such as the national "Just Say No to Drugs" campaign. To the extent that young people perceive health risks and/or strong social disapproval with the use of drugs, they are less likely to use them. Rates of disapproval of occasional marijuana use among twelfth-graders began to drop around 1992; at about the same time, rates of occasional marijuana use among these students began to increase (see also Bennett et al., 1996:155).

The use of marijuana is essentially a group activity, lending itself to occasions that promote friendships and participation in a social setting. Marijuana is usually smoked in intimate, or primary, groups as part of a pattern of their social relations. Marijuana use contributes to long-term social relations, to a certain degree of value consensus within a group, to a convergence of values as a result of progressive group involvement, and to the maintenance of a group's cohesive nature, among other things (Goode, 1993:190-192). These are similar to the benefits that alcohol sometimes offers to middle-class groups that use alcoholic beverages as "social lubricants" at a party. The group nature of marijuana use is also sometimes necessary because interpersonal contacts are needed in order to get a supply of marijuana, to learn the special technique of smoking to gain maximum effect, and to furnish psychological support for continuing to engage in an illicit activity.

Illegal Drug Use: Heroin

Patterns in the use of heroin, a narcotic, are slightly different from those of marijuana for a number of reasons, including the physical consequences of prolonged heroin use, the usual method in which the drug is used, and that law enforcement has made the criminal-law control of narcotic drug use a higher priority over the years than the social control of non-narcotic drugs.

People have used heroin for thousands of years, but patterns of heroin use have changed over time. In the nineteenth century, for example, about two-thirds of the users were women, and addiction in the medical profession was widely acknowledged (Morgan, 1981). The average age of addicts was then between 40 and 50, and some investigators believed that addiction was a problem of middle age, as most addicts took up the habit after the age of 30 (Lindesmith and Gagnon, 1964:164-165).

Heroin use expanded in the United States during the middle of the twentieth century. The first documented widespread use in large cities was reported after 1945 (Hunt and Chambers, 1976:53). It remained at low levels through the 1950s, then increased rapidly during the 1960s (see the review in Clinard and Meier, 1995: Chapter 8). Levels of use seemed to reach a peak in most cities during 1968 and 1969. By 1971, all large cities—those over one million in population—had experienced their peak, although smaller city use continued to increase during the 1970s. Patterns throughout the 1980s suggested that the levels of addiction present in the late 1970s appeared to level off, with estimates of the number of heroin addicts in the early 1980s being close to those believed to exist in the late 1970s (Trebach, 1982; Trebach, 1987). Although heroin addiction is not a growing problem in the 1990s (Reuter, 1995), there are still as many addicts today as there were two or three decades ago. And although the number of addicts may not be increasing, heroin appears to have become popular among young celebrities, especially in the music industry. The deaths of such musicians as Kurt Cobain and Shannon Hoon and the overdose of members of Hoon's "Blind Melon" band all suggest that heroin may be gaining adherents once again.

Not all heroin users are addicts. Some estimates suggest there may be about 500,000 heroin addicts (persons who use heroin every day) with an additional 3.5 million "chippers" (occasional users) in this country (Trebach, 1982:3-4). The existence of so many occasional heroin users suggests that the addiction process is not simply a result of the physical properties of heroin; other factors are involved. Addiction takes place over time and appears to be facilitated by the intravenous method of administering the drug. There are disagreements on the exact causes of addiction, but there is no mistaking the difficulty of overcoming the addiction once it occurs. Rates of relapse are very high with most forms of heroin-addiction treatment.

The United States may lead all countries in the number of heroin addicts, although such estimates are always extremely speculative. An international survey of research scientists and physicians in 25 countries published in 1977 reported that the largest number of opiate addicts in the general population was in the United States with 620,000, followed by Iran with 400,000, Thailand with 350,000, Hong Kong with 80,000, Canada with 18,000, Singapore with 13,000, Australia with 12,500, Italy with 10,000, and the United Kingdom with 6,000 (Trebach, 1982:6-7).

Heroin use among persons under 20 years of age is not common. The National Institute of Drug Abuse (NIDA) national survey of high school youth mentioned earlier typically finds that very few students report ever having tried heroin. Recent estimates place the figure at 2 percent or less depending on the grade of the student (Johnston, Bachman and O'Malley, 1995). Figures of reported heroin use among young adults are also very low—1 percent or less.

Addiction to opiates is now heavily concentrated among young, urban, lower-class males from large cities, particularly among blacks and Puerto Ricans. The high heroin addiction rates among blacks is partly a product of the concentration of heroin distribution traffic in many black urban areas. This facilitates the development of a street-addict subculture. The proportion of all addicts who are black is perhaps 30 percent, with the highest concentration in the northeastern part of the United States (Chambers and Harter, 1987).

The linking of the disease AIDS to the use of contaminated needles has generated substantial fear among heroin addicts. The extent of AIDS among addict populations is not known but may be very high. We do know that the percentage of addicts who have AIDS in Europe has been increasing in recent years, prompting such countries as Switzerland to set up areas in cities where addicts can obtain sterilized needles free from legal intervention. The Centers for Disease Control and Prevention estimates that most of the new AIDS cases in the United States will occur among those sharing dirty needles, not among homosexuals.

Programs of clean-needle exchange are controversial. Critics charge that such practices may encourage illegal drug use, there is some deterrent effect from the possibility of AIDS. Supporters of such programs claim that addiction exists largely independent of AIDS and that even prolonged use of heroin does not result in major health problems, unlike the use of many other drugs. As a result, these supporters suggest that addicts have more to fear from AIDS than from their drugs; and of course, AIDS can be spread to non-addicts.

These were the issues in 1996 in New Jersey when an advisory council on AIDS recommended that the state allow needle exchange programs and the sale of syringes with a prescription at pharmacies (*New York Times*, April 4, 1996, p. B8). The council also recommended that such programs offer other services, such as AIDS education and counseling and referrals to drug-treatment programs. The stimulus for the council's recommendation was that intravenous drug use accounted for 51 percent of the state's AIDS cases from the early 1980s through December 1995.

Along with the concern over AIDS, some have worried about the impact of changes in the economics of heroin. An increase in the world supply of heroin in the 1990s has had the effect of lowering the price of the drug in many markets, including the United States. This price reduction has rendered the drug more available to a larger number of potential users than in previous decades. There is no evidence, however, that the number of addicts has increased as a result of this change in the heroin economy. In fact, there is reason to believe that it is neither economics nor criminal law that prevents most people from using heroin; rather, it is the distinct possibility and fear of addiction.

Illegal Drug Use: Cocaine

Although cocaine was first isolated in the later 1800s, there was relatively little cocaine use in the United States until the 1970s and 1980s. Long-regarded as a "desirable drug" because of its euphoric effect, the dominant pattern of cocaine use was sporadic and infrequent. The main reason for its infrequent use at that time was its short supply in the United States. As a result, its cost was very high, thereby limiting its availability to people of high income.

The supply of cocaine is related to the way in which the drug is obtained and processed. Cocaine derives from coca leaves that are best grown in the high mountain jungles of Columbia and Peru. The leaves must be harvested and treated chemically to release the cocaine. Inciardi (1986:73-74) describes the processing:

> At [secret, near-by] jungle refineries, the leaves are sold for $8 to $12 a kilo [2.2 pounds]. The leaves are then pulverized, soaked in alcohol mixed with benzol . . . and shaken. The alcohol-benzol mixture is then drained, sulfuric acid is added, and the solution is shaken again. Next, a precipitate is formed when sodium carbonate is added to the solution. When this is washed with kerosene and chilled, crystals of crude cocaine are left behind. These crystals are known as coca paste. The cocaine content of the leaves is relatively low—0.5% to 1.0% by weight as opposed to the paste, which has a cocaine concentration ranging up to 90% but more commonly only about 40%.

Once processed, the cocaine is taken to port cities in South America, then to supply points in the United States. High-speed boats and aircraft are used to smuggle the drug into the country, and a sophisticated system of distribution delivers the drug to users. At each point of the manufacturing and distribution process, the cocaine is diluted with, among other things, baking soda, caffeine, and powdered laxatives. Eventually, it has an average purity of 12 percent and sells on the street for about $100 per gram. With this process, 500 kilograms of coca leaves worth about $4,000 to the grower results in eight kilos of street cocaine worth about $500,000.

The supply of cocaine changed in the 1980s. Improved roads in the coca-growing regions in Columbia permitted the use of large trucks to bring out more leaves from the high mountain jungles. As a result, there was much more exported cocaine than ever before.

This increased availability served to introduce many new users to the drug and, in turn, produced new use patterns. Some forms of the drug are now cheaply obtained. As a result, cocaine is found among all segments of the population and in all areas of the country.

By 1985, a new form of cocaine, called "crack" (or crack-cocaine), was introduced into many urban areas. It is called crack presumably because of the crackling sound it makes when smoked. The substance is manufactured by soaking cocaine hydrochloride and baking soda in water and then applying heat. This results in relatively small crystals about the size of peas. Crack had been available prior to the mid-1980s, but it became popular when it was offered as an alternative to cocaine.

There are a number of reasons for the popularity of crack (Inciardi, Lockwood, and Pottieger, 1993:7). First, it can be smoked rather than snorted, thus more rapidly absorbed into the body. It offers a very quick "high." Second, crack is cheaper than cocaine. A gram of cocaine for snorting might cost $60 or more depending on its purity, but the same gram can be transformed into anywhere from five to thirty crack rocks. For the user, individual rocks can be purchased for as little as $2, depending on the size. This has helped spread the drug to the young and to poor people. Third, crack is easily hidden and transportable, which facilitates illicit transactions.

Powder cocaine, the "champagne" of drugs, produces a relatively short euphoric experience, which is a main reason why some people use multiple doses, often up to 10 doses per day (Cox et al., 1983). The user is said to suffer no ill side effects, such as hangover, physical addiction, lung cancer, risk from dirty syringes, or burned-out brain cells (Inciardi, 1986:78). The cocaine euphoria is immediate and almost universally regarded as pleasurable. Because it seemed to have few negative side effects, cocaine developed a reputation as being an "ideal" drug. In 1974, one of President Jimmy Carter's assistants claimed that "cocaine . . . is probably the most benign of illicit drugs" (Walters, 1996).

There may be as many as 1.5 million cocaine users in the United States, most of whom are occasional users. The annual Monitoring the Future survey of drug use found that the proportion of high school seniors who had used cocaine had reached a peak of about 12 percent in 1985 and had declined since that time (Johnston, Bachman and O'Malley, 1993:83). By 1995, only 6 percent of high school seniors had ever tried cocaine and only 1 percent had used it during the previous month (Johnston, Bachman and O'Malley, 1995). The figures are even smaller for the use of crack cocaine. Judging from what people are spending on illegal drugs, a subject to be discussed shortly, it appears that cocaine use—and the use of other illegal drugs—may be declining in the United States. A Rand Corporation study, drawing from several sources, reported a general decrease in the use of illicit drugs in the United States since the mid-1980s (Reuter, 1995). The most likely explanation for this reduction is not law enforcement efforts, but is probably related more to increased social disapproval and the perceived health hazards, including the fear of disease such as AIDS. It is also the case that illegal drugs are expensive. The cost exerts its own preventative effect.

Indicators of increased illicit drug use in younger age categories suggest that the reversal of drug use declines may be over in the United States, but these estimates of use among junior- and high-school youth show relatively small increases, so it is not possible to extrapolate trends from such statistics.

How Much Do Illegal Drugs Cost?

America's users spend a great deal of money on their illegal drugs, as their illegal status helps keep prices high. When any commodity is illegal, there likely will be no competing manufacturers, as well as no competitive system of distribution and sales. Everything must move underground. Supplying drug users is a risky proposition. The price goes up to compensate for the risks.

It is obviously difficult to determine how much users of illegal drugs spend, but some estimates have been offered. A study by Abt Associates, Inc. released in 1995 reported that the amounts are very high (Office of National Drug Control Policy, 1995). In 1993, for example, it was estimated that Americans spent $49 billion on the following drugs: $31 billion on cocaine, $7 billion on heroin, $9 billion on marijuana, and $2 billion on other illegal drugs and illicitly sold legal drugs. These estimates do not include "income in kind" payments. Other forms of exchange also create value. Dealers often keep drugs for personal use, users sometimes help dealers in exchange for payment in drugs, and some users perform sex for drugs, particularly for crack cocaine. When these additional values are added to cash payments, the total spent on illegal drugs increases an estimated $10 billion or more.

By any measure, these costs are staggering. Such figures are even higher when one considers that they are part of the underground economy where no overhead is assessed and no taxes paid. They also do not include the costs of making drugs illegal, the main expenditure being the cost of drug enforcement.

The Abt study also estimated trends in illegal drug use from 1988 to 1993 by estimating the supply. Measured in metric tons per year, the supply of drugs reported by the study has actually decreased along with the price of such drugs. So, the amount of cocaine on American streets in 1993 was less than that in 1988. There was a similar trend with prices and purchases; Americans spent about $64 billion on illegal drugs in 1988 but only about $49 billion in 1993.

The Relationship Between Crime and Drugs

People arrested for crimes frequently test positive for recent drug use (Bureau of Justice Statistics, 1995). Data collected from male arrestees in 1992 in 24 cities showed that the percentage of those testing positive for drugs ranged from 42 percent to 79 percent and for females the range was from 38 percent to 85 percent. Such figures are generally consistent with estimates obtained from the annual survey of victims in the National Crime Victimization Survey. According to the 1992 survey, about half of the victims were unable to determine whether the offender had used drugs, but in those crimes where victims believed they could make a determination, nearly 60 percent reported that the offender was under the influence of alcohol and/or drugs at the time of the crime.

Such figures point strongly to a relationship between drugs and crime, but they are not helpful in determining exactly what the nature of that relationship might be. We know that drugs are related to crime in different ways. Some crimes are defined in terms of drugs (e.g., the manufacture of illegal substances), the effects of some drugs that may be related to the commission of crimes (e.g., alcohol-based assaults), or to the lifestyle of certain drug users (e.g., committing a crime to obtain money to buy an illegal drug).

Drug-Defined Crimes

There are a number of current laws that prohibit the manufacture, sale, and consumption of particular drugs, such as heroin. In addition to illicit drugs, there are other drugs whose consumption and manufacture are merely controlled, such as alcohol and prescription medicines. Narcotics, for example, are drugs that can lead to physical dependency or addiction and are controlled and limited to medical use. The concept of "addiction" usually entails the development of tolerance, or the need for greater amounts of the drug to induce the same effect. The nonmedical use of most narcotics (other than nicotine and caffeine) is illegal in the United States. Other drugs, such as Darvon, are illegal for general use but they may be prescribed by a physician for medical purposes.

Narcotics are not the only legally prohibited drugs. Other drugs, such as hallucinogens—a category that includes marijuana, hashish, and LSD—are also illegal even though they are not narcotics. Hallucinogens are mood-altering drugs and although there are some medical uses for them, such as the treatment of certain eye disorders, their manufacture and sale are presently illegal. Stimulants (e.g., amphetamines) are closely regulated by law, and some are used for medical purposes. Still other drugs are legal, such as alcoholic beverages, but their sale is limited in terms of age (those over 21 years old), times (Sunday sales are not permitted in some jurisdictions), and places (e.g., taverns but not in a moving vehicle).

The Federal Bureau of Investigation (1995:164) recorded more than a million arrests in 1994 for drug violations. About two-thirds of the arrests were for possession rather than manufacture or sale, and most of the possession arrests were for marijuana. In fact, nearly half of all drug arrests were for possession of marijuana.

Drug-Related Crimes

Drug-related crimes are those in which a drug's effect contributes to the commission of a crime. Alcohol, for example, has been found to be related to certain violent crimes, including assault and murder. In his classic study of homicide, Wolfgang (1958) found that alcohol was involved in about two-thirds of the homicides he investigated. In nearly 40 percent of the cases, both the offender and the victim had been drinking. Alcohol is also a factor in many instances of domestic violence and assaults. Oliver (1994:15-16) summarizes the results of a number of studies that link alcohol and drugs with violent conduct, including homicide, assault, and robbery. It is clear that the use of alcohol and certain drugs facilitates the commission of other crimes.

The effects of drugs may also be related to crime in another sense. Some crimes are motivated by the need of the offender to obtain money to support continued drug use. Heroin addicts, for example, require substantial sums of money to purchase their drug, but the typical heroin addict is unable to raise the sums needed for a number of compelling reasons (see Stephens, 1991). First, because heroin is illegal, the price is high; dealers are willing to risk arrest and imprisonment, but the rewards must be significant. This drives the price up. Second, most addicts do not have the kind of legitimate occupations that will generate enough income for their drugs. They do not have high levels of education or sophisticated job skills. Third, the lifestyle of the addict revolves around taking, enjoying, tolerating, or withdrawing from drugs. As a result, most addicts have neither the money, abilities, nor time to cope with their addiction without resorting to crime. Stealing (and, for some women, prostitution) requires little long-term commitment and if successful, provides an immediate return with which to obtain their drug.

Drug-Using Crimes

Many drug-users are recreational or occasional users of drugs, but others exist in a lifestyle that centers around drugs. Some criminologists have long observed that one of the most undesirable consequences of drug laws is that they drive drug users underground and into contact with more serious criminals. Because of their participation in a drug-using subculture, they are exposed to further criminal opportunities. Some of these opportunities will be important in providing money to purchase more drugs.

The distinction between "drug user" and "drug distributor" is often blurred. Although the terms "kingpin" and "pusher" suggest that those who manufacture or distribute illegal drugs are different from those who use them, this distinction is difficult to maintain on the streets. Many heroin addicts will also distribute the drug to other users in exchange for a personal supply of the drug, and most marijuana smokers appear to be both users and dealers with their friends.

Current Drug Policies and How We Got There

The overall policy in the United States with respect to drugs is one of legal repression. That is, the United States relies primarily on the criminal law to control the supply of many drugs and to bring drug users together with treatment programs to reduce demand. The criminal law is at the core of the basic policy regarding drugs, although many of the goals of this policy cannot be achieved through the law.

Current drug policy reflects the repressive actions taken in earlier years. In 1971, President Nixon appointed National Security Advisor Henry Kissinger to coordinate drug control efforts in the Departments of State and Justice (Walters, 1996). Turkey was targeted as a point of intervention because about 80 percent of the world's heroin came from there. France also received attention because most of the Turkish heroin was refined there. President Nixon's efforts were directed mainly toward reducing the supply of illicit drugs. The creation of the Drug Enforcement Agency (DEA) in 1973 was the culmination of his efforts, but he did not end heroin addiction. By the early 1970s, Mexican suppliers were able to offer addicts low-quality "black tar" heroin to meet their needs.

President Nixon pursued an aggressive policy, but the Carter administration was relatively inactive in drug matters, although the president did call on Congress to decriminalize marijuana possession. One of his drug advisors, Dr. Peter Bourne, even went so far as to recommend the decriminalization of cocaine in 1977. President Carter maintained the DEA but did not reinforce either its resources or message.

Drug efforts during the Reagan and Bush presidencies were sporadic but concentrated generally on interdiction. The use of military personnel, primarily the Coast Guard, and a reliance on the DEA constituted the main weapons against drugs, although treatment was not neglected completely. First Lady Nancy Reagan, for example, was instrumental in facilitating a series of drug-treatment programs utilizing space in local hospitals. These so-called "care units" were short-term programs of usually one month or less. When President Bush took office in 1988, he continued the theme, begun in the Reagan years, of "Just Say No!" to drugs.

The Office of National Drug Control Policy (ONDCP), founded in 1988, is the component of the federal government charged with directing the "war on drugs." The national strategy, as articulated by the ONDCP, defines drugs as essentially a legal problem, although there are many medical and social dimensions as well. Public policy, however, seems to demand a meaning of illegal drugs that essentially captures both their undesirable characteristics and our faith in the law to reduce or eliminate them.

The ONDCP states that the overarching goal for the current drug control strategy is the reduction of the number of drug users in the United States (The Office of National Drug Control Policy, 1995). The strategy outlines various major goals that are categorized as demand reduction (to reduce the demand for drugs), domestic law enforcement (to reduce drug-related crime), and international goals (to increase international cooperation, such as the effort to reduce international drug trafficking). Although not all the specific objectives within each of these broad categories would entail the use of law enforcement (e.g., expansion of treatment facilities for addicts), the law is the primary weapon in drug control strategy.

The most recent version of the drug control approach was introduced on April 30, 1996, by President Clinton. The plan maintains a focus on reducing both supply and demands for illicit drugs; about two-thirds of the budget for the plan deals with reducing supply, about one-third with increasing treatment and preventative efforts. There is particular attention to methamphetamines, an addictive stimulant whose use has been increasing in some parts of the country. The current plan calls for mandatory minimum sentences for the sale of methamphetamines, sentences equivalent to those presently imposed for crack cocaine.

The Clinton ONDCP policy is a product of a particular political time and climate, though the policies of previous administrations were very similar. The Bush and Reagan presidencies, for example, also laid heavy emphasis on the use of law enforcement and military personnel to interdict drugs from coming into the United States. President Clinton attempts to balance a bit more than did Bush and Reagan the extent to which the focus should be on reducing demand for drugs rather than attempting only to reduce the supply. But the difference is a matter of degree.

Drugs, Race, and Ethnicity

American awareness of drug taking, and the subsequent rise of a legal response to this behavior, began in the 1800s, at a time when many patent medicines contained what would later be considered illegal drugs, particularly opiate derivatives (Inciardi, 1986: Chapter 1). These drugs, as well as raw opium, were widely used in the nineteenth century in the United States, particularly by women who took them for "female disorders." At that time, many of the drugs could be easily and legally purchased. Two important drugs are derived from opium—morphine, a potent drug that was isolated initially in 1804, and heroin, which is about three times more powerful than morphine, first isolated in 1898. In fact, heroin was originally manufactured by pharmaceutical chemists to be sold over drugstore counters as a cough remedy. Cocaine was first isolated in the late 1850s, but it did not become popular in the United States until the 1880s, when it was proclaimed a wonder drug and sold in wine products as a stimulant (Morgan, 1981:16).

Even the intravenous ingestion of morphine was not uncommon at the time. The 1897 edition of the Sears Roebuck catalog, for example, contained hypodermic kits that included a syringe, two needles, two vials, and a carrying case. The cost: $1.50. Extra needles were available for 25 cents or $2.75 per dozen (Inciardi, 1986:5-6).

As shocking as this may seem by today's anti-drug standards, it was not this kind of drug taking that was of major public concern. That concern was later motivated not by the drugs themselves but by the kinds of people who used them. Some of the initial laws against drugs were directed at particular groups of opiate users, such as the Chinese and Mexicans. Patterns of opiate use were quite different around the turn of the century than they are in present-day cities.

One of the earliest laws on opiates was passed in 1875 in the city of San Francisco. It prohibited the smoking of opium in then-popular opium dens (Brecher, 1972). The law was fueled by the public fear that Chinese men were luring white women into these dens for sexual purposes. Few Americans understood that opium dens occupied roughly the same position in Chinese culture as that of the saloon in white American culture. Although there were some opium addicts, most Chinese used opium infrequently and mainly on social occasions.

This first law displayed a number of characteristics that would be found in many of its successors: It prohibited the use of a particular drug associated with a particular group, without apparent regard to the physiological properties of the drug. In other words, it was not the physical effects of the opium or opiate derivatives that concerned lawmakers, but—in this case—the use of the drug by the Chinese.

The racial nature of the law was reflected in a number of its ingredients. The law ignored opium and other products made from opium that were used by whites in over-the-counter substances and in different forms (i.e., liquid, powder, or pill form). Instead, it focused on the smoking of opium in specially designated areas (i.e., opium dens). In other words, one could consume opium, but not by smoking and not in dens.

Federal drug legislation followed this city ordinance in 1888. As with the San Francisco city law, the federal legislation attempted to restrict opium trading and smoking. As with the city ordinance, the federal law did not prohibit the use of opium itself, only how it was consumed; nor did it prohibit the sale and use of opium in the form that involved most whites nor restrict the actions of whites engaged in opium trade.

There was apparently little concern with drug addiction in the late 1800s, at least no more than with drunkenness. But social awareness of addiction increased in the first quarter of the twentieth century. That concern eventually generated legislation, such as the Pure Food and Drug Act of 1906 and the Harrison Act of 1914. The intent of the Pure Food and Drug Act was to regulate the manufacture of patent medicines and over-the-counter drugs that contained heroin and cocaine, but the effect was to make such substances illegal. The Harrison Act was initially a revenue measure designed to make drug transactions a matter of public record so that taxes could be paid on them. But it became a major piece of legislation that defined narcotic drug taking as illegal (which included cocaine as a narcotic, although it is not a narcotic) and defined as criminals all those who took those drugs.

One might think that the intent of the legislation was to control addiction, but it was not merely the fear of addiction that fueled this legislation. Samuel Gompers, president of the American Federation of Labor from 1886 to 1924, reportedly used racist imagery to accelerate drug legislation. Walter Hill writes:

> Gompers conjures up a terrible picture of how the Chinese entice little white boys and girls into becoming "opium fiends." Condemned to spend their days in the back of laundry rooms, these tiny lost souls would yield up their virgin bodies to their maniacal yellow captors. "What other crimes were committed in those dark fetid places," Gompers writes, "when these little innocent victims of the Chinamen's wiles were under the influence of the drug, are almost too horrible to imagine. . . . There are hundreds, aye, thousands, of our American girls and boys who have acquired this deathly habit and are doomed, hopelessly doomed, beyond the shadow of redemption." (Hill, 1973:51)

Subsequent legislation broadened the definition of illegal drugs to include marijuana and hashish. Because it does not dissolve in water, marijuana cannot be injected; it must be taken orally by smoking and eating, and its effects are variable and slow. As a result, research on the medical use of marijuana never materialized to the degree of research on the opiate drugs and cocaine. Even today, although there is reason to believe that marijuana might be useful in some limited medical situations, it does not have the cloak of medical legitimization worn by many other drugs. Noteworthy, though, was the passage of referendums in 1996 in both Arizona and California to allow marijuana use on a doctor's order to ease pain, such as that associated with cancer. Early in 1997, Attorney General Janet Reno announced that federal agents would withdraw drug-prescribing privileges and perhaps prosecute criminally physicians who "pushed" marijuana for their patients on the basis of the new California and Arizona statutes. Reno maintains that the referendums represented illegal intrusion by the states into a matter controlled by federal law.

As with other drugs that were subsequently made illegal, marijuana use was associated initially with marginal social groups. Large-scale use around the turn of the century was reported among migrant workers in the U.S. Southwest. Eventually, as marijuana users migrated to urban areas, its use spread to other urban immigrant groups, such as African Americans. Some occupational groups were closely associated with marijuana; jazz musicians, for example, reportedly had especially high rates of marijuana use through the 1920s and 1930s. Spurred by the vigorous campaign of Harry Anslinger, Commissioner of the Treasury Department's Bureau of Narcotics, marijuana legislation was not long in coming. The use of marijuana outside the mainstream of white, middle-class society, and the lobbying efforts of the Bureau of Narcotics resulted in the Marijuana Tax Act of 1937.

The racist motivation of this early legislation is unmistakable, as is the fear generated by certain drugs. Throughout the twentieth century, it has been the characteristics of users, not those of the drugs, that have been the better predictors of drug laws. The inmates who rioted in the federal prisons in 1995 over the penalty disparity between crack and powder cocaine may not have been informed about the racial nature of drug laws, but they probably would not have been surprised by it either.

The Prohibition Experience

During the first part of this century, the United States experienced a major effort to control drugs by the use of criminal law. The first—and most important—was the enactment of the Eighteenth Amendment to the Constitution, popularly known as "Prohibition." It prohibited the production, sale, and distribution of alcohol for purposes of consumption and remained in effect from 1920 to 1933. Prohibition resulted from the efforts of groups of citizens who became moral crusaders seeking to persuade others of the sins of alcohol consumption and the need to enact the law to solve the problem. Public drinking, often done in taverns and largely concentrated among lower-class citizens, was the immediate target for temperance groups. These groups believed strongly that alcohol consumption was bad both for people and their behavior. Drinking was also condemned as a reflection of the absence of moral values.

Motivated less by racial than by class and moral differences, prohibition was controversial at the time and has remained so today. It is claimed by some that Prohibition was a failure, that it was unable to stop the consumption of alcoholic beverages, and that in various ways, it made drinking problems worse. Others claim that Prohibition, while not successful in every respect, did accomplish much to reduce problems associated with heavy drinking.

Regardless of one's position on the consequences of Prohibition, our interest lies in the use of the law to solve drug problems, including those related to alcohol, marijuana, heroin, and cocaine. There are a number of arguments that have been raised against a legal solution to drug and alcohol problems. The major ones are summarized here with respect to Prohibition, but most of them are applicable as well to the legal prohibition of other drugs. These arguments, adapted from McWilliams (1993:70-79), are listed as follows:

1. *Prohibition created disrespect for law.* Prohibition was immediately unpopular among many different types of individuals, particularly those involved in the manufacture, distribution, sale, and consumption of alcoholic beverages, who found obvious and self-interested fault with the legislation. But so too did many others, including those who did not drink frequently or heavily. Their objections reflected a different position on the use of alcohol. Those who did not believe that drinking was wrong, and those who violated the law because of that belief, may have broadened their negative feelings about Prohibition toward other laws as well. As a result, many otherwise law-abiding citizens broke the law.

2. *Prohibition eroded respect for organized religion.* The Prohibition movement was essentially a middle-class Protestant movement. Bolstered by Biblical pronouncements regarding the misuse of alcohol, as well as a faith in the ability of Protestantism to create a better world, Prohibitionists justified their actions not only in terms of reducing a social problem (i.e., alcoholism), but also on the basis of high moral principle (Timberlake, 1963: Chapter 1). Prohibitionists made much of the terrible toll drinking took upon the drinker's family and employer. What they might have underestimated was the number of people who drank alcoholic beverages without the kind of costs incurred by such heavy drinkers as alcoholics. And as Prohibition failed, it undercut organized religion, which was considered responsible for its unsuccessful policy.

3. *Prohibition greatly expanded the power of organized crime.* Organized criminal syndicates existed in the United States prior to Prohibition, but their activities were confined to local areas and their operations limited. With the advent of Prohibition, these syndicates expanded their horizons and increased their power by meeting the demands of those segments of the public eager to drink. Some syn-

dicates, such as those in Chicago, became very wealthy and their leaders extremely powerful, not only in matters of organized crime but in legitimate politics as well.

4. *Prohibition corrupted the criminal justice system.* Police, judges, and correctional personnel were contaminated by organized crime's exploitation of Prohibition and the money earned from it. Criminal justice officials were often bribed to look the other way in regard to bootleggers and others involved in the illegal alcohol trade. In some instances, the high profits that syndicates generated underwrote a long-lasting relationship with criminal justice officials that would extend well beyond the period of Prohibition.

5. *Prohibition overburdened the criminal justice system.* The caseload of criminal justice systems in many jurisdictions escalated as a result of Prohibition. Although this is almost inevitably true for any newly outlawed behavior, the volume of alcohol cases was extremely high during the 1920s, particularly in the larger cities. And as criminal justice officials attempted to deal with the growth of cases of bootlegging, illegal distribution, and illegal sales, these alcohol-related cases kept officials from dealing with other, more serious crimes.

6. *People were harmed financially, emotionally, and morally by Prohibition.* In 1919, those legitimately involved in alcohol production, distribution, and sales were put out of work. It happened quickly, although not without warning, as many jurisdictions had enacted "local options" that prohibited saloons and alcohol by the drink. Nevertheless, the ripple effect of Prohibition sometimes drowned those in the restaurant, sporting, and entertainment industries. It took several decades for these industries to rebound after Prohibition, in large part because the end of Prohibition coincided with the beginning of the Great Depression.

7. *Prohibition caused physical harm.* It is often overlooked that Prohibition in fact physically harmed some people. With only illegally manufactured distilled spirits to drink, there were those who consumed beverages that were poorly made. Some of the people who made illegal alcohol, often in their bathtubs and under less than sanitary and scientifically controlled circumstances, manufactured it incorrectly, putting together concoctions that were deadly. Consumers had no way of knowing the quality of the alcoholic beverages they were consuming.

8. *Prohibition changed the drinking habits of the country—for the worse.* Before Prohibition, Americans were mainly beer drinkers. Some consumed wine, but few were frequent distilled liquor drinkers. After Prohibition, however, more people drank hard liquor. Perhaps as a protest against the law, drinking became more open; the advent of the liquor flask can be traced to Prohibition. Alcohol became something to take along because one could not depend on finding a source at one's destination. Prohibition also changed drinking habits; whereas before, most beer drinking was done at home, now it became more popular in public places.

9. *Prohibition contributed to cigarette smoking as a national habit.* The original use of tobacco can be traced to the first colonists, but pipe and cigar smoking were the most popular forms of tobacco usage until about the turn of the century. Cigarettes grew in popularity after the Civil War, though there was both health and moral concern about their use. This concern led to legislation prohibiting cigarette smoking, particularly among young people. By 1921, cigarettes were illegal in 14 states and bills were pending in 28 others (McWilliams, 1993:77). During Prohibition, smoking had became a symbol of independence, glamour, and sophistication. By 1930, cigarettes were legal virtually everywhere—and as their consumption doubled between 1920 and 1930, they became as irresistible as alcohol (Troyer and Markle, 1983:34).

10. *Prohibition prevented the treatment of drinking problems.* When the Prohibitionists succeeded in making alcohol illegal, there was no standard of moderate drinking; any drinking was considered deviant. As Timberlake (1963:184) notes, "In trying to impose a rigid standard of sobriety on the entire nation by law they had undertaken something that the working classes would not accept and that they themselves would often not obey." Prohibition greatly undermined the notion of moderation, itself an important restraint on drinking.

11. *Prohibition caused "immorality."* Prohibition did not stop drinking, although it did put a dent in it. Not everyone violated the law, but many did. Drinking moved underground; it flourished in speakeasies, which were often not only taverns but also places of "ill repute," where the indulgence of other vices was possible, such as gambling, the use of other drugs, and prostitution. The availability and consumption of drugs other than alcohol also increased during Prohibition, largely because drinking had been outlawed.

12. Prohibition was very expensive. It is difficult to estimate accurately the costs of Prohibition. The total cost would include money used to find alternative employment for those put out of work by Prohibition and the criminal justice costs of enforcing the laws. One such estimate is that Prohibition cost one billion dollars at a time when assembly line workers at the Ford Motor Company were earning $5 a day.

Modern Legal Prohibitions

Prohibition was an expensive and disappointing experience for the United States. Although it probably did curtail drinking for many, including those who had problems with their drinking prior to its enactment, the overall costs of the policy appeared to outweigh the benefits. One lesson learned from Prohibition was the importance of using the law in instances in which public opinion is consistent with its dictates. Just like unpopular wars, unpopular laws are likely to encounter substantial difficulties in seeking their goals.

Conventional images of the law as a powerful entity that can coerce conformity without popular support are incorrect. It is too simplistic to assert that law comes about because most people want it, but it does seem to be the case that there are many laws that cannot exist independently of the people whose behavior they regulate. Prohibition exemplifies this principle, and current drug laws may be another illustration of it.

The Controlled Substances Act of 1970 brought together under one law all of the previous federal statutes in an attempt to provide coherence to the variety of drug laws. Most legislation at the state level dealt mainly with increasing the penalties associated with state drug laws. Possession of even small amounts of marijuana could result in severe penalties, including life imprisonment in some states. Since 1970, penalties in many jurisdictions have abated but only for marijuana. Penalty increases have been fast and furious for most other illegal substances, particularly heroin, cocaine, and methamphetamines.

In the 1980s and 1990s, fueled by public fears of a drug "menace," many states and the federal government instituted mandatory penalties. These statutes were part of a larger movement to reform criminal justice sentencing procedures by reducing judicial discretion over sentencing. Many states shifted from indeterminate to determinate sentencing, with some establishing a set of sentencing guide-lines to determine actual disposition. The effect in many states, as well as in the federal system, has been to lengthen actual time served in prison and to alter the demographic and offense-pattern compo-sition of prison inmates.

In 1980, 57 percent of all state and federal prisoners were incar-cerated for a violent crime. Thirty percent were in prison for prop-erty offenses, 8 percent for drugs, and 5 percent for public order crimes (Beck and Gilliard, 1995). By 1993, only 45 percent of state and federal prisoners were incarcerated for violent crimes, 26 per-cent for drugs, 22 percent for property offenses, and seven percent for public order crimes. In 13 years, the composition of inmates had changed because of alterations in sentencing practices that placed higher priority on drug offenders. Today, there are more inmates who are incarcerated for violent crimes than for any other offense, but there are fewer of them than in 1980; whereas, the number of drug offenders has more than tripled during this time. The new drug laws have been a substantial contributor to prison overcrowding throughout the United States.

During this time, there was clear recognition that drug usage was related to other, more general conditions, and in fact, that those conditions—often called "root causes"—should really be the focus of intervention efforts. When asked to prepare a report on the root causes of drug abuse, William Bennett, the Drug Czar during Presi-dent Reagan's administration, sidestepped the issue. The request recognized that drug use was related to larger problems of poverty, inadequate education, and a host of other social ills. Bennett replied, "We have a drug problem . . . [but] we don't have the time or author-ity to fix the housing or jobs or poverty problems" (Baum, 1996:302). Looking at the root causes of drugs would only dilute the focus on drugs, Bennett reasoned, and going beyond that focus was outside the mandate of the drug office. In addition, of course, focusing only on drugs was a good deal easier than trying to deal with the other social conditions that give rise to them.

The Consequences of the New Drug Laws: The New York State Example

Shortly after the new mandatory penalties and use of sentencing guidelines, states began to experience an increase in the number of admissions to corrections programs for drug offenses, as intended by the legislation. But the numbers were higher than anticipated, and corrections systems were not prepared to deal with the issue of addiction on such a large scale. Although many prisons had some kind of drug treatment program, most of them were not sufficiently organized or large enough to be of much use.

The New York experience is illustrative of the effects of the more stringent drug law penalties of the 1970s and 1980s. Drug penalties were greatly increased by legislation enacted in 1973 under then-Governor Nelson Rockefeller. The effect was to increase dramatically the number of admissions to New York's correctional programs. The figures increased steadily over the next 20 years. In 1974, for example, there had been a total of 713 new prison commitments for drug felonies. By 1992, however, there were more than 11,000 drug felony commitments, with a cumulative total of about 75,000 such commitments.

In the early 1980s, drug offenders accounted for roughly 10 percent of all new court commitments to the New York Department of Corrections. New York prisons had been populated mainly by persons who had committed violent crimes. By 1989, however, persons committing violent crimes totaled no more than 40 percent of the prison population, and drug offenders comprised about 45 percent. These figures are higher than the national figures cited earlier, but New York (particularly New York City) has long been known as the heroin center of the United States. There are more addicts in New York City than in any other city—or state.

The impact of the law is reflected in a "snapshot" of the New York correctional population provided by Thomas Coughlin (1993), the New York State Corrections Commissioner. On May 22, 1993, there were 22,000 inmates doing time for drug crimes out of a total correctional population of 64,000. In other words, about 35 percent of all of New York's inmates were in prison for drug crimes. Of the 22,000 inmates, 600 were convicted of a felony that, were it not for determinate sentencing, could have resulted in a local jail sentence or probation. More than 15,000 of these inmates were second felony offenders, which meant that there was no judicial discretion to impose a sentence other than state prison.

These effects were perhaps predictable but terribly frustrating to corrections officials who must administer the system. New York law now mandates an identical 8- to 25-year maximum sentencing range for a person who commits a forcible rape and for a person who sells a dollar's worth of cocaine. Clearly, the law is not meant to reflect the impact of these crimes on their respective victims.

An International Policy Alternative: The Netherlands Approach to Drug Control

Drugs have long been regarded as a problem in the Netherlands, as in many other countries, but a different approach has been taken. The Netherlands has a population of 15 million people, 90 percent of whom live in cities. The largest city is Amsterdam, with a population of 700,000. There are an estimated 21,000 addicts in the Netherlands, 7,000 of whom are clients of methadone maintenance clinics. It appears that cocaine use is relatively low and has been stable over recent decades, and the use of "crack" cocaine is infrequent. Cocaine use is mainly experimental or recreational. Marijuana is the most frequently used illicit drug. According to a report by the Dutch Ministry of Justice and the Ministry of Welfare, Health and Cultural Affairs, the main objective of the Netherlands' drug policy is to restrict as much as possible the risks of drug use to the users themselves, their immediate environment, and society as a whole. Principle attention is directed toward the users. The policy appears to conceive of drug use in medical rather than legal terms. The law is obviously considered important in dealing with drugs in the Netherlands, but considerable value is likewise attached to strongly organized informal social control. Although risks to society are taken into account—and it is here where the law is most useful—the government attempts to ensure that drug users are not further harmed by prosecution and imprisonment. The Dutch policy continuously seeks to strike the right balance between protecting drug addicts and protecting the community.

This philosophy can be contrasted with American policy. In the United States, drug policy is driven by a similar goal, the reduction of use; but unlike in the Netherlands, the U.S. policy conceives of drug use as it does other crimes, as a freely chosen behavior that can be reduced by legal coercion. There is no recognition that conceiving drug use only in legal terms denies its medical and social context. There is also no recognition in U.S. policy that the use of the law can do harm to users.

The possession, transport, trafficking, manufacture, and sale of illicit drugs in the Netherlands is identified in the 1919 Opium Act, first revised in 1976. The consumption of illicit drugs is not illegal. The act attempts to distinguish users from traffickers of drugs. Possession of illegal drugs does not automatically involve a serious penalty in the absence of evidence of intent to sell.

The Dutch Code of Criminal Procedure has a provision called the "expediency principle," which provides the Public Prosecutions Department with the power to refrain from instituting criminal proceedings if there are believed to be weighty public interests against doing so. In the words of the Code, prosecution is to be avoided in certain cases "on grounds deriving from the general good." Guidelines have been established for detecting and prosecuting offenses under the Opium Act. Similar guidelines also exist for other offenses, such as the illegal possession of firearms, pirate broadcasting, and exceeding the speed limit. The guidelines contain recommendations of penalties to be imposed and set out the priorities to be observed in detecting and prosecuting offenses. International drug trafficking has the greatest priority, possession of drugs the lowest. Whether possession cases should be prosecuted and if so, to what degree, is a matter of discretion for the prosecutor. The Dutch Government directs responsibility for drug use to communities.

A major part of the Netherlands anti-drug strategy is drug education. Information on the risks of drug use and the use of alcohol and tobacco are to be presented together. School prevention programs, using the latest information pertaining to drug risks, are directed toward potential drug users. Knowledge about the health risks of using certain drugs is often sufficient to prevent the drug's use. But drug education is not enough, and parents and the general citizenry are also requested to help potential drug users to identify drug risks.

Research conducted by the Dutch government on the lifestyles of heroin addicts in the Netherlands has generated a new appreciation for the complexity of drug taking. While some people who use drugs will eventually become addicted to them, others are able to take drugs, including opiates, on an occasional, experimental, or recreational basis. This is similar to the observation about heroin use in the United States. There are clearly many different types of users with many different lifestyles. This Dutch research has also called into question the possibility of prevention of addiction by means of drug information only. Preventing occasional users from becoming frequent users or addicts is considered extremely important. The idea that preventing problems that accrue from the use of drugs is accordingly given at least equal emphasis as preventing the initial use of drugs.

A related problem is the spread of diseases, such as AIDS, among intravenous drug users. The Dutch government has instituted a clean-needle exchange to remove dirty needles from circulation. Needle exchanges are run from methadone maintenance programs, as well as by various municipalities. The report indicates that in 1992, 1,000,000 syringes were exchanged in Amsterdam alone. While there is no illusion that needle exchange programs will alone contain AIDS cases among drug addicts, it is one avenue toward reduction. But, in addition to needle exchanges, "persuasive face-to-face counseling, in order to change addicts' risky behavior in favor of safer practices, is essential."

In view of the greater sensitivity to various forms of drug taking, the report also says that "the Dutch government believes that drug use should be shorn of its taboo image and its sensational and emotional overtones. The image of the user and addict should be demythologized and reduced to its real proportions, for it is precisely the stigma, paradoxically enough, that exercises such a strong attraction on some young people."

The primary weapon against drugs in the Netherlands is interpersonal intervention. Drug treatment for those who are addicted is considered essential. This treatment is administered outside of the Dutch criminal justice system. The central agency for this work is the Medical Consultation Bureaus for Alcohol and Drug Problems (CADs). The CADs are autonomous non-governmental institutions, the entire costs of which are paid by the government. In the words of the report:

> The CADs are also active in the field of probation; one aspect is the initial reception of drug addicts in police stations, where an effort is made to establish contact that may lead to the acceptance of further aid during and after detention. Although the CADs primarily provide non-residential mental health care, their services are oriented toward social work, as the majority of their staff (approximately 900 in all) are social workers. The objectives of indi-

vidual CADs may vary from kicking the habit (drug-free), to stabilizing the functioning of addicts by supplying the substitute drug methadone on a "maintenance basis" (stable dosage). "Reduction based" methadone programs are also applied (gradually reduced dosages to nil). A variety of methods is used, including psychotherapy, group therapy, material assistance, family therapy, counseling, and advising groups of parents. An increasingly important area of the CADs' work is prevention, including AIDS control (i.e., needle-exchange, information and education).

The Dutch approach thus employs a conception of drug taking, especially addiction, that does not fit the kinds of problems that the law typically addresses. Drug use is considered to be a community problem, and the solution must be sought via non-legal means. Even those addicts who are in the Dutch criminal justice system are seen as candidates for intervention. In December 1993, the State Secretary for Welfare, Health and Cultural Affairs and the Minister of Justice presented a plan to Parliament to take more addicts out of the justice system and to offer them help. This approach will reduce the pressure on the justice system. The plan explicitly acknowledges that the policy will be effective only if there are sufficient monitoring facilities and/or after-care projects for the reinsertion of these persons into society.

What Kind of a Problem Is 'Drugs?'

The Netherlands approach is an example of a policy that conceives of drug usage as a problem more appropriate for other institutions and other social control mechanisms than law. Although most people in the United States would identify illicit drug taking as a problem, there is disagreement on what kind of problem it is. To some, drugs are a problem for criminal law, like theft, interpersonal violence, and fraud. To these people, the main weapon against drugs is the criminal justice system. To others, drugs represent more of a social or medical problem, one better addressed by community action, better parenting, and medical treatment. The appropriate policy follows from how one defines the problem.

Interestingly, although it might be expected that criminal justice officials advocate only a legal solution for drugs, this is not always the case. To inform policymakers about the law enforcement position on drugs, a "Law Enforcement Summit" was held in May 1995, involving the leaders of more than 50 law enforcement agencies. Several federal judges and George Shultz, former Secretary of State, spoke. Schultz denounced the Drug War as wrongheaded and not making sense economically.

Baltimore Mayor Kurt Schmoke, the main speaker, was invited because the city of Baltimore had decided to formulate its drug problem in terms that emphasized the fact that drugs are a social, not a legal, problem. Joseph McNamara, former Chief of Police of Kansas City and San Jose, asked Schmoke how a medical approach used in Baltimore went over politically in that city. The response was said to be as follows:

> I go to meet with people in the community, and I ask them three questions: Do you think we've won the Drug War? And people just laugh. Do you think we're winning the Drug War? And people just shake their heads. And the third question is, if you think we keep doing what we're doing now, in 10 years, will we have won the Drug War?

Clearly, it was a rhetorical question.

After this meeting, the Baltimore Police Commissioner announced that his department would de-emphasize arrests for possessing small quantities of drugs (*Baltimore Sun,* January 24, 1996). Instead, the Commissioner said the police would focus their energy on gun possession and gun violence. The Commissioner was careful not to call his policy change an instance of decriminalization, but it was clearly based on the view that the war on drugs cannot be won by relying only on criminal law. "What impacts on the quality of life in this city," proclaimed a mayor's office spokesperson, "is not people taking drugs, but the violence associated with the drug trade."

Using the Baltimore approach as a focal point, the Law Enforcement Summit concluded with a survey of participants, in which more than 90 percent of those attending agreed that the legal war on drugs was a failure, a battle that could not be won with available resources. "The group was unanimous in saying," according to McNamara, "more treatment and more education would be more effective than more arrests and prisons." Furthermore, McNamara reported that "the group was unanimous in calling for a blue-ribbon panel to study the harm done by the Drug War and alternative methods of dealing with drugs."

The consequences of the drug war extend well beyond the immediate circumstances of making, selling, and using illegal drugs. One such consequence is the corruption that infests the criminal justice system as a result of the high profits in certain drugs. McNamara (1995) identified specific examples. The former police chief of Detroit was sent to prison for stealing drug funds. A number of sheriffs throughout the country have been convicted of dealing in drugs. The former untouchables, the "feds," now have officers in jail for drug offenses. The DEA agent who arrested General Noriega, the former leader of Panama who was implicated in drug trafficking, was arrested and imprisoned for stealing laundered drug money. In another case, an FBI agent stole drugs from the evidence room and mailed samples to regional drug dealers so they could determine the purity of the product and the appropriate price. McNamara (1995:43) tells of other scandals:

> In New Orleans, a uniformed cop in league with a drug dealer has been convicted of murdering her partner and shop owners during a robbery committed while she was on patrol. In Washington, D.C., and in Atlanta, cops in drug stings were arrested for stealing and taking bribes. New York State troopers falsified drug evidence that sent people to prison.

Drugs are not only outlawed, they are outlawing and corrupting, much like alcohol during Prohibition. Clearly, the war metaphor has generated bad police practices, partly because everything is fair in war. The rationalization of crooked cops is that criminals are the enemy and should not profit. Some police feel justified in using questionable or illegal methods against drug dealers and users because, as McNamara says, "It's a war, after all."

The consequences of the drug war are far-ranging and subtle. Increasingly, local and federal police agencies and other criminal justice organizations are being met with suspicion and distrust in the community. Some of this distrust involves high-profile cases, such as the Rodney King and O.J. Simpson cases. In the Rodney King case, the police were clearly involved in illegal activities against a defendant, whereas in the Simpson case, allegations of police misconduct by a racist police officer may have been instrumental in Simpson's acquittal. But a further cause of this distrust is related to the perceived unfairness of law enforcers, most of which is concentrated in groups against which the police have been the most aggressive: the inner areas of large metropolitan cities, mainly populated by African Americans. Confidence among whites has not declined as much, largely because the kinds of drugs that are the objects of current law enforcement are not found in white neighborhoods.

Further evidence of the ineffectiveness of current drug laws is reflected in a recent poll of policy administrators. Every three years or so, the National Institute of Justice conducts the National Assessment Program, which attempts to identify the needs and problems in criminal justice agencies around the nation. Almost all police chiefs and sheriffs (95 percent) claim that drug possession and sales are creating workload problems, primarily because of the increased number of cases (McEwen, 1995). In most communities, the drug problem is coming to dominate law enforcement operations. More than 75 percent of police departments have created special community programs and crime units focusing on drugs. Not only is the war on drugs not being won, it has not even achieved a stalemate.

Decriminalization Does Not Solve the Problem of Drugs

One way to deal with the problems caused by the criminalization of drugs is to declare a truce: decriminalize drugs that are now illegal. Although such a policy might go a long way to reduce some problems, it leaves untouched those that gave rise to much legislation in the first place. Drug use has many undesirable consequences both for users and society at large, regardless of the particular substance. The use of some drugs involves health risks which are serious and of long-term duration. Some drug use interferes with the building and development of satisfying social and personal relationships with others. Some drug use interferes seriously with an individual's ability to find and hold meaningful employment, as well as reducing work productivity. Some drug use is associated with the commission of other crimes, some of which are the direct result of drug use (e.g., when the crime was committed because the offender was "high") while others are indirectly related to drugs themselves (e.g., an assault over a drug transaction). Some drug use is associated with a lifestyle from which most people wish to escape—polydrug use (alcohol, marijuana, tobacco, and others), poverty, discrimination, and living in crowded conditions.

Furthermore, the call to decriminalize often disguises troubling questions. Are all drugs to be legal? Even crack-cocaine (Inciardi and Saum, 1996)? Does decriminalization mean that now-illegal drugs can be sold openly on the marketplace, like cigarettes and alcohol? Would some drugs be regulated, much like prescription drugs now, and if so, which drugs would be handled this way?

Critics of decriminalization find important moral and practical messages in law that are not found elsewhere. Attacks on the policies of Mayor Schmoke of Baltimore, whose approach was detailed earlier, illustrate the criticisms. Bennett et al. (1996:166) observe that emergency room admissions for serious health problems associated with drugs and drug overdoses rose significantly during the time when Schmoke was Mayor of Baltimore. While Bennett and his colleagues cannot demonstrate that the increases were a direct result of the Baltimore policies, they do find that "it is at least fair to say that his [Schmoke's] policies did not prevent Baltimore from becoming far and away the national leader in drug-related emergency room admissions."

The consequences of drug use are not borne only by the users. Illicit drugs cost society billions of dollars each year: Employers lose money through reduced productivity and accidents on the job; banks lose money when addicted borrowers default on loans and forge checks; crime victims can lose not only money but their lives in attacks by people under the influence of drugs; criminal justice officials expend millions of dollars annually in processing drug- and alcohol-related cases through the police, courts, and corrections systems; the health care system is put under increasing strain by accidents caused by drug use; and people in sensitive occupations put many other lives at risk when they operate machinery, such as construction equipment and public transportation vehicles. Monetary estimates cannot account for the loss of human capital and the toll drugs and alcohol have taken on interpersonal relationships. The costs from drugs are so great overall that society has a strong impetus to somehow regulate their use.

We must also be sensitive to important differences among different kinds of drugs. Alcohol is a drug, but it differs from illegal drugs in some important ways. For example, alcohol is often taken socially and in moderation with no serious negative physical or social consequences. Red wine, for example, has been linked with reduced heart disease when it is used in relatively small quantities. There is also much more social support for the use of alcohol or tea, and these drinks are often consumed for reasons different from other drugs, such as the simple desire to quench one's thirst. Marijuana and LSD, on the other hand, are consumed to produce one effect only: getting high. Once the euphoria is no longer attained, for whatever reason, many marijuana users terminate their use.

Legalization of marijuana, heroin, cocaine, and other illegal drugs does not provide an easy—or perhaps any—solution to the nation's drug problems. Mario Cuomo, former Governor of New York State, draws an analogy to a poisoned lake near a village (Cuomo, 1995:148):

> Imagine a village where more and more of the young people were being driven crazy by drinking from a poisoned lake in the hills. They storm the village night after night, creating mayhem. More and more of them are locked up. More and more executed. The villagers have to pay for more and more police and jail cells. Wouldn't someone say "Let's dry up the lake; let's find a new source of clean water?"

This analogy considers the problem to be one of both supply and demand. The issue is two-fold: there is a poisoned lake, and the village's youth want the water. The law may be able to address, even if imperfectly, the former problem, but it is unlikely to be effective in dealing with the latter. The reasons for drug use are many, including experimentation, escapism, mood alteration, and habit. The law is unable to exert influence over virtually any of these reasons, let alone exert control over them.

But there are other issues. No one currently advocates legalizing drugs for children. Even under the most permissive system of law, therefore, there will be at least one group for whom the law will be used to prohibit drugs. This is essentially the system we presently have and enforce with respect to alcohol and tobacco. Most people would also agree that the law has not been effective in keeping alcohol and tobacco away from children who really want them. And it may be that the law is as effective as it can be short of draconian measures that would be unsuitable in a free society. Furthermore, to say that alcohol is different from illicit drugs is not to condone its use. It is for this reason that many were disturbed in 1996 when the alcohol beverage industry appeared ready to end its self-imposed ban on advertising distilled spirits. In June 1996, a television station in Texas began showing ads for Seagram's whiskey, the first such ads in the media since the 1940s. Some media advertising specialists believe that the distillers want to put pressure on beer companies which run up a $626 million advertising bill annually. If networks refuse hard liquor ads, then a campaign could be begun to ban beer commercials. Others claim that the distillers' long-term strategy is to get on television now so that when further technological advances occur in home electronics they will be guaranteed a place. Some distillers already advertise on the Internet.

It should be recognized too that the law has produced some important advances against illicit drugs. Interdiction measures have reduced the supply of certain illegal drugs, thereby reducing their use either by making them physically difficult to obtain or by increasing the price to render their use impractical. Yet although the law can slow the supply of drugs, there can never be enough law enforcement to stop that supply. Unless there is a change in the original conditions that bring about the decision to use illicit drugs, there will always be some groups eager to supply them for a profit. It is unrealistic to think that the law can solve the drug problem alone, as long as large numbers of people choose to use drugs.

Decriminalization is likely to increase the use of certain drugs. Herbert Packer (1968) points out that the demand for some drugs is elastic, and the demand for other drugs is inelastic. By this, he means that the demand for some drugs can fluctuate widely over time, whereas the demand for other drugs is more stable and predictable. For example, most people do not use heroin because they do not wish to become addicts, not because they fear the law. The overall demand for heroin is therefore likely to remain relatively constant, regardless of its legal status. The demand for heroin is said to be inelastic. A drug like marijuana, on the other hand, which does not produce physical dependency, is likely to have a more elastic demand. Decriminalization will tend to increase use, because the law usually exercises a significant restraint on use both through its deterrent effect and by reducing the supply of the drug. Furthermore, there may be fewer other nonlegal sources of control for marijuana.

Decriminalization is more likely to increase use—at least experimental use—of marijuana than heroin, if only because the law has a more significant control over marijuana than heroin.

There are some important trade-offs in the use of law to control drug behavior. Rand Corporation analysts, for example, estimate that a 25 percent reduction in funds currently used to cut the supply of cocaine would result in an 8 percent increase in cocaine use (Everingham and Rydell, 1994; Rydell and Everingham, 1994). If some of those saved funds were then spent on treatment programs, the current number of cocaine users could be substantially reduced, more than compensating for the 8 percent increase in use. Clearly, there is a need to balance those resources devoted to reducing supply and those to reducing the demand for cocaine. But it does not follow that all funds currently pouring into law enforcement to reduce supply should be diverted to treatment. Not all users will avail themselves of treatment, and not all those who do will finish treatment successfully. The law will be part of the overall system of control over illicit drugs for some time to come.

Conclusion

The campaign against drugs cannot be won if the law is the only weapon and complete repression is the only objective. The history of drug laws reflects a history of racist imagery, selective application, and uneven enforcement. No one doubts that drugs can ruin the lives of users and those around them, that drugs represent a loss to employers and communities, or that children need to be discouraged from drugs at an early age. None of these, however, render drugs a legal problem, as opposed to a family, community, or social problem. The real problem of drugs is their ubiquity in American life, our dependency on chemicals in subtle, everyday situations, and our inability to resolve our ambivalence about them: They are both wonderful and terrible—sometimes at the same time. This is a problem for which the law is inappropriate.

These are hardly new ideas, but until recently they have been heard only from the left end of the political spectrum. In recent years, political conservatives have also been expressing doubt about the effectiveness of a drug policy based on legal repression. Conservative skepticism about current drug policies increased significantly when the well-known conservative magazine *National Review* published a special issue on drugs in 1996, the title of which said it all: "The War on Drugs is Lost." The *Review's* editor, William F. Buckley, avowed that not only was the law ineffective but it was counterproductive. Furthermore, the war has been far too expensive; more than $75 billion a year is spent on it, money that could be put to better use. The problem of drugs and the law had been dealt with before in the pages of *National Review.* In the July 10, 1995, issue, Michael S. Gazzaniga, Director for the Center of Neuroscience at the University of California at Davis, suggested that people cannot be deterred by the law from using drugs, because the physiology of humans and the physical properties of drugs make the lure of drugs irresistible to some uncertain number of persons.

There are several policy alternatives, including regulation (manufacture and sale under controlled circumstances) and decriminalization (no regulation, whereby drugs are treated as any other legal commodity). Regulation is essentially the current policy with respect to alcohol and tobacco. Manufacture in accordance with government safety standards and distribution can both be accomplished competitively to keep prices down. Sales could be governed by laws as to time, place, and consumer. Furthermore, many of these decisions could be made at the local level to conform to local custom and social standards. In some places, alcohol would be sold only in state-run stores and on certain days, and sale to minors would be illegal.

Drug policy continues to search for the most appropriate role for law. A national citizens' group advocating changes in the criminal justice system made the following recommendation in 1996: "Replace the war on drugs with a policy of harm reduction where the police work with public health and other professionals to stem substance use. Substance abuse would be treated as a public health challenge rather than a criminal justice problem" (Donziger, 1996:200-201). The notion of "harm reduction" means that the law should work cooperatively with other institutions to address problems. In this case, it refers to the importance of treatment facilities for addicts, the use of health professionals to administer drugs to addicts as part of a larger program of treatment, and needle exchange programs. Also recognized is the use of law to compel treatment for those who need and would benefit from it through such devices as drug courts.

Current skepticism about the role of law in controlling drugs is not motivated only by frustration with the law's apparent inability to reduce the supply of illegal drugs (Inciardi and Saum, 1996). Rather, those who would decriminalize drugs have supplied a number of arguments, some sociological, others practical and philosophical. They include a review of the harmful consequences of employing law enforcement to control drug use, the inefficiency in deploying precious police resources, and the use of the law in circumstances in which it has little chance of overall success. Whether such reasons are persuasive depends, in part, on one's conception of the law and to what purpose it should be implemented.

References

Baum, Dan. 1996. *Smoke and Mirrors: The War on Drugs and the Politics of Failure.* Boston: Little, Brown.

Beck, Allen J., and Darrell K. Gilliard. 1995. *Prisoners in 1994.* Washington, DC: Bureau of Justice Statistics.

Bennett, William J., John J. DiIulio, and John P. Walters. 1996. *Body Count: Moral Poverty . . . and How to Win America's War Against Crime and Drugs.* New York: Simon and Schuster.

Brecher, Edward M. 1972. *Licit and Illicit Drugs.* Boston: Little, Brown

Bureau of Justice Statistics. 1995. *Drugs and Crime Facts, 1994.* Washington, DC: Department of Justice.

Chambers, Carl D., and Michael T. Harter. 1987. "The Epidemiology of Narcotic Abuse among Blacks in the United States, 1935-1980." Pp. 191-223 in *Chemical Dependencies: Patterns, Costs, and Consequences,* Carl D. Chambers, James A. Inciardi, David M. Peterson, Harvey A. Siegal, and O.Z. White (eds.). Athens: Ohio University Press.

Clinard, Marshall B., and Robert F. Meier. 1995. *Sociology of Deviant Behavior,* 9th edition. Fort Worth, TX: Harcourt Brace.

Coughlin, Thomas A. III. 1993. "Rockefeller Drug Laws—20 Years Later." Testimony Before Assembly Committee on Code. Albany: New York State Legislature.

Cox, Terrance, Michael R. Jacobs, A. Eugene Leblanc, and Joan A. Marshman. 1983. *Drugs and Drug Abuse: A Reference Text.* Toronto: Addiction Research Foundation.

Cuomo, Mario. 1995. *Reason to Believe.* New York: Simon and Schuster.

Donziger, Steven R., ed. 1996. *The Real War on Crime: The Report of the National Criminal Justice Commission*. New York: HarperPerennial.

Everingham, Susan S., and C. Peter Rydell. 1994. *Modeling the Demand for Cocaine*. Los Angeles: Rand Corporation.

Federal Bureau of Investigation. 1995. *Crime in the United States, 1994*. Washington, DC: Department of Justice.

Goode, Erich. 1993. *Drugs in American Society*, 4th edition. New York: Knopf.

Hill, Herbert. 1973. "Anti-Oriental Agitation," *Society*, 10:43-54.

Hunt, Leon Gibson, and Carl D. Chambers. 1976. *The Heroin Epidemics: A Study of Heroin Use in the United States, 1965-1975*. New York: Spectrum Publications.

Inciardi, James A. 1986. *The War on Drugs*. Palo Alto, CA: Mayfield.

Inciardi, James A. 1987. *The Great Drug War*. New York: Macmillan.

Inciardi, James A., Dorothy Lockwood, and Anne E. Pottieger. 1993. *Women and Crack-Cocaine*. New York: Macmillan.

Inciardi, James A., and Christine Saum. 1996. "Legalization Madness." *The Public Interest*, 123:72-82.

Johnston, Lloyd D., Patrick M. O'Malley, and Jerald G. Bachman. 1993. *National Survey Results on Drug Use From the Monitoring the Future Study, 1975-1992, Volume 1, Secondary School Students*. Washington, DC: NIH Publication 93-3597, Government Printing Office.

Johnston, Lloyd, Jerald Bachman, and Patrick O'Malley. 1995. *Monitoring the Future: 1995*. Ann Arbor: University of Michigan.

Lindesmith, Alfred R., and John H. Gagnon. 1964. "Anomie and Drug Addiction." Pp. 162-178 in *Anomie and Deviant Behavior: A Discussion and Critique*, Marshall B. Clinard (ed.). New York: Free Press.

McEwen, Tom. 1995. *National Assessment Program: 1994 Survey Results*. Rockville, MD: National Criminal Justice Reference Service.

McNamara, Joseph. 1995. Address at the 9th International Conference on Drug Policy Reform. Santa Monica, CA, October, 1995.

McWilliams, Peter. 1993. *Ain't Nobody's Business If You Do*. Los Angeles: Prelude Press.

Ministry of Welfare, Health and Cultural Affairs. 1994. *The Drug Policy in The Netherlands*. Amsterdam: The Netherlands.

Morgan, H. Wayne. 1981. *Drugs in America: A Social History, 1800-1980*. Syracuse, NY: Syracuse University Press.

National Commission on Marijuana and Drug Abuse. 1972. *Marihuana: A Signal of Misunderstanding*. Washington, DC: Government Printing Office.

Office of National Drug Control Policy. 1995. *National Drug Control Strategy: Executive Summary*. Washington, DC: The White House.

Oliver, William. 1994. *The Violent Social World of Black Men*. New York: Lexington.

Packer, Herbert A. 1968. *The Limits of the Criminal Sanction*. Stanford: Stanford University Press.

Reuter, Peter. 1995. *Cocaine: The First Decade*. Los Angeles: The Rand Corporation.

Rydell, C. Peter, and Susan S. Everingham. 1994. *Controlling Cocaine: Supply vs. Demand Programs*. Los Angeles: Rand Corporation.

Stephens, Richard C. 1991. *The Street Addict Role: A Theory of Heroin Addiction*. Albany: State University of New York Press.

Timberlake, James H. 1963. *Prohibition and the Progressive Movement, 1900-1920*. New Haven, CT: Yale University Press.

Trebach, Arnold S. 1982. *The Heroin Solution*. New Haven, CT: Yale University Press.

Trebach, Arnold S. 1987. *The Great Drug War*. New York: Macmillan.

Troyer, Ronald J., and Gerald E. Markle. 1983. *Cigarettes: The Battle Over Smoking*. New Brunswick, NJ: Rutgers University Press.

Walters, John P. 1996. "Illegal Drugs and Presidential Leadership." *Wall Street Journal*, September 26:23.

Wolfgang, Marvin E. 1958. *Patterns of Criminal Homicide*. Philadelphia: University of Pennsylvania Press.

4

Homosexuality

Homosexuality is a topic about which there is considerable controversy in the United States. Much of the controversy revolves around the extent to which homosexuality is immoral, a debate that has spilled out of the churches and into the legislatures. To some, there is substantial moral harm from homosexuality which justifies using legal control; to others, homosexuality is an entirely private matter that should not be of concern to the criminal law. Homosexuals have faced both moral and legal censure. To be sure, most of the topics of current controversy—same-sex marriages, the role of homosexual personnel in the military, the ordination of homosexuals in churches, the identification of homosexuality as a protected category of citizens against discrimination, the ability of homosexuals to adopt and raise children—do not appear to touch on matters that involve criminal law. But law always lurks in the background, giving meaning to the issue and, in some instances, definition to a particular topic.

There is much that is confusing about homosexuality, and only some of this confusion can be addressed scientifically. One observer, for example, views the origin of homosexuality like the development of any other habit:

> What deters young people from becoming emotionally committed to this form of release is doubtless its negative evaluation by peers and social rewards that are contingent on normal heterosexual relations. The few who turn into "true" homosexuals are presumably like the few drinkers who turn into confirmed alcoholics: they do so both because they drink too much and because they cannot

make the normal adjustments in life. Once the homosexual habit
is fixed by the reinforcement of frequent gratification, it becomes
extraordinarily difficult to break. (Davis, 1976:255-256)

Such a view is obviously too simplistic to persuade many observers today, but even more surprising is the tone of disapproval
it conveys. Homosexuality, in this view, is merely a bad habit like
alcoholism, and we are told that we are lucky that only a few persons
are so afflicted.

Strong opinions and polarized thinking have come to dominate
discussions of homosexuality. To some, homosexuality is a lifestyle
variation, freely chosen and largely, if not totally, immoral. To others,
it is a biological condition over which the individual has no more
control than of one's eye or skin color. Because neither science nor
religion has yet resolved these opposing conceptions, it is entirely
understandable that the law has come to be used to both threaten
and protect heterosexual interests.

Whether homosexuality is viewed as choice or as condition is
particularly important, because such conceptions have consequences for the use of law to regulate homosexuality. Criminal law
cannot punish in the absence of intent to produce wrong-doing, and
for this reason, the law recognizes various exceptions to criminal
responsibility, such as compulsion, duress, and insanity. If homosexuality is the result of a conscious choice, as some believe, the law
can be appropriately used. Yet, there is confusion even about the
meaning of the term "homosexuality," which can refer both to a
sexual orientation or preference and to sexual conduct between
members of the same sex.

A note on usage: In this chapter, we follow the strict meaning of
the term homosexuality; the prefix "homo" means "same," not male.
Thus, we intend the term to refer both to male homosexuality and
lesbianism, although most of the writing and research on this topic
has been done with respect to male homosexuality. This lamentable
situation is reflected in the discussion in this chapter, but our intent
is to treat both male and female homosexuality together.

Defining Homosexuality

There are several different definitions of "homosexual" that
have given rise to different theories of the origin of homosexuality

and differences in the estimates of the number of individuals who are homosexual. Homosexuality can be reflected in attitudes expressing sexual or erotic preference, the presence of a homosexual self-concept, or in actual sex behavior with members of one's own sex, whether male or female. These three connotations of the term homosexual—homosexual behavior, homosexual preference or orientation, and homosexual identity or self-concept—have each different implications for our conception of homosexuality and its appropriateness under law.

Homosexual Behavior

Between males, homosexual behavior can be carried out physically in a number of ways: sodomy (anal), fellatio (mouth-genital), and mutual masturbation. Homosexual behavior between women can consist of oral stimulation of the clitoris (cunnilingus), mutual masturbation, and the use of objects such as vibrators or an artificial penis. People who engage in homosexual behavior, males and females, come from all social classes, have varying degrees of education and a wide range of occupations and professions, have varied interests and avocations, and may be either married or single.

Homosexual behavior may seem to be the most obvious indicator of whether someone is a homosexual, but people can engage in homosexual behavior and still not consider themselves to be homosexual. They may participate in homosexual acts yet remain primarily attracted to persons of the opposite sex. On the other hand, some married males may feel more attracted to persons of their own sex and derive from them most of their sexual stimulation. The degree to which a person combines high levels of homosexual attraction and homosexual behavior may stem from one's participation in a homosexual subculture and the extent to which one is a member of that subculture. For this reason, there is no such thing as *a* homosexual but rather differing degrees of a person's involvement with homosexuality at certain levels of behavior and attraction.

How common are homosexual experiences? No one knows for sure, but one estimate was obtained in an extensive survey of adult sexual behavior: Laumann and his colleagues (1994:294) report that 2.7 percent of their sample of males and 1.3 percent of the females reported having sexual relations with someone of the same sex during the past year.

Homosexual Preference or Orientation

Homosexual preference refers to the subjective feeling that a person of the same sex is more sexually attractive than a person of the opposite sex. The idea of considering homosexuality as sexual or erotic preference enables us to understand a number of different sexual behavior patterns (Langevin, 1985:2-3). According to Kinsey et al. (1948), in one of the best known studies of sexuality in the United States, 37 percent of a random sample of American males had what they considered to be a homosexual experience at some time during their lives. But only 4 percent were exclusively homosexual and expressed an erotic preference for men throughout their adult lives. The others likely engaged in homosexual acts out of a desire for something different or while living with males in such situations as an all-male school or prison. In addition, there are some men who have had homosexual relations with male prostitutes—or have been male prostitutes themselves—though their involvement in this behavior is not necessarily the consequence of sexual preference (Luckenbill, 1986). Similarly, there are some women who have had sexual relations with female prostitutes, but not all of these women are necessarily lesbians. Some, like the males, are bisexual; others are simply adventurous. Having had homosexual relations does not constitute being a homosexual, at least in the sociological sense of the term.

Homosexual Identity or Self-Concept

Yet another view of homosexuality derives its meaning from the self-conception of those who identify themselves as homosexuals. Sociologists have traditionally been more interested in the origins and consequences of the development of a homosexual self-concept than in homosexual behavior.

Using a self-concept measure yields different estimates of the prevalence of homosexuality. Although Kinsey's respondents were purposefully recruited and did not constitute a probability sample of adults, the sample of Laumann et al. (1994:293) was a representative sample: 2.8 percent of the men and 1.4 percent of the women reported some level of homosexual identity.

A few decades ago, little was known about the self-concept of homosexuals and the process by which it arose and changed. Sociologists knew that not all people who had homosexual preferences came to develop a corresponding self-concept, but the reasons seemed to extend beyond the powerful stigma that was associated with disclosing a deviant identity.

Sociologists believed that the key to this self-concept was in the process by which homosexuals made public their orientation: the "coming-out" process. Analogous to debutantes who "come out" in polite society to publicly introduce their membership in the elite, the coming-out process for homosexuals entailed a public disclosure of homosexual orientation and a willingness to participate in public life as a homosexual. Once one left the closet, there was little possibility of turning back. The sociological literature on the coming-out process is particularly extensive, in part because it deals with an intensely moving, high-risk public proclamation. The coming-out process further strengthens homosexual orientation that has already developed and been recognized by the individual as such.

Causes of Homosexuality

To ask about the origins of homosexuality means exploring the origins of all sexual preference. How is it that some people come to prefer sex with persons of the opposite sex, whereas others prefer it with members of the same sex? There remains much confusion about the origins of homosexuality, with some speculating that it has a genetic basis, others that it has a psychological one. According to a recent poll, for example, many psychiatrists believe there is a biological basis to homosexuality (Vreeland et al., 1995), a view that has become very popular among homosexuals as well. Still others adhere to a more sociological foundation, which argues that homosexuality is learned, just as heterosexuality is learned. Although no one has as yet definitively resolved such disputes, we can at least identify them.

The Biological Perspective

The biological perspective has gained support in recent years with research that has suggested, but no more than that, that homosexual orientation may be connected to disruptions in physical development or may reside in a particular gene. Some researchers have explored the chemical and hormonal bases of homosexuality. Roper

(1996), for example, believes that homosexual orientation may be determined by testosterone action on the brain. A reduction in testosterone levels results in reduced proliferation of hypothalamic nuclei, which are said to play a vital role in psychosexual orientation.

LeVay also believes that brain development may determine whether a person develops homosexual tendencies, and like Roper he has sought the answer in the hypothalmus. LeVay pinpointed a cell group called INAH3 (derived from "third interstitial nucleus of the anterior hypothalmus"). He points out that the INAH3 group is twice as large in men as in women. In autopsies of 19 homosexual and 16 heterosexual men who had died of AIDS, LeVay found that the cell group was two to three times larger in the heterosexual men than in the homosexuals and that in fact the group was altogether absent in some of the gays. He notes that the likelihood of such an outcome occurring by chance is about one in one thousand. This finding, nonetheless, has to be regarded as no more than a very tentative explanatory possibility; indeed, LeVay notes some of several possible interpretations:

> What might lie behind these apparent correlations between sexual orientation and brain structure? Logically, three possibilities exist. One is that the structural differences were present early in life — perhaps even before birth — and helped to establish the men's sexual orientation. The second is that the differences arose in adult life as a result of the men's sexual feelings or behavior. The third possibility is that there is no causal connection, but both sexual orientation and the brain structure in question are linked to some third variable, such as a developmental event during uterine or early postnatal life. (LeVay and Hamer, 1994:46)

The presence of the AIDS virus also represents a possible confounding variable, though the same phenomenon was found in a few non-AIDS cases autopsied. In the end, though, the conclusion remains that the researcher at the moment "cannot decide among the possibilities with and certainty." (LeVay and Hamer, 1994:46)

Other researchers have explored the genetic bases of homosexuality by examining the extent to which homosexuality is affected by genetic influences. A research team led by Dean Hamer has conducted perhaps the best-known work on this topic. Hamer and his associates (1994) concluded that there is a possibility of a genetic basis to sexual orientation, especially in the region of human DNA known as "Xq28."

Hamer's research was conducted at the National Cancer Institute, using a sample of 114 gay men. The investigators were intrigued that the families of 76 of these gay men included a higher proportion of homosexual male relatives than found in the general population. Because most of the homosexual relatives were on the mother's side of the family, the researchers concentrated on the X chromosome, which comes from the mother. "Using an approach called DNA linkage analysis, we found that a small region of the X chromosome, Xq28, appeared the same in an unexpectedly high proportion of gay brothers" (Hamer and Copeland, 1994:21). Specifically, DNA from 40 pairs of homosexual brothers was examined. The laws of inheritance indicate that two brothers have a 50–50 chance of inheriting the same single copy of their mother's X chromosome (the chromosome with the suspected DNA "marker" for homosexuality). Thus, it was expected that, on average, 20 of the 40 pairs of brothers would have this chromosome. Instead, the researchers found that 33 pairs of brothers shared five different patches of the same genetic material, suggesting that they had all inherited the same X chromosome from their mother.

Hamer's research team concluded that there may be at least one gene that is inherited by a son from his mother that helps to determine whether the son is predisposed to be heterosexual or homosexual. Presumably, a common version of the gene increases the likelihood that the son will be heterosexual, and an uncommon version of the gene increases the likelihood that the son will be homosexual.

Hamer's work continues to expand, as new families are located and the sample is enlarged. To date, this research suggests a possible genetic basis for male, but not female, homosexuality. A recent study examined families that contained either two gay brothers or two lesbian sisters, as well as heterosexual siblings (Hu et al., 1995). The researchers reported the existence of a linkage between the Xq28 markers and the sexual orientation for the gay male families but not for the lesbian families. The researchers point out that although the results suggest some kind of X-chromosome linkage, they failed to find evidence of any direct inheritance (Hamer and Copeland, 1994:104).

The Learning Perspective

The learning perspective represents an alternative, but not com-pletely separate, explanation of homosexuality. Because there is much we have to understand about the origins of homosexuality, it is possible that both biological and learning mechanisms are at work.

The learning of sexuality involves the acquisition of sexual norms and orientations, and this learning occurs throughout the lifecycle. Many sociologists believe that although it has a biological basis, sexuality is a social construction "that has been learned in interaction with others" (Plummer, 1975:30). It is not dictated by body chemistry or anatomical structures, but by experiences, social situations, and social expectations. "Male" and "female" are socially constructed categories, as is the conduct that arises from these roles.

One learns to be erotically responsive to some persons or objects but not to others. The process is not automatic, which is why some people are aroused by some objects that others do not respond to. One can learn that virtually anything is a sexual stimuli if it is paired with an appropriate sexual response. The sex drive, in other words, "is neither powerful nor weak; it can be almost anything we make it" (Goode and Troiden, 1974:15). The social meaning of sexuality, then, is attained in the same manner as the meaning of other social acts—as part of the overall socialization process that begins early in life (Akers, 1985:184-185). Sexuality is learned over a period of time and according to general principles of learning and social inter-action. In other words, people learn to become homosexuals through the same general processes by which they learn to become hetero-sexual. It is the *content* of this learning that differs.

Virtually any object or person is capable of providing sexual satisfaction, but sexual behavior is always embedded in a web of normative constraints and other regulations that define only certain objects and persons as acceptable. Rewards and punishments from early childhood help the individual to define acceptable sexuality. Most people learn to adopt heterosexual roles and to derive sexual satisfaction from objects and people considered to be "conven-tional," that is, within the norms of their group.

But the learning of sexuality is not a uniform experience, because sexual socialization is an imperfect process and some individuals will come to derive sexual satisfaction from objects and people out-side the group's normative structure. This can be expected for at least two reasons. First, the area of eroticism is an ambiguous one for socializers. Many parents and others feel uncomfortable about offering sex education that includes sex-specific information. For most socializers, the topic of sex is embarrassing. This seems to be particularly true for parents and children, as neither seems comfortable thinking of the other as sexual beings.

Second, the area of sexuality covers much ground, from appropriate partners to appropriate time, objects, places, and ages. In fact, sexual norms are among the most complicated of all social norms because of the different combinations of contingencies that one must learn. A woman, for example, might learn that males are appropriate sexual partners but only in certain relationships (e.g., after marriage) and certain places (e.g., private). It is not surprising, therefore, that there are instances in which the socialization process fails to adequately prepare individuals for sexual growth and maturation within the group. Some individuals will find themselves open to sexual alternatives, such as using a prostitute for sexual gratification or engaging in aberrant sexual practices, such as sadism or masochism. For the same reason, it is not surprising that some people come to be attracted to members of the same sex. Even taking into account the complexity of sexual norms and the ambiguity of the socialization process, by far most people are socialized to become heterosexual.

Beyond these general statements, it is not possible at the present time to provide a definitive answer about the causes of homosexuality—or heterosexuality, for that matter. We continue to investigate the process of the acquisition of sexual orientation, and subsequent work may reach the conclusion that although sexual orientation is facilitated by certain chromosomal structures, it is basically a learned perspective.

Most homosexuals tend to lean toward the biological view to explain their own orientation, to some because it absolves them of the responsibility that may be imposed on them for having chosen this form of life; to others because they believe that heterosexuals have no right to condemn them for an inborn condition. But adherence to this biological view is not entirely motivated by a desire to deflect social stigma or counter condemnation. Many homosexuals report that their experiences were such that they had some inkling that they were "different" early in life. Many stories identify a turn-

ing point where homosexuals received an insight into the fact that
they were not like others in their sexual orientation, seemingly before they had a chance to learn many sexual norms at all. One writer
recounts how he refrained from recess in elementary school because
he didn't like to play soccer (Sullivan, 1995:3-4):

> [A] girl sitting next to me looked at me with a mixture of curiosity
> and disgust. "Why aren't you out with the boys playing football?"
> she asked. "Because I hate it," I replied. "Are you sure you're not
> a girl under there?" she asked, with the suspicion of a sneer. "Yeah,
> of course," I replied, stung and somewhat shaken.

There seems to be little point in trying to discover the causes of
homosexuality by relying on such authorities as the medical profession. The Committee on Public Health of the New York State Academy of Medicine declared authoritatively in 1964 that
"homosexuality is indeed an illness," and that "the homosexual is
an emotionally disturbed individual who has not acquired a normal
capacity to develop satisfying heterosexual relationships" (New
York Academy of Medicine Committee on Public Health, 1964; Geis,
1979:28). A decade later, however, the American Psychiatric Association would proclaim that homosexuality is not an illness and that
homosexuals are not in need of special services by virtue of their
being homosexuals.

Public Opinion and Homosexuality

Psychiatrists are not the only people who change their minds.
There are unmistakable signs of increased public tolerance of homosexuality, although the degree of shift is not dramatic. Surveys
record different degrees of approval and disapproval of homosexuality, though the difference is often attributable to how the questions
are worded. Yet, however questions are worded, most people in the
United States still disapprove of homosexuality. A Kinsey Institute
survey in 1970 asked more than 3,000 adult respondents selected on
a national basis about a variety of sexual acts, including homosexuality. The single most disapproved act involved homosexuality
among partners who had no special affection for each other (Klassen, Williams, and Levitt, 1989:18). Of the respondents, 88 percent
indicated that this was "always wrong" or "almost always wrong."

Fewer respondents found homosexual acts between parties who were in love as "always wrong" or "almost always wrong," but the percentage was still high: 79 percent.

In another national survey, investigators asked young men about their attitudes toward homosexuality and found that 89 percent found sex between two men to be "disgusting," and only 12 percent thought they could be friends with a gay male (Marsiglio, 1993). These views were related to perceptions of the traditional male role, religious fundamentalist beliefs, and upbringing by a parent with few formal years of education.

Evidence indicates that the level of public disapproval of homosexuality has declined from previous decades (Stephan and McMullin, 1982). The percentage of people who favor legalizing homosexual relations between consenting adults, for example, increased slightly from 43 percent in 1977 to 47 percent in 1989 (cited by Posner, 1992:202). This means, of course, that more than half of the respondents do not favor such measures. In 1986, 54 percent agreed that homosexual relations between consenting adults should be illegal. This negative opinion was even stronger for older age groups, but there is also evidence that the majority of college students have negative views of homosexuality (Endleman, 1990:52). In the 1986 poll, 51 percent believed that the Constitution of the United States does not protect private homosexual acts (Gallup Poll, 1986), a position that was consistent with an important U.S. Supreme Court ruling that same year.

The modest but measurable increase in tolerance of homosexuality among the general population has occurred in most groups, although there remains stronger condemnation of homosexuality among religious Christians than among others. The issue there remains a divisive one, whether over a broad topic, such as the morality of homosexuality in general, or a narrow one, such as the appropriateness of allowing known homosexuals to become clergy. And, in spite of increasing tolerance, a substantial majority of Americans do not agree that homosexuality is just another lifestyle. When 70 percent of a sample of Americans responds to a poll that homosexuality is immoral (Shapiro, 1994), one might reasonably question whether all respondents are using the same definition of "morality."

There has long been an uneasy relationship between homosexuality and Christianity. Historically, most of the objections to homosexual behavior that have been raised in the larger society can be traced to religious prohibitions (Greenberg, 1988). One common objection is that homosexual conduct cannot lead to reproduction or to the development of a "normal" family. Homosexuality certainly cannot lead to human reproduction, but reproduction is increasingly seen as only one purpose for sex. Most heterosexual people also engage in sexual relations for purposes other than human reproduction. Indeed, the purpose of birth control is precisely to avoid reproduction. Even the Roman Catholic church, though it discourages birth control devices, endorses timed birth control to avoid ovulation, the so-called "rhythm" method.

Some Christians have accepted homosexuals as full church members, but others oppose such increasing religious liberalization. During the 1990s, the issue that was contested most strenuously was whether homosexuals could be ordained as clergy. The Episcopal Church, like many Protestant denominations, had been wrestling with the question for a number of years, largely without resolution. When an openly gay man was ordained in May 1990, the Church had to confront the issue in a more direct manner. Six years later, a special church court ruled that there was no church doctrine against ordaining non-celibate homosexuals (*Des Moines Register*, May 20, 1996, p. 1A). The court ruled further that the Episcopal Church was in a period of indecision about homosexuality, which triggered a series of debates as local churches wrestled with the meanings of the ruling. For some, the decision was evidence of further liberalization; for others, it represented a reasonable compromise on the issue, so that local churches could decide for themselves whether to ordain homosexuals. The matter is likely to be a topic of controversy for some time.

The Regulation of Homosexuality

Religious objections to homosexuality are part of a larger context of social regulation of sexuality. One of the most distinctive features of human societies is the variety and strength of controls that govern sexual behavior. Sex is one of the most strongly regulated acts of human beings; even in relatively permissive societies, sexual activity receives special social attention. Even those individuals who regard sex between consenting adults as natural and private have had to recognize the powerful social pressures, norms, attitudes, and taboos on sex, independent of legal restrictions.

Homosexuality is perhaps most visible in social settings that encourage sexuality but are one-sexed in composition, such as in the military, boarding schools, prisons, and other one-sex societies in which sexuality may be encouraged—or tolerated—but where there is no opportunity for heterosexual activity. This is not to say that homosexuals are merely heterosexuals who do not have a heterosexual outlet; homosexuality is obviously much more complex than that. But it should be recognized that homosexuality is often neither a permanent nor invariant orientation, and that many people are able at different times to adapt to changing sexual circumstances.

Legal prohibitions regarding sexuality, of course, do not take into account such variation, although social norms are able to accommodate situational contingencies. Laws against unwanted sexual aggression (e.g., rape), specific forms of sexual behavior (e.g., sodomy), and sexuality with commercial intent (e.g., prostitution) apply to everyone in all social situations. The social regulation of sexuality, however, is more complicated because it is often difficult to determine the content of norms and where or when they might apply.

The Social Regulation of Sexuality

As pointed out earlier, sexuality is not just a biological fact or condition; it is a learned one. This means that people learn sexual content in the larger and more general process of socialization. There is much that people must learn: appropriate norms, objects, relationships, times and places for sex, situations, partners—indeed, everything that is sexual. This learning takes place over an extended period of time, but it suffers from a serious handicap in our society: People do not like to talk much about sex in personal and intimate terms. Sex is considered impolite and intensely private in some groups. Many believe that sex should be discussed only in the context of a family, though many parents find the subject difficult to address. As a result, the sexual socialization process tends to be imperfect and overburdened with misinformation or non-information concerning sexuality, the result of which much is misunderstood. The process involves not only sex education but the communication of norms and values that pertain to the sex act in its social and religious context. This is obviously a very subtle process.

One reason that the norms governing sex hold such power is that sexual drive itself is powerful. Sexual gratification is not required for individual survival in the same way as the alleviation of hunger, thirst, or fatigue. As a result, restrictions on sexuality are often more absolute than those governing, for example, ingesting food which would be more likely to permit exceptions necessary for survival (Davis, 1976:223). When one includes the fact that sexuality is experienced mentally and visually, as well as behaviorally, and that sexual behavior can take many different forms, one can realize that there is an enormous variety of sexual behaviors to regulate.

Sexual norms are linked with reproductive norms because sexual intercourse has the potential to create a new human being. This means that the social regulation of sexuality is often considered part of the social regulation system that relates to the bearing and rearing of children. Child rearing is obviously a fundamental societal need, and every society has an interest in ensuring that child bearing and rearing are performed in a way that is believed to most benefit the society. This is why many modern discussions of homosexuality often revolve around family issues, as well as why there is a strong temptation to use the criminal law as a backup to existing social attitudes.

Religious and Legal Regulation of Sexuality

There are a number of sexual acts that appear to demand a legal response, such as those with involuntary partners and those with children regardless of their consent. Our concern in this chapter is not with such acts, which would affect both heterosexuality and homosexuality and about which there is widespread agreement. Rather, we are concerned with consensual homosexual relations involving adults. One question is whether, and to what extent, the law should be involved in regulating the sexual relations of consenting adults, whether the behavior is homosexual or heterosexual. Despite one's opinion on that issue, the fact is that sexual acts associated with homosexuality have been subject to criminal law in the United States and elsewhere, and this situation has existed for a long time.

Early religious codes were very influential on the content of laws regarding homosexuality, but this influence was not as simple as it might seem. Ancient Jewish regulations on sex were subsequently adopted by the Christian Church. These regulations were incorporated into ecclesiastical laws that influenced thinking about homosexuality during the medieval ages and later provided the basis for the legal condemnation of homosexuality in English common law (see Katz, 1976 and 1983). There were a number of prohibitions in the Old Testament concerning a variety of acts and conditions, but all of them died out except for homosexuality. The prohibition against homosexuality was retained in the Christian tradition.

Before this time, the concept of homosexuality did not exist as it does now. The Hebrews and the Greeks had no word for homosexuality. Ancient Greek and Roman cultures permitted sexual activity with either sex, although exclusive sexuality with the same sex may have been rare and considered a bit unusual (McWilliams, 1993:605). In their now-famous survey, Ford and Beach studied 76 folk societies and found that among 49 of them, or 64 percent, "homosexual activities of one sort or another are considered normal and socially acceptable for certain members of the community" (Ford and Beach, 1951:130).

Some observers hold that the negative position of the Christian church on homosexuality has been longstanding and consistent (Soards, 1995). Other writers claim that homosexuality was tolerated in the Christian tradition until the mid-thirteenth century, at which time the church adopted a more negative view (Boswell, 1980). This is not to say that homosexuality was encouraged in earlier periods. Soards (1995:38-40) points out that regulations in Spain about 700 A.D. held that homosexuals were to be castrated, an edict reinforced later by declarations of the king of Spain at the Council of Toledo. By the twelfth century, homosexuals were ordered to show through confession and penance that they were worthy of redemption from their "shameful sin of sodomy."

Homosexuality did not play a prominent role in ecclesiastical debates during the Reformation, but by the twentieth century, Protestant thought underwent a marked change from earlier positions. Increasingly, homosexuality was referred to as a moral perversity. Theologian Karl Barth (cited in Soards, 1995:43) described homosexuality as a "physical, psychological, and social sickness, the phenomenon of perversion, decadence, and decay, which can emerge when man refuses to admit the validity of the divine command." A similar transformation took place in the Latter-Day Saints (Mormon) Church, in which homoeroticism was tolerated until the mid-1950s, when the Church expressed strong condemnation (Quinn, 1996).

Eventually, the language of illness and therapy began to replace and challenge the tone of moral condemnation. Much of this change occurred in the context of "hate the sin, love the sinner," an approach that has generated confusion among many Christians, if only because the distinction between "homosexual" and "homosexual behavior" is no sharper than it is between "heterosexual" and "heterosexual behavior." In each instance, peoples' sexual orientation does not provide enough information to define or categorize them. Furthermore, it may make little sense—except perhaps to a few—to proclaim that one has a sexual orientation that is not acted upon. In those instances where there is a separation of sexual behavior from sexual orientation (e.g., as with priests under a vow of celibacy), it is recognized that the individual has had to make a remarkably strong and unusual commitment. To some, including, ironically, fundamentalist Protestants, such a separation is itself often seen as unnatural.

The most basic division in debates about homosexuality "is between those who maintain that homosexuality is proscribed by Scripture and by God's design for human sexuality and those who argue that the love of God surely must embrace the lifestyle of those who discover that by nature they are homosexuals" (Baird and Baird, 1995:18). Those who adhere to the former view are more punitive than those who express the latter, more charitable view. Combatants often appeal either to Scripture or church law or policy for guidance. Some assert that the Bible's few explicit prohibitions on sex between men (there are none against sex between women) is evidence that such behavior is permissible (Bawer, 1996:240-242), whereas others derive no such insight from the absence of categoric prohibition.

But although religious disapproval of homosexuality has seemingly increased over time, legal censure has declined. As with the religious courts, early legal prohibitions were strict. Emperor Justinian condemned homosexual offenders to death in 538 A.D., and this portion of the Justinian Code served as the basis for the punishment of homosexuality in Europe for 1,300 years.

During most of this time, homosexual acts were dealt with by ecclesiastical, but not government, courts in England, often with torture followed by death. By 1533, the jurisdiction of such offenses was vested in royal courts, and the English statute enacted at that time provided for death "without benefit of clergy." Claiming "clergy" was typically allowed for offenses deemed less serious. The offender had to demonstrate an ability to read, a condition at the time found almost exclusively among church officials. Later, a particular biblical passage ("the hanging verse") had to be recited, and illiterate offenders often had trouble memorizing the verse beforehand. This punishment remained until the nineteenth century when it was reduced to life imprisonment. In France, as late as the mid-eighteenth century, homosexuals were burned at the stake. The Napoleonic Code, enacted after the French Revolution, omitted explicit mention of homosexual acts, a situation that still prevails in many European countries.

During the course of this century, other European countries maintained strong legal prohibitions against homosexuality, but they were infrequently enforced. Today, although laws seek to protect young people from homosexual acts and to protect "public decency," most continental European countries do not consider homosexual acts committed in private by consenting adults to be criminal (Geis, 1979). Even in those countries where the behavior is defined by law as criminal, violators are generally not prosecuted.

Much of this trend can be traced to the 1950s, when a British governmental committee was charged with the task of examining the laws relating to homosexual behavior and prostitution. The committee was created because there was concern that the penalties for many sexual acts were too severe. Under the British law of 1956, for example, sodomy with a person under age was punishable by life imprisonment; the sentence for the same crime committed with adults was imprisonment. The Wolfenden Report, which its committee issued in 1957, recommended the cessation of penalties for homosexual acts between consenting adults. After long debate, penalties in England for homosexual acts in private between adults over 21 were removed in 1965. Sanctions remained for acts with those under age and for persons who procure others for homosexual acts.

As in Europe, American laws were heavily influenced by religious admonitions. The law of criminal sodomy in colonial Connecticut's statute, for example, followed closely the wording of Leviticus (18:22):

> That if any man shall lie with mankind, as he lieth with woman-kind, both of them have committed abomination; they shall be put to death, except it shall appear that one of the parties was forced or under 15 years of age. . . . (cited in Dworkin, 1987:153)

Other American statutes maintained a similar moral outrage, if not the precise wording of Biblical injunctions. The 1837 North Carolina statute makes reference to "the abominable and detestable crime against nature, not [to] be named among Christians" (cited in Dworkin, 1987:153). Although many state laws would not subsequently contain such preachy embellishments, it was clear that sodomy was generally considered to be both a crime against law and against nature. Perhaps reflecting the depth of feeling on the issue, it was not until 1962 that Illinois became the first American state to repeal the criminal sodomy statute.

As of June, 1995, there were operative sodomy laws in Alabama, Arkansas, Arizona, Florida, Georgia, Idaho, Kansas, Louisiana, Maryland, Minnesota, Mississippi, Missouri, Montana (where there is litigation pending), North Carolina, Oklahoma, Rhode Island, South Carolina, Tennessee (where there also is litigation pending), Utah, and Virginia (Eskridge, 1996:135). Texas and Michigan have had lower court decisions invalidating their sodomy laws, and Massachusetts' sodomy law has been partially invalidated.

Legal Changes

The changes in European laws preceded those concerning homosexual acts in the United States. The law has been used to regulate homosexuality, but there has been tremendous variation in the nature of that regulation. The laws of many states now make homosexual acts a crime only if committed publicly (as it is with heterosexual acts), effectively exempting all homosexual acts engaged in private. In the United States, it is not a crime to *be* a homosexual but rather to commit a homosexual *act*, such as sodomy, fellatio, and mutual masturbation. However, by identifying sexual activities associated mainly with homosexuality, the intent of the legislation is clear.

Soliciting for homosexual acts is also generally a crime, as is soliciting for heterosexual acts. Practically speaking, the only homosexual acts that are punished are between males and not between women. Although some states provide for relatively high penalties (up to 10 years, with a few states providing from 30 to 60 years), such felony laws are very rarely if ever enforced. Where there are arrests, they are usually for solicitation, a misdemeanor with less than a one-year penalty. It must also be recognized that though laws are seldom enforced, they remain on the books and represent a strong, official symbolic expression of disapproval.

As recently as 1986, the U.S. Supreme Court ruled on the constitutionality of state laws against sodomy. In August, 1982, Michael Hardwick was cited for carrying an open bottle of beer in public. He never showed up in court, and the police obtained a warrant for his arrest. A police officer went to Hardwick's apartment, was invited in by a guest, and subsequently saw Hardwick—who was in his own bed at the time—and another male engaging in an act of sodomy. The Georgia statute prohibited sodomy, which was defined as an act where one "performs or submits to any sexual act involving the sex organs of one person and the mouth or anus of another." After the police arrested Hardwick under this law, the case was referred to the local prosecutor who refused to take it to court, indicating that he did not normally prosecute under sex statutes unless the display was public. But Hardwick decided to push the matter as a "test case" of the sodomy statute.

Hardwick's lawyers reasoned that what was involved was a sexual act between two consenting adults. Hardwick lost at trial but won in a court of appeals, leading the state of Georgia to take the case to the U.S. Supreme Court. The case reached the Court in 1986. In a closely voted 1986 decision (5-4), the court ruled that state laws against sodomy were not unconstitutional. The deciding voter, Justice Powell, is reported to have later regretted his decision, perhaps more than any other he had made during his time on the U.S. Supreme Court (Toobin, 1996). Hardwick is currently in prison for life.

In spite of the *Hardwick* ruling, the sodomy statutes in a number of states have been repealed, most of them during the past two decades. One of the most significant decisions was *Commonwealth v. Wasson*, decided in 1993, in which the state Supreme Court in Kentucky ruled that statutes prohibiting sodomy violated the state constitution. The *Wasson* decision, the exact opposite of *Hardwick*, was justified on the grounds that the constitutionality of sodomy statutes can also be addressed at the state level, because states as well as the federal government have constitutions.

There are other laws that relate to homosexuals. For example, all states at the time of this writing prohibit marriage by people of the same sex. The implications of this prohibition are more far reaching than the nature of the relationship between two homosexuals, because they extend to the legal consequences that often include the non-recognition of the union for purposes of fair housing and insurance benefits. The issue of same-sex marriage is one that we will address shortly.

The Consequences of Legal Regulation

Few homosexuals regard themselves as criminals or deviants, as being "sick" or immoral. The negative views of others as expressed in stigmatizing efforts, however, are not without their effect. Many homosexuals believe it is necessary to conceal their homosexuality from others. They report that they sometimes feel guilty for their behavior and fear negative social sanctions from such persons as family, friends, and employers with whom they wish to continue to associate. Often, the homosexual may be outwardly gregarious and popular but inwardly feel rejected and alone (Harry, 1982).

There is little doubt that most homosexuals have experienced negative stigma because of their homosexuality, and there is little doubt that such censure has much of its roots in legal measures to control homosexuality. Most of this stigma has been generated in social situations by heterosexuals and has ranged from mild expressions of disapproval to assault, or "gay bashing." Between these extremes, homosexuals have experienced ridicule and scorn, moral condemnation, and social avoidance. Some say that many of these sanctions reflect homophobia, the fear and misunderstanding of homosexuality. Whatever their origins, the sanctions experienced by homosexuals have been substantial, although variable, during different historical periods. There is no known society that values homosexuality, though some have tolerated it at different times, in different individuals, and under different circumstances.

One consequence of both legal and social regulation in the 1990s is the increased militancy of some homosexuals. Not content to be the objects of society's disapproval, some gays have declared a new view of homosexuality as non-deviant, acceptable behavior. Bolstered by recent biological work that suggests a chromosomal basis for at least some portion of sexual preference, militant gays have attempted to "take back" the conception and language of homosexuality from the larger society (Browning, 1994). Groups such as Queer Nation often protest conventional normative definitions by affirming gayness.

These very activities, however, demonstrate the power and impact of the stigma on homosexuality. Gay men and women are often put in the position of asserting that they are "normal" and everyone else is out of step. On the one hand, militant gays deny that homosexuality is deviant; on the other, they experience substantial discomfort trying to live in a heterosexual world that generally disapproves of them. Not wishing to accept the larger community's social and legal definitions of their sexuality, many of them rebel against the labels in ways that often accentuate their differences rather than their similarities. Such efforts are not individualistic responses but represent a collective reaction that stems from a political movement.

The Gay Movement and Gay Communities

The gay movement became politically visible on June 28, 1969, when patrons of Stonewall, a gay bar in New York City's Greenwich Village, refused to cooperate with police who were carrying out a routine raid. The patrons, composed mostly of flamboyant drag queens and prostitutes, escalated their protests against the police into nearly five days of rioting that eventually involved hundreds of sympathetic supporters. The rioting appeared to accomplish little; no laws were changed, gays continued to be "bashed," and homosexuals continued to be regarded as socially and sexually marginal people. The significance of this resistance was in the imagination it sparked in gay people throughout the country and elsewhere. Many gays became eager to reject the social stigma and shame heaped upon them by conventional society (Bawer, 1996:4-15). Stonewall became synonymous with any resistance to that oppression.

Although resistance to social stigma and legal repression had existed prior to Stonewall, the rioting galvanized gay opinion like no other event. Gays had witnessed the success of the women's movement, which grew out of similarly felt oppression. But gays and lesbians had obstacles beyond traditionally held prejudices, reinforced by two of the most powerful institutions of social control in society: religion and the law. The women's movement had to confront antiquated tradition and stodgy beliefs about gender roles but not moral condemnation or night sticks, as did the gay movement.

Only the cleverest and most energetic strategies would stand a chance against such puissant foes. Yet,

> gays developed a territorial base, with a matrix of bars, associations, publications, theaters, churches, writers, comedians, professional services, and eventually political representatives. Gayness became a sort of ethnicity with its own codes of recognition, rituals, parades, sacred days, even its own flag with a rainbow motif. (Gitlin, 1995:142-143)

The first generation of gays after Stonewall worked hard to produce such a community, but the effort was thought to require extremism and aggressiveness. It was to be a public community, which meant that homosexuals would have to be enticed to come out of the closet. Gay pride marches, celebrations of Stonewall, and organized events by such groups as Queer Nation were meant to shock, annoy, retaliate, and educate—all at the same time. There was a portion of the gay community that "developed a radical direct-action movement among men and women who are no longer interested in dwelling only within the safe ghettos of gaydom" (Browning, 1994:25). The closet was defined as only a temporary haven from the political realities of the movement and the drive for eventual freedom.

As in the women's movement, the gay movement produced a gulf among different generations, antagonisms among leaders and followers over points of ideology, and gender segregation. The movement was and continues to be far from monolithic. Some leaders oppose discrimination in any form; others preach the politics of sexual identity in which gayness must be affirmed as something special and distinctive. Some gays are willing to live peaceably in the absence of overt discrimination; others want no less than a social recanting of previous wrongs done to gays. Some wish only that gay bashing would be eliminated; others are more militant in demanding retributive—and in some cases—retaliatory justice.

The women's movement can appeal to both men and women and, hence, can lay theoretical claim to a large segment of potential supporters in the population, but the gay movement cannot assert itself on the basis of numbers only. Rather, it has to rely, ironically, on the moral strength and legal correctness of its position. Such a strategy involves a tricky balancing act, in which previously denigrated acts and conditions are reclaimed from the oppressors and reaffirmed. The first target has been language. The words "gay," "homosexual," and "lesbian" had served their purpose well for those before Stonewall, but they seemed old-fashioned in the 1990s. These were terms for the closet, not public discourse. More suitable to the militants were the previously hated expressions of "queer," "faggot," and "dyke." By claiming such words as their own and providing them with positive meaning, the movement believed that it would liberate the terms from their oppressors. Frank Browning (1994:34) summarizes the strategy:

> Steal back all the hateful epithets thrown at gay people over the decades, turn them inside out, and celebrate them. If homophobes and fundamentalist preachers rant on about homosexuals recruiting the young because it's the only way to replenish their unholy ranks, then steal the language back. Yes, queer people want to recruit the young, not by kidnapping young men as Chicago serial killer John Wayne Gacy did, but by being mentors and role models who would show gay and lesbian adolescents that they are not alone, that they are not freaks, that they need not continue committing suicides at three times the rate of straight teenagers.

So gay activists took one of two directions. The first direction was found in the first-generation gay activist after Stonewall, a militant who exaggerated gayness for effect. "Fag power, Dyke Power, Que-e-e-e-r Nation!" was the shout. Or "We're Queer! We're Here! Get Used to It!" signs, outrageous clothes, public displays of sexuality—anything that was acceptable to get across the message that the days of passivity—the closet—were over. The militant, dissatisfied with continued discrimination and social censure, would demand equality by highlighting the differences between gays and straights. One writer recounts that some gays were able to read a manifesto that advised:

The next time some straight person comes down on you for being angry, tell them that until things change, you don't need any more evidence that the world turns at your expense. You don't need to see only hetero couples grocery shopping on your TV. . . . You don't want any more baby pictures shoved in your face until you can have or keep your own. No more weddings, showers, anniversaries, please, unless they were our own brothers and sisters celebrating. And tell them not to dismiss you by saying, "You have rights," "You have privileges," "You're overreacting," or "You have a victim's mentality." Tell them, "GO AWAY FROM ME, until YOU can change." (Browning, 1994:27)

While most gays would reject this statement as little more than an understandable but politically ineffective tantrum, rage is an important component of the gay agenda. Unmistakable gains have been attained politically and socially, and many gays have experienced what one writer called "virtual equality" (Vaid, 1995), a condition of being almost there, almost equal. By the mid-1990s, gays were said to be "virtually normal" (Sullivan, 1995). But "virtually" would be insufficient for many.

The second, more recent direction was that of the subdued activist who saw political extremism as part of a short-term agenda. More meaningful change would involve direct education, modeling, and quiet conformity. The gay educator didn't want to shake the boat, only to make sure there was room for everyone on board. He or she was interested in the more subtle, longer-term strategy of convincing straights that gays were very much like them in most of the ways that count. The moderate was convinced that the key to social change was political activism which, in turn, required a resolution of the basic conflict in the gay movement. The question needing resolution was whether gays were different from straights of whatever race and gender such that they required special status, or whether gays were just like everyone else except in sexual orientation.

The presentation of this conflict now determines the direction of the gay movement. What is required is not merely agreement on a political strategy but discussion and resolution of many issues, involving the extent to which homosexuality is deviant and according to whom, the degree to which gays can be accepted in straight society, and the role of law in liberating or repressing them.

Two Recent Issues

As public opinion expresses more toleration toward homosexuality, two recent issues continue to polarize people. These issues are the acceptability of same-sex marriages and the extent to which homosexuality should be considered a protected status for purposes of law and public policy.

Same-Sex Marriages

As with many issues concerning homosexuality, people are in conflict over both the appropriateness and legality of same-sex marriages. The issue took on more political urgency in 1995 when a special commission appointed by the Hawaiian legislature recommended the legalization of same-sex marriages. The legal proceedings had begun in 1990, when a Hawaiian lower court heard a case in which three gay couples claimed that that state's constitution afforded them the right to obtain marriage licenses. One of the couples, Ninia Baehr and Genora Dancel, had met only a few months before they decided to get married. The couple had strong emotional feelings about each other, but they were specifically motivated when Baehr sustained a serious ear infection and her medical bills mounted. "I wanted to get her on my insurance, but only married people can do that," said Dancel, a television station engineer (Barrett, 1996). When denied the licenses, the couples filed a lawsuit against the state of Hawaii. The case, *Baehr v. Lewin,* first reached the state Supreme Court in 1993, at which time the court agreed with the couple.

The following year, the state legislature passed a law defining marriage as a union solely between a man and a woman. The Hawaiian Supreme Court delayed rehearing the *Baehr* case until a special commission report was issued. The commission in December 1995 recommended legalizing same-sex marriages, saying in effect that there was no reason not to recognize them.

The matter is noteworthy for a number of reasons, not the least of which is that no case concerning gay marriages has progressed so far in the court system of any state or the federal government. Although the case originated in Hawaii, the issue has had national significance because the "full faith and credit clause" of the U.S. Constitution requires other states to recognize Hawaiian marriages.

In other words, if you are married in Hawaii, you are married in the other 49 states as well, unless states pass laws specifically withholding recognition and the courts allow such statutes to stand. This is the same situation for divorces; a divorce in one state is recognized in all other states.

As a result of the Hawaiian ruling, some states introduced legislation withholding recognition of same-sex marriages. Utah, which has a long history of dealing with non-traditional marriages, passed a law in 1995 that denies recognition of marriages that do not conform to Utah law. In 1996, South Dakota defined marriage in that state as a union between a man and a woman. Legislation of this sort is typically justified with the rationale that the state has an interest in encouraging heterosexual marriages to best guarantee a satisfactory environment for raising children.

Similar legislation has been considered in a number of states, but the outcome of that legislation is far from certain. The Iowa House of Representatives, for example, approved a bill on February 20, 1996, withholding recognition of same-sex marriages from other states. The Iowa Senate subsequently refused to take up the measure, effectively killing it, at least during that legislative session. The outcome of legislation in other states is likely to take several years to reach a conclusion, but a federal law was enacted in 1996, when the Senate and the House of Representatives passed a bill rejecting same-sex marriage.

A different outcome occurred in Oregon. When the Oregon State Employees' Benefit board denied medical, health, and life insurance benefits to the partners of three lesbian state employees, they and their partners sued the state (McCall, 1996). A Portland judge ordered the state to pay the benefits, as the couples had "conducted themselves as members of a family," and each had "enjoyed a long-term and committed relationship identical to marriage." The state of Oregon may appeal the ruling.

Attitudes Toward Same-Sex Marriages. The divided opinions among legislators paralleled those found among Iowa citizens. When the *Des Moines Register* (April 12, 1996, p. 1M) asked in a public opinion poll whether the state should recognize same-sex marriages, 41 percent of the respondents said it should outlaw such marriages, compared to 46 percent who thought that the state should neither condone nor condemn them. Another 9 percent believed such marriages should be recognized, and 4 percent were unsure. It is noteworthy that there were so few people who were unsure and relatively few who approved such unions. Of even more interest is the number of respondents—46 percent, the largest single group—who believed that the state should not be involved in such matters.

National poll figures concerning attitudes on same-sex marriages differ from the Iowa results in the degree of opposition to such marriages. A poll conducted by NBC News reported that 60 percent disapproved of recognizing same-sex marriages, and just 26 percent approved of them. The rest of the respondents were undecided. Similar results were obtained by a Gallup poll released on April 4, 1996. Overall, two-thirds of respondents indicated that same-sex marriages should not be sanctioned by law, compared to 27 percent who said they should be legally recognized. Even among those who believed that homosexuality is or should be an "acceptable lifestyle," 43 percent were opposed to legally sanctioned gay marriages.

The Issues. There are two kinds of marriages, civil and religious. Civil marriage is a kind of legally sanctioned relationship available to all within a political jurisdiction, subject to constitutional standards and procedures. Religious marriage involves church recognition of a union and is subject to the rules and policies of individual churches, as well as those of the state. The boundaries of what constitutes an acceptable civil marriage have changed considerably through our history. There was a time when African Americans and Asian Americans were not permitted to marry at all; until 1967, laws in some states provided for criminal prosecution of those who married someone of the "wrong" race; and in earlier times women who married were considered the implicit property of their spouses. All of these policies under civil marriage have changed.

There are also differences between civil and religious marriages, but such differences do not invalidate the marriage. The Roman Catholic Church, for example, does not recognize a second marriage after divorce, although the marriage will be recognized under civil law. It is also the case that many gay couples have been "married" in religious ceremonies conducted in churches and temples in many states. The issue with respect to the Hawaii case is not whether individual churches will recognize same-sex marriages, but whether they will be recognized in the civil realm.

Most objections to same-sex marriages reflect negative social attitudes toward homosexuality. Furthermore, some people are concerned that official recognition of same-sex marriage might be construed as a societal endorsement of homosexuality and perhaps even sodomy. Such a concern, of course, assumes that the issuance of a marriage license entails something more than merely filling out a form. State issuance of licenses to ride a bicycle on public streets, operate a chauffeur service, or run a restaurant is not an endorsement of those activities; it is merely an effort to make them more orderly and controlled. It is debatable whether state-sanctioned same-sex marriage would make society more civilized, as argued by Eskridge (1996), but it is certainly the case that obtaining a marriage license is easier than obtaining a driver's license, which includes long lines and a test. State interest in marriage has demonstrated no such concern or barriers.

One persuasive argument is that the equal protection clause of the Fourteenth Amendment requires that only in cases of "compelling state interest" should the government be legally allowed to prohibit marriage among consenting adults. The issue is sex discrimination, because to prohibit homosexual marriage is by definition to limit the choice of marriage partners. A woman cannot marry a woman, and a man cannot marry a man. Appiah (1996:54) points out the following:

> Some will object that this is preposterous: the current law treats men and women equally in requiring both to marry someone of the other gender. But, by that line of reasoning . . . we could defend anti-miscegenation laws: for all those require both whites and blacks to marry within their "races."

Clearly, this is a line of reason that has long been rejected in the United States, but the legal system has yet to fully embrace its implications for homosexuality.

Homosexuality as a Protected Status

The law is a powerful resource that can be used to confer political advantages on groups. It is not surprising to find that it has been used to restrict and regulate homosexual conduct. Because it is a resource, of course, the law can be used by homosexuals as well as other groups, such as in the case of anti-discrimination legislation. The importance of such legislation is unmistakable to those affected by it. One letter writer responding to a newspaper editorial on same-sex marriages took issue with the position that gays were asking for special rights:

> I am a 43-year-old gay man in a committed relationship who is raising an 18-year-old straight son. Currently I do have special rights because I am gay. I have the right to be fired from my job and be denied housing in 41 states without legal recourse simply because I am gay. I have the right to be denied custody of my son in most legal jurisdictions, regardless of my parenting capabilities. I have the right to be denied visitation of my lover in a hospital's intensive care unit because we are not legally considered to be family. I have the right to incur large legal bills and suffer great uncertainty in an estate settlement if he dies before I do, despite any wills that we might prepare. I also have the very special right to have my lover (a non-American) deported, as he is in the U.S. on a temporary work permit; if we were able to legally marry, a green card could be easily obtained.
>
> I don't want these special rights or any others. I just want the right to be able to lead a happy, healthy, peaceful and legally committed life with the person that I happen to love. I want the right to marry him. These rights seem to be the same rights that any loving, committed couple desire and deserve. In my mind, they have a "family values" ring to them. (*Wall Street Journal,* March 22, 1996, p. A13)

Because rights are not absolute and must be interpreted within moral and political contexts (Dworkin, 1977), what sometimes appears to be a right for one group looks like the deprivation of a right for another. And this is more than an academic discussion.

On November 3, 1992, Colorado voters were asked to consider a referendum which, if passed, would alter the state's constitution. The amendment stated the following:

> Neither the State of Colorado, through any of its branches or departments, nor any of its agencies, political subdivisions, municipalities or school districts, shall enact, adopt or enforce any statute, regulation, ordinance or policy whereby homosexual, lesbian or bisexual orientation, conduct, practices or relationships shall constitute or otherwise be the basis of or entitle any person or class of

persons to have or claim any minority status quota preferences, protected status or claim of discrimination.

The amendment passed by a vote of 53 percent to 47 percent. This passage meant that all state and local government units were barred from providing any protection to homosexuals, lesbians, and bisexuals against discrimination. It also resulted in substantial legal maneuvering. First, a suit was filed asking a court to declare the amendment unconstitutional. A state court invalidated the amendment, allowing ordinances or policies prohibiting discrimination based on sexual orientation to remain intact in Denver, Boulder, Aspen, and several other Colorado cities.

The central argument was whether homosexuals were entitled to the category of protected status. Colorado state officials argued that the amendment merely denied "special rights" to homosexuals and put them in the same legal and social position as everyone else. Members of the homosexual community and others argued that the amendment itself was discriminatory since it removed homosexuals, but no other group, from legal protections in housing, insurance, health benefits, welfare, private education, and employment.

It was on the basis of this argument that the case eventually wound its way to the Colorado Supreme Court (see *Evans v. Romer*, 854 P.2d 1270, Colo. 1993). There, the justices ruled the law was unconstitutional because

> the Equal Protection Clause of the United States Constitution protects the fundamental right to participate equally in the political process. . . . Any legislation or state constitutional amendment which infringes on this right by "fencing out" an independently identifiable class of persons must be subject to strict judicial scrutiny.

An appeal was made to the U.S. Supreme Court which subsequently ruled on May 21, 1996, in a 6-3 vote, that the Colorado amendment was indeed unconstitutional.

The Supreme Court decision, of course, did not settle the larger issue of whether homosexuals constitute a group in need of special protection. At issue was one basis for the same-sex marriage case in Hawaii. The attorney for Baehr and Dancel in the Hawaiian case argued that his clients should be permitted to marry because, among other reasons, homosexuals constituted an oppressed group that could not be denied equal protection of the law, in this case the marriage law (*Wall Street Journal*, June 19, 1996, p. A5). Continued legal action and social debate is guaranteed.

Conclusion

Homosexuality has been tolerated in many societies, but it has never been respected or held as an ideal of sexual relations. In such societies as ancient Greece and Rome, homosexuality was permitted but not praised. There is no reliable way, however, to gauge public opinion in such societies, nor is it possible to know accurately whether homosexuality, although tolerated, was viewed negatively or positively. Finding instances in which homosexuality was tolerated is quite different from claiming that it was esteemed.

Viewing homosexuality negatively, however, does not necessarily mean that it is an appropriate candidate for criminalization. All sexual behavior is socially regulated and some is legally regulated. Recent changes in opinion and law may reflect fundamental changes in the way in which homosexuality is regarded, but the process of greater open-mindedness is indeed slow. The Wolfenden Report that recommended the decriminalization of homosexuality in Great Britain in the 1950s generated considerable controversy. Though the recommendation was eventually enacted into law, the British public continued to oppose the legislation. A Gallup Poll taken after the Report was issued showed that 38 percent of the respondents favored the legislation, 15 percent were uncertain, and 47 percent were against it (Williams, 1960).

It is doubtful that legal prohibitions can be more effective than religious and historical restrictions in regulating sexual conduct. Yet curiously, there are contemporary legislators who seem to find more power in the law than it can legitimately possess. In the summer of 1994, the family of a deceased woman were shocked to witness a man in a funeral home fondling her dead body. Their outrage, along with the fact that the Iowa criminal code did not prohibit such behavior, prompted action at the next legislative session. A law prohibiting sexual acts with a corpse was championed by the chair of the Senate Judiciary Committee, who reported that he was surprised to learn of the law's failure to prohibit this behavior, a situation that represented to him an obvious omission. "From time to time," he said, "we find that even though the Iowa code is as large as it is, some individuals have a way of finding that one niche it doesn't cover" (*Des Moines Register,* February 22, 1996, p. 2B). It could be argued that the reason there is not more of this kind of aberrant behavior is not that most people are deterred by the law, but that most find such behavior highly objectionable, regardless of its legal status.

Laws exist to achieve social rather than individual regulation, whereas religious edicts are often the arena of disagreements. The norms that govern sexual behavior are usually powerful and broad. Some societies also have a system of laws that bolster these social restrictions. The difficulty is that although social regulation varies from group to group, legal prohibitions apply to all within a political jurisdiction. This means that the law may not be consistent with the content of the sexual norms of any given individual's group. In some cases, the law may be just the opposite of the group's edicts. Homosexuality has been subject to legal prohibition for a long time in the Western legal tradition, but the content and perhaps intent of that law has changed over time. So too has public opinion, which in the end is a formidable force in the efforts to shape that law.

References

Akers, Ronald L. 1985. *Deviant Behavior: A Social Learning Approach,* 3rd edition. Belmont, CA: Wadsworth.

Appiah, K. Anthony. 1996. "The Marrying Kind." *New York Review of Books,* 43 (June 20): 48-54.

Baird, Robert M., and M. Katherine Baird, eds. 1995. "Introduction." *Homosexuality: Debating the Issues.* New York: Prometheus Books.

Barrett, Paul M. 1996. "How Hawaii Became Ground Zero in Battle over Gay Marriages." *Wall Street Journal,* June 17, 1996, pp. 1A, 5A.

Bawer, Bruce. 1996. *Beyond Queer: Challenging Gay Left Orthodoxy.* New York: Free Press.

Boswell, John. 1980. *Christianity, Social Tolerance, and Homosexuality.* Chicago: University of Chicago Press.

Browning, Frank. 1994. *The Culture of Desire.* New York: Simon and Schuster.

Davis, Kingsley. 1976. "Sexual Behavior." Pp. 219-261 in Robert K. Merton and Robert Nisbet (eds.), *Contemporary Social Problems,* 4th ed. New York: Harcourt Brace Jovanovich.

Dworkin, Andrea. 1987. *Intercourse.* New York: Free Press.

Dworkin, Ronald. 1977. *Taking Rights Seriously.* New York: Oxford University Press.

Endleman, Robert. 1990. *Deviance and Psychopathology: The Sociology and Psychology of Outsiders.* Malabar, FL: Robert Krieger Publishing.

Eskridge, William N. 1996. *The Case for Same-Sex Marriage: From Sexual Liberty to Civilized Commitment.* New York: Free Press.

Ford, Clellan S., and Frank A. Beach. 1951. *Patterns of Sexual Behavior.* New York: Harper and Row.

Gallup Poll. 1986. "Sharp Decline Found in Support for Legalizing Gay Relations." *The Gallup Report,* Report Number 254, November: 24-26.

Geis, Gilbert. 1979. *Not the Law's Business.* New York: Schoken.

Gitlin, Todd. 1995. *The Twilight of Common Dreams.* New York: Henry Holt.

Goode, Erich, and Richard T. Troiden, eds. 1974. *Sexual Deviance and Sexual Deviants.* New York: Morrow.

Greenberg, David F. 1988. *The Construction of Homosexuality.* Chicago: University of Chicago Press.

Hamer, Dean, and Peter Copeland. 1994. *The Science of Desire: The Search for the Gay Gene and the Biology of Behavior.* New York: Simon and Schuster.

Harry, Joseph. 1982. *Gay Children Grown Up: Gender Culture and Gender Deviance.* New York: Praeger.

Hu, Stella, Angela M. L. Pattatucci, Chavis Patterson, Lin Li, David W. Fulker, Stacy S. Cherny, Leonid Kruglyak, and Dean H. Hamer. 1995. "Linkage Between Sexual Orientation And Chromosome Xq28 In Males But Not In Females". *Nature Genetics,* 11: 248-256.

Katz, Jonathan, ed. 1976. *Gay American History: Lesbians and Gay Men in the U.S.A.* New York: Cromwell.

Katz, Jonathan. 1983. *Gay/Lesbian Almanac: A New Documentary.* New York: Harper and Row.

Kinsey, Alfred C., Wardell B. Pomeroy, and Charles E. Martin. 1948. *Sexual Behavior in the Human Male.* Philadelphia: Saunders.

Klassen, Albert D., Colin J. Williams, and Eugene E. Levitt. 1989. *Sex and Morality in the U.S.* Middletown, CT: Wesleyan University Press.

Langevin, Ron. 1985. "Introduction." Pp. 1-13 in *Erotic Preference, Gender Identity, and Aggression in Men: New Research Studies,* Ron Langevin (ed.). Hillsdale, NJ: Lawrence Erlbaum Associates.

Laumann, Edward O., John H. Gagnon, Robert T. Michael, and Stuart Michaels. 1994. *The Social Organization of Sexuality: Sexual Practices in the United States.* Chicago: University of Chicago Press.

LeVay, Simon, and Dean H. Hamer. 1994. "Evidence for a Biological Influence in Male Homosexuality." *Scientific American,* 270: 44-45.

Luckenbill, David F. 1986. "Deviant Career Mobility: The Case of Male Prostitutes." *Social Problems,* 33: 283-293.

Marsiglio, William. 1993. "Attitudes toward Homosexual Activity and Gays as Friends: A National Survey of Heterosexual 15- to 19-Year Old Males." *Journal of Sex Research,* 30: 12-17.

McCall, William. 1996. "Judge: Same-Sex Partners of State Workers Must Get Benefits." *Corvallis Gazette-Times,* August 10, p. 1.

McWilliams, Peter. 1993. *Ain't Nobody's Business If You Do.* Los Angeles: Prelude Press.

New York Academy of Medicine Committee on Public Health. 1964. "Homosexuality," *Bulletin of the New York Academy of Medicine,* 40: 576.

Plummer, Kenneth. 1975. *Sexual Stigma: An Interactionist Account.* London: Routledge and Kegan Paul.

Posner, Richard A. 1992. *Sex and Reason.* Cambridge, MA: Harvard University Press.

Quinn, D. Michael. 1996. *Same-Sex Dynamics among Nineteenth Century Americans: A Mormon Example.* Urbana: University of Illinois Press.

Roper, W. G. 1996. "The Etiology Of Male Homosexuality." *Medical Hypotheses,* 46: 85-88.

Shapiro, Joseph P. 1994. "Straight Talk about Gays." *U.S. News and World Report,* July 5: 47.

Soards, Marion. 1995. *Scripture and Homosexuality: Biblical Authority and the Church Today.* Louisville, KY: Westminster John Knox Press.

Stephan, G. Edward, and Douglas R. McMullin. 1982. "Tolerance of Sexual Nonconformity: City Size as a Situational and Early Learning Determinant." *American Sociological Review,* 47: 411-415.

Sullivan, Andrew. 1995. *Virtually Normal: An Argument about Homosexuality.* New York: Knopf.

Toobin, Jeffery. 1996. "Supreme Sacrifice." *The New Yorker,* July 8: 43-47.

Vaid, Urvashi. 1995. *Virtual Equality: The Mainstreaming of Gay and Lesbian Liberation.* New York: Anchor Doubleday.

Vreeland, Carolyn N., Bernard J. Gallagher III, and Joseph A. McFalls, Jr. 1995. "The Beliefs of Members of the American Psychiatric Association on the Etiology of Male Homosexuality: A National Survey." *Journal of Psychology,* 129: 507-517.

Williams, J. E. Hall. 1960. "Sex Offenses: The British Experience." *Law and Contemporary Problems,* 25: 354-364.

5

Abortion

Abortion was decreed by the U.S. Supreme Court in the 1973 case of *Roe v. Wade* to be a constitutionally protected right during the first three months of pregnancy. But voluntary abortion remains high on the list of behaviors regarded by some as involving "a victim without a crime." The alleged "victim," of course, is the legally aborted fetus. As we shall see, a person's view about whether abortion, even though it is legal, involves a victim depends on what that person believes rather than what that person knows or can scientifically prove.

The fiercely debated issue of abortion provides a special understanding of the semantic, political, and historical aspects of the more general subject of crimes without victims and victims without crimes. Questions surrounding abortion arouse strong passions in many people, and the subject has moved from being primarily a concern of criminal law and medical practice to one that occupies center stage in national politics.

Appointees to the Supreme Court have to field many questions in the U.S. Senate Committee on the Judiciary by those who are determined to know how each candidate will rule if a case that has outlawed or restricted abortion were to come before the court. Depending on what they learn about the person's views on abortion, many senators will vote for or against confirmation.

Both major political parties have to face up to the fact that, according to a 1996 New York Times/CBS Poll, 37 percent of the U.S. population favors abortion for those who want it, 41 percent believes that abortion should be available but under stricter limits than now exist, and 21 percent thinks that abortions should not be permitted. The problem that politicians face is how many of these people will allow their opinions about abortion to dominate their decision of who to vote for. The best guess is that the 21 percent opposing abortion are more likely to be persuaded to vote for a candidate because of his or her views on abortion and that the 78 percent who favor abortion are likely to find other issues more significant when voting.

In its 1992 convention in Houston, the Republican Party adopted a staunchly anti-abortion platform, declaring that "the unborn child has a fundamental individual right to life which cannot be infringed." The platform also called for a "human rights constitutional amendment" and "legislation to make clear that the Fourteenth Amendment's protections apply to unborn children." In 1996, the Party reaffirmed its position at its San Diego convention, but in an appendix to its platform noted its recognition that there are "divergent points of view on issues such as abortion." The political difficulty is that because large majorities (often by a 2-1 split) of Republican partisans do not approve of a constitutional amendment on abortion, Republican candidates often have the delicate task of softening their abortion stand without alienating their constituents who are intensely opposed to abortion.

In contrast, the Democratic party platform took the following position: "Democrats stand behind the right of every woman to choose, consistent with *Roe v. Wade*, regardless of ability to pay, and support a national law to protect that right." For a number of reasons, mostly political, the issue of abortion did not figure prominently in the 1996 presidential election campaigning.

Both sides in the abortion debate are well aware that the public responds more readily to evocative slogans. Thus, one side began to call itself "pro-life" (after all, who can be against life?), and the other side defended its position as "pro-choice" (after all, who in a democratic society can be against free choice?). In the semantic arena at least, the pro-life group gained a tactical edge, because it is apparent that those things that we are allowed to "choose" will always be limited by many conditions, such as our ability to pay for what we want. In addition, there is an edge of selfishness attached to favoring "choice" over "life."

As Dallas Blanchard (1994:1) observes, "Each side wants to seize the high ground of the ethical/moral debate while appealing to as wide a constituency as possible." Pro-lifers, he further notes, maintain that pro-choice advocates are really "pro-death," and pro-choicers insists that pro-lifers are "anti-women."

The Arguments Against Abortion

Those who object to abortions take their stand on a powerful, yet unprovable, position. At moment of conception, they maintain, a human being has come into existence. To deliberately void that human being is murder. This view can be held on religious grounds, as a moral position, or as a matter (to some) of pure common sense. From this premise comes the conclusion that abortion must be outlawed, because all decent people are obligated to oppose murder.

There is also an undertone of denunciation of immoral behavior in the advocacy of some of those who favor the pro-life position. They believe that the possibility of a legal abortion contributes to casual sexual encounters between unmarried people and to carelessness in the use of birth control. But more fundamentally, they believe that a woman who becomes pregnant has the duty—not as a penalty but as an obligation to the unborn child—to carry the fetus to term. Pro-life proponents point out that if for any reason the child is not desired, there are usually plenty of other couples willing to adopt the infant and raise it as their own. Some propose a national registry of people willing to adopt children that could be distributed to doctors and clinics that treat pregnant women. They also advocate tax credits to defray adoption costs.

Pro-lifers sometimes circulate statements from people whose parents had considered abortion but decided against it. Such statements typically express how grateful the person is to be experiencing life and they will often document that person's achievements in order to argue that, without him or her, others' lives would have been depleted. Among the arguments against this kind of reasoning is that the same statement could be made about any instance of sexual intercourse that could have but did not produce a conception. The child of such an event could have made an equally significant contribution to society. Second, opponents can argue, no mention is made of unwanted but unaborted children who live abominable lives. Impoverished, ill-educated, and basically unloved, they may grow up and in the worst-case scenario, murder somebody; hence, it could be argued that had this fetus been aborted, an innocent victim might have been spared.

At times, efforts of some anti-abortion forces to impose their position have gone to extremes, as pro-life advocates have become increasingly infuriated and frustrated. A few have taken the law into their own hands; there have been murders of doctors who perform abortions and of women who work in abortion clinics. Such actions are deplored by most leaders on both sides as intolerable acts, and it is arguable whether they turn more people against the pro-lifers or whether they so frighten potential abortees and doctors that they give up the practice (Simonds, 1996).

The Arguments for Abortion

The pro-choicers insist that their view of the situation leads them to the conclusion (which they cannot prove) that human life does not begin until actual birth. Proponents of this view claim that those who differ with them are perfectly free to avoid abortions for themselves, but that they have no right to impose their undemonstrable beliefs on others.

The pro-choice people regard the necessity to carry an embryo for nine months and to give birth to a child as an unreasonable imposition on someone who does not want to do so. If the use of birth control (which avoids pregnancy) is not against the law, they argue, then why should a slightly later prebirth procedure that accomplishes the same thing be outlawed? To say that a woman's right to abortion is unacceptably selfish, they further argue, is like saying that using anesthetics in childbirth is selfish.

The fight—*battle* is probably a better term—over abortion shows no signs of abating, and it is difficult to think of a compromise that would appease either side. The pro-life group, generally the more vociferous of the two because it is seeking change in the status quo, pickets abortion clinics and lobbies to jettison the rules that permit abortions. It advocates that, at a minimum, individual states should be allowed to legislate on abortion. It is not easy to envisage how precisely such a situation might work out. Clearly, some states would enthusiastically embrace a ban on abortion, but others would not. This would presumably allow those who could afford it to seek out a pro-abortion jurisdiction to accomplish what they need.

Religion and Abortion

The most intense debates over abortion are often related to religious doctrine, most notably that of the Roman Catholic Church which, with its 55 million adherents, includes 23 percent of the American population. A major religious debate centers around the idea of "ensoulment," a concept that seeks to define the exact moment when a fetus becomes a human being with a God-given right to life. After all the constitutional arguments have been heard, the abortion issue inevitably comes back to a fundamental question: how does one view the fetus?

The historical record shows that in early times, Catholic doctrinal authorities held that abortion during the early months of pregnancy did not constitute an ecclesiastic offense. St. Augustine established early Christian dogma on abortion with his fourth-century pronouncement that the soul was not present until the time of fetal quickening; therefore, abortion prior to that time did not constitute the destruction of human life. This view was enunciated by Gratian in *Decretus* (c. 1140), a systematic treatise that formed the kernel of the *Corpus Juris Canonici,* and by the proclamations of Innocent III, head of the church from 1198 to 1216, and those of his immediate successors. The dividing line between "early" and "late" pregnancy was 40 days after conception for a male fetus and 80 days for a female fetus, numbers based on the time it takes to discern genital development in spontaneously aborted fetuses. In practice, because it was impossible to determine the sex of the fetus, 80 days became the latest time for sanctioned abortions (Asma, 1994).

The early Catholic church position on ensoulment was codified as official doctrine during the Council of Trent in the mid-sixteenth century (Schroeder, 1941:385). After persisting for more than two centuries, however, the position was abandoned in 1869, when Pope Pius IX put forward the doctrine of "immediate ensoulment" of the fetus and declared that both early and late non-spontaneous abortions were acts of homicide.

The position of the Roman Catholic church was emphatically restated by Pope John Paul II in his 1995 encyclical *Evangelium Vitae* (The Gospel of Life), which condemns abortion and euthanasia, "crimes which no human law can claim to legitimate." The Pope wrote, "I declare that direct abortion, that is, abortion willed as an end or as a means, always constitutes a grave moral disorder, since it is the deliberate killing of an innocent human being." He warned against the "profound crisis of culture," which he said was caused by the exaltation of the freedom of individuals at the expense of their personal responsibility, a matter which the Pope believed has created "a veritable structure of sin." Experimentation with human embryos, including experiments for the purpose of fertilization outside the human body, were also condemned. Nonetheless, the Pope reassured penitent women who have undergone abortions of God's mercy and the church's care (Bohlen, 1995:A4; John Paul II, 1995).

Catholic leaders and their supporters maintain that pro-abortion views are built on a foundation of selfish expediency and the taking of divine prerogatives into one's own hands. But the Roman Catholic position does not find favor among all the leaders of religious denominations in the United States. Some believe that its adoption into law would direct women intent on abortions to quacks and extortionists rather than having their situation handled by reputable and competent medical practitioners. (*Roe v. Wade* permits abortion during the first trimester but only by qualified medical personnel.) Others say their own theological learning fails to substantiate the view that abortion is a violation of religious doctrine.

Nor are the ranks solid within the Catholic Church. Before his death, Cardinal Cushing of Boston maintained publicly that "Catholics do not need the support of civil law to be faithful to their religious convictions, and they do not seek to impose by law their moral views on other members of society" (Lader, 1965:60). Cardinal Cushing's attitude typifies what has traditionally been the generally flexible position that the Catholic Church has taken on social issues in the United States (Buddle, 1992). However, the subject of abortion has come to be defined in terms of a moral absolute which leaves little room for the kinds of compromises that typically mark church-state relationships.

The question of abortion becomes even more complicated when a pregnancy is caused by the rape of the potential mother. A consistent pro-life position has been that regardless of how the child was conceived, a woman is still morally obligated to bear the child. Prochoicers often oppose this issue with specific examples: if the impregnated victim of rape is a 13- or 14-year old girl, should she also bear this responsibility?

Similar issues of consistency arise for adherents of the pro-life position in regard to their views on capital punishment. Generally, abortion pro-lifers tend to a greater extent to favor capital punishment than pro-choice advocates, as both positions are in line with a more conservative political and social ideology. They usually argue that these two views are not incompatible: the fetus is an innocent human being, but the murderer has forfeited his or her right to life. In that sense, the name "pro-life," like "pro-choice," is applicable to only one particular issue.

Abortion Before It Became Legal

Despite religious objections to abortion, it was widely available in the United States before the nineteenth century. The primary abortionists were midwives and herbalists, who typically advertised their services in newspapers (Rothman, 1989). In the mid-nineteenth century, however, the medical profession launched a crusade to drive these practitioners out of business, branding them as immoral and incompetent. This has been viewed as part of an effort to extend physicians' monopoly over medical services, a campaign marked by a basic contradiction: Doctors maintained that abortion was morally wrong, but they also insisted that only they could determine when it was necessary (Luker, 1984). Organized medicine adopted a "messianic tone . . . to recapture what it considered to be its ancient and rightful place among society's policymakers and savants." One medical spokesperson proclaimed that "the hospital was a temple in which presided a god" and portrayed physicians as disciples of "missionary work" (Mohr, 1978:163-164). Religious groups and arguments played little role in the creation of the anti-abortion statutes in the nineteenth century. Rather, it was largely physicians, newly organized into professional associations, who conducted the crusade (Dworkin, 1993:45). The campaign succeeded. Between 1859 and 1900, many states enacted laws that allowed abortions to be performed only when the pregnancy threatened a woman's life and then only by a medical doctor (Tribe, 1991).

Doctors soon found themselves with patients who wanted abortions but did not meet the legal standards. This group included teenagers, unmarried women, women with "too many" children, women who for personal reasons (such as a demanding job or an unhappy marriage) did not wish to bear or raise a child, and women who (for any number of reasons) did not wish to carry a child for nine months and then place it out for adoption. Women who had the wherewithal and the proper connections were given legal, allegedly "therapeutic" abortions. The less fortunate had to resort to illegal back-alley operators, who sometimes botched the surgeries so badly that their patients died (Freeman, 1962; Howell, 1969).

Between 1939 and 1964, according to one estimate, about one in every five pregnancies in the United States was terminated by an illegal abortion—about 1,000,000 criminal abortions per year (Bates and Zawadzki, 1964). Many of the criminal abortions were performed on married women with children, and many were done by licensed medical doctors. Frederick J. Taussig (1936:422), an authority on abortion, stated that he knew of "no other instances in history in which there had been such frank and universal disregard for a criminal law."

In most American jurisdictions, before abortion was declared legal, criminal sanctions were applied not to the woman having an abortion but to the person who performed it. Just as prostitutes rather than their customers tend to be brought to court, it was the practitioner and not the patient who bore the weight of the law if caught. Most often, this happened only when the after-effects of the abortion caused serious enough injury to bring the "victim" to the attention of medical authorities. Under such conditions, she sometimes was persuaded to testify for the state against the abortionist. When a 23-year-old Florida woman was convicted in 1971 for submitting to an abortion, she was believed to be the first woman in the English-speaking world to have been prosecuted for this offense by the criminal justice system. She was sentenced to a two-year term of probation and given a week to leave Florida (Nordheimer, 1971).

Statisticians of crime often observe that if all women who committed the criminal offense of having an abortion were counted in the tallies of illegal behavior, the female crime rate would have come much closer to that of males, and generalizations about criminal tendency by gender would have to be thoroughly altered.

The Decriminalization of Abortion

In 1973, the U.S. Supreme Court in *Roe v. Wade*, citing a woman's right to privacy, legalized abortions performed by a physician during the first trimester of a woman's pregnancy. A companion decision, *Doe v. Bolton,* declared that physicians had the right to determine whether to perform an abortion (Faux, 1988).

It is not a simple matter to pinpoint the reasons that led to so sweeping a change in the legal status of abortion. Certainly, the increased vigor of the women's movement played a very large role. That movement has had deep roots in an affluence which afforded increased opportunity for women to achieve outside the home. Also, revived Malthusian fears of overpopulation disaster led abortion to be redefined in some instances as part of the war waged on a potentially worldwide problem. Birth control pills, which allowed a greater degree of interference with conception than ever before, called into question the inviolability of the birth process, as it could have been prevented all so casually even before it began. The public nature of birth control also brought into the limelight cognate and once taboo subjects. Inserting a diaphragm is a very private process. Birth control pills, on the other hand, can simply lie on the kitchen counter, waiting to be gulped down with orange juice at the family breakfast. A gynecologist at the time observed:

> The climate for accepting even a discussion of the abortion issue has been enhanced by the progress made in birth control. Five years ago, birth control was a dirty word. Now it's socially acceptable, and that means that abortion can be discussed as well. (Edelson, 1965)

Note, in a similar vein, the sudden public attention to condoms which not too long ago were never discussed in "polite" society and never in "polite" terms. With the advent of AIDS, condoms are now sold from dispensers in college dormitory restrooms and in restaurants, among other places, and are openly discussed in newspapers and on television—even though the media do not allow them to be advertised. It used to be that teenage boys proclaimed loudly to the pharmacist that they wanted to buy cigarettes, then whispered that they also needed some condoms. Today, the reverse may well occur.

Post-Roe Court Rulings and Laws

The forces opposed to a permissive abortion policy have been able to chip away at the doctrine, but they have so far been unsuccessful in having it overthrown. The major Supreme Court opinions on abortion since *Roe v. Wade* came in 1989 in *Webster v. Reproductive Health Service* and in 1992 in *Planned Parenthood of Southeastern Pennsylvania v. Casey.* In addition, Congress enacted a law, vetoed by the president, which outlawed abortions after 20 weeks of pregnancy; and the nation's courts have consistently upheld the requirement that minors must obtain permission from a parent, guardian, or judge if they wish to have an abortion.

The Webster *Decision (1989)*

The *Webster* decision supported a Missouri statute that prohibits the use of public facilities for abortions, except to save the mother's life, and disallows public funding for abortion counseling. The Missouri law also requires a doctor to determine and inform a pregnant women whether her fetus of 20 or more weeks gestation is viable and could potentially survive.

The court reasoned that prohibiting the use of public funds and facilities for abortion "leaves the pregnant woman with the same choices as if the state had chosen not to operate public hospitals at all" (Webster, 1989:509). Nothing in the constitution, the court decreed, required the state to enter or remain in the business of performing abortions. Justice Scalia dissented only because he believed that the court should have gone further and turned its back on the *Roe v. Wade* decision, and that its ruling would "needlessly prolong this court's self-awarded sovereignty over a field where it has little proper business since the answers to most of the cruel questions posed are political and not just juridical" (Webster, 1989:532)

On the other side, also in dissent, Justice Blackmun took strong issue with the restrictions the *Webster* decision placed on free access to abortion in the first trimester:

> The plurality discards a landmark case of the last generation, and casts into darkness the hopes and visions of every woman in this country who has come to believe that the constitution guaranteed her the right to exercise some control over her unique ability to bear children. The plurality does so either oblivious or insensitive to the fact that millions of women, and their families, have ordered their lives around the right to reproductive choice, and that this right has become vital to the full participation of women in the economic and political walks of American life. . . . The plurality

would clear the way again for the state to conscript a woman's body.... (Webster, 1989:557).

The Casey Decision (1992)

The *Planned Parenthood v. Casey* decision found the Supreme Court justices divided 5 to 4 in favor of upholding a Pennsylvania law that mandates a woman seeking an abortion to hear a lecture or watch a film about fetal development and then wait a day before undergoing an abortion. The waiting period imposes a cost on some women who have to travel long distances to reach an abortion facility. The waiting period has also at times been used to trace the abortion seekers' license plates and telephone their parents to announce that their grandchild is about to be murdered. In the lecture, the doctor is required to provide information on the alternatives to the abortion, the medical risks of abortion and of carrying the child to term, and the probable gestational age of the "unborn child." It further requires physicians to inform their patients of the availability of printed materials published by the state describing the fetus, the medical assistance benefits for prenatal care, childbirth, and neonatal care and information regarding the father's legal responsibility to assist with child support (Wells, 1995).

The *Casey* decision also permits public disclosure of the records of an abortion clinic, but the court ruled that the requirement in Pennsylvania that a married woman must inform her husband of a contemplated abortion was not constitutionally valid (see also O'Hara, 1992).

Intact Dilation and Evacuation

On the legislative front, the Congress in 1996 passed and President Bill Clinton subsequently vetoed a bill that would have outlawed a rarely used technique to end pregnancies after 20 weeks of gestation. The bill represented the first measure enacted by Congress since *Roe v. Wade* that would ban a specific abortion procedure. The surgery, called "intact dilation and evacuation" by its proponents and "partial birth abortion" by those opposed to it, involves partially extracting the fetus feet first. It can be used when problems arise later in pregnancies that either threaten the mother or indicate fetal disorders or, of course, it can be employed to end a pregnancy for whatever other personal reasons.

The President held a White House press conference during which he insisted that the procedure was a "potentially life-saving, certainly health-saving" measure for "a small but extremely vulnerable group of women and families in this country, just a few hundred a year"—or about 1.5 percent of the total number of abortions annually. President Clinton had been overruled by Congress in his request that the procedure be permitted when it could save the life of a woman or prevent serious risk to her health. The President was flanked by five women who had undergone late-term abortions and who tearfully testified to how important this had been for them. Opponents insisted that the procedure is a gruesome "partial birth" abortion and argued that the President had "rejected a very modest and bipartisan measure reflecting the values of the great majority of Americans" (Purdum, 1996).

Abortion in Other Countries

Despite some chipping away at the edges of the *Roe* decision, American abortion policy is one of the most permissive in the world. In most European nations, a woman alone cannot decide to have an abortion. In England and Switzerland, for example, two doctors must certify the existence of legal grounds for the procedure. In Greece and Germany, a woman must seek a second opinion from a doctor other than the one who is to perform the abortion. When the abortion is to occur late in the pregnancy, many countries require the woman to present her case to a committee for approval. In Israel, only women under 17 or over 40 are allowed to have abortions legally, unless the child was conceived out of wedlock, there is a risk of genetic damage, or the abortion is deemed necessary to protect the mother's health. In Sweden, a society generally considered to be one of the most sexually permissive in the world, abortion is possible on demand but only up to the 18th week of pregnancy, in contrast to the 24th week in the United States (Wilson, 1994).

In contrast to the United States, the medical profession in England more than held its own against abortion law and the courts. A stringent prohibition against abortion was enacted in England in 1803 (Lord Ellenborough's Act), but physicians often ignored it, and their actions were in turn ignored by law enforcement agencies. In a test case in 1938, the English courts legitimized physicians' control of abortion and ruled that medical doctors could rely on their professional judgment without interference (*Rex v. Bourne*, 1938). The case involved a 14-year-old girl who had been raped by two soldiers and had become pregnant. Bourne, a London surgeon, performed an abortion and informed the legal authorities, asking for a trial that would clarify the law. At the trial, Bourne testified that the birth of a child probably would have destroyed the young girl's physical and mental health.

The judge noted that Bourne had acted "as a member of the profession devoted to the alleviation of human suffering" and forcefully led the jury to acquit Bourne with a summation observation: "I think that . . . if the doctor is of the opinion, on reasonable grounds and with adequate knowledge, that the probable consequences of the continuance of the pregnancy will be to make the woman a physical and mental wreck, the jury are quite entitled to take the view that the doctor, who, in these circumstances, and in that honest belief, operates, is operating for the purpose of preserving the life of the woman."

The Abortion Act of 1967 sought to restrict abortions in Britain to a limited number of conditions. The looseness of the definitions in the act, however, permitted many physicians, particularly those not working in the National Health Service, to interpret it very broadly; and the authorities were unwilling to interfere with this exercise of professional power. In Britain, therefore, doctors were able to keep the courts out of what they regarded as their professional realm. In the United States, on the other hand, doctors deferred to the law and the courts in areas where they could have legitimately claimed strong professional pre-eminence. In part, of course, this was a consequence of the inability of American doctors to present a united front on the moral elements associated with performing abortions on (or for) their patients.

Today, there are about 180,000 abortions each year in Britain, a figure that has risen since the 1987 Abortion Act, though statistically it remains markedly lower than in such countries as the United States, Australia, and Italy (Fisher, 1995).

Fathers, Minors, and Abortion

A side struggle in the abortion controversy concerns the right of the male who has fathered a fetus, be he husband or otherwise, to have a say in whether the fetus should be carried to term. That issue becomes more complicated if the sire argues that the conception occurred with an understanding that a birth would ensue and that he is willing to bear full financial and personal responsibility for the upbringing of the child. Primarily for debate purposes, the matter can be further complicated if the male is able to prove that he is no longer capable of having children of his own because, let us assume, he had an irreversible vasectomy soon after the woman conceived.

Further questions arise in regard to minors. One position favors the view that minors should not be allowed to undergo an abortion unless their parents give their consent. Support for this position is based on the view that underaged girls do not possess the maturity to make so vital a decision. There is also a belief that parental involvement should be a significant element in the decision. Those opposing this position say that parents are often a large part of the problem and are unlikely to contribute to a sound solution. When the pregnancy is the result of sexual assault within the family, then the issue of involving parents in the abortion decision becomes considerably more problematic.

The majority of state legislatures—38 out of 50—insist that parents provide prior consent if a minor seeks an abortion, but they also offer an alternative: If she so chooses, a minor may obtain that permission from a juvenile court judge who will have to determine if the girl is sufficiently informed and mature enough to make a satisfactory decision. The United States Supreme Court endorsed such laws in its 1979 ruling, *Belloti v. Baird*. In 1996, the Court tacitly re-endorsed this approach by refusing to hear a case from South Dakota whose laws allowed approval only from parents for an underaged girl to have an abortion (*Janklow v. Planned Parenthood, Sioux Falls Clinic*, 1996). A lower court had declared parts of the South Dakota law unconstitutional, decreeing that "the state can impose regulations designed to ensure that a woman makes a thoughtful and informed choice," but that this can be done "only if such regulations do not unduly burden her right to choose whether to abort" (*Planned Parenthood, Sioux Falls Clinic v. Miller*, 1996).

In 1996, the California Supreme Court faced the same issue, brought before it primarily because the state has a constitutional provision upholding the right to privacy, and the federal position on privacy is based on court rulings. In the case of *American Academy of Pediatrics v. Lundgren* (1996), the California court upheld the state statute under which a doctor could be prosecuted criminally if he performed an abortion on an unemancipated minor who did not have the prior approval of a parent, guardian, or juvenile court judge. The court declared that minors do not have the same rights as adults to privacy (the basis of the *Roe* decision) and noted that under state law they must obtain parental permission for most medical and dental treatment, for a permanent tattoo, for marriage, and for a driver's license.

About 30,000 unmarried teenagers now obtain abortions in California each year. It was estimated that about 14,000 of them would look to judges for permission, though some might prefer to have the child rather than go through the abortion approval process. Justice Joyce Kennard, who dissented in the California case, noted that teenagers who do not want to face their parents might perceive court involvement as "unbearably intimidating, dangerous or humiliating" and may therefore "risk their lives with illegal or self-induced abortions or opt for bearing a child they cannot care for." If California's experience is similar to that in Pennsylvania and Massachusetts, which have equivalent provisions, each of the petitions to the judges would be granted (Barnes, 1995). On the other hand, the law can react strongly when it is disobeyed. In late 1996, for example, a 40-year-old woman who drove a 13-year-old Pennsylvania girl to New York—where there are no parental notification laws—for an abortion without informing the girl's mother was fined $500 and sentenced to 150 hours of community service. The woman's 19-year-old stepson, who had impregnated the girl, was convicted of statutory rape.

Those who object to the law point out that the approval process adds an additional two-week waiting period prior to the abortion, and that with passing time the operation becomes somewhat more complex and dangerous, therefore endangering young women.

How Many Abortions Are There?

The legalization of abortion produced dramatic divisions within the world of medicine. Within five years following *Roe*, 75 percent of the more than 1,000,000 abortions annually in the United States were not being performed by private doctors in hospitals or in their offices but in 250 of the nation's 500 abortion clinics (Forrest, Tietze and Sullivan, 1978). Some gynecologists and obstetricians refuse to perform abortions because they have moral objections to the procedure. Many do not want to gain a reputation among colleagues or in the community as abortionists. Other doctors resent being put into a position in which patients can treat physicians as hirelings, mere providers of a service on demand (Imber, 1986). Finally, doctors do not perform abortions because they fear harassment or physical harm from militant anti-abortionists.

Perhaps in some small measure because of the tightening restrictions surrounding the obtaining of an abortion, the number of abortions has been inching its way down since *Roe v. Wade*. In 1994, the latest year for which figures are now available, there were 1.2 million abortions, down about 2 percent from the previous year and down substantially from the 1990 high of 1,429,577. The 1994 decrease was the fourth year in a row that the number of abortions has declined in the United States. The ratio of abortions to live births is also slowly declining. In 1994, there were 321 abortions for every 1,000 live births, the lowest ratio since 1976. About one in five women who had abortions in 1994 was under the age of 19.

One commentator on the decline relates it to the following four causes: (1) teenagers are postponing sexual intercourse; (2) the increased effectiveness of the pro-life forces, marked by greater sensitivity and professionalism in their efforts to persuade pregnant woman to give birth and retain the child or place it out for adoption; (3) the new restrictive state laws, especially those that deny payment to welfare mothers for abortion procedures; and (4) the decline in the number of physicians who will perform abortions (Mathewes-Green, 1995). The growing use of condoms to avoid the HIV virus and the increasing social acceptance of unmarried women bearing children also probably contribute to a reduced rate of unwanted pregnancies. In 1992, 30 percent of all births were to unmarried women, up from 18 percent in 1980. Further, the changing age structure in the United States plays into a reduced abortion rate, since there now are fewer women in the prime childbearing ages of 20 to 29, so that the number of possible pregnancies has declined (Bosanko, 1995). On the other hand, our comparatively lenient policies undoubtedly contribute to the larger percentage of the female population that undergoes abortion in the United States than in most countries. Figures for 1990, the latest international statistics available, show the U.S. abortion rate at about 27.4 per 1,000 women. For Canada, the rate was 14.6, for Germany 5.8, and for Italy 12.7 (Seis, 1996:A20). Within the United States, different states report highly varying abortion rates, with the lowest in Wyoming and the highest in Nevada (Henshaw and Van Vort, 1994).

Determining Abortion's Impact

A review of the history of abortion in the United States and Great Britain indicates that abortion on demand, within some limits, rules the day, at least for the moment. What *is*, however, bears no necessary relationship to what *ought to be*. Our task here is to explore the implications both of criminalized abortion policies and those regarded as more liberal. We will look at these issues from the viewpoints of the major parties to the question and discuss matters not previously covered here: first, the prospective mother; second, the unborn fetus or child; third, the medical profession; fourth, the churches; and, finally, the society in general.

Woman and Abortion

Abortion patterns in the United States when the behavior was illegal have been carefully investigated by the Kinsey Institute. Its research was based on interviews with 5,293 white, nonprison women, most of whom were in the upper 20 percent in socioeconomic status. The women had 4,248 conceptions. These resulted in 2,434 live births, 667 spontaneous abortions, and 1,067 illegal abortions, or about one abortion for every two live births. The estimate was believed to be on the low side, on the assumption that some of the women probably underreported on the question of abortion (Gebhard, et al., 1958). Reviewing the Kinsey results and other studies, sociologist Alice Rossi (1967:27) concluded that at that time, it was "highly probable that one in every two or three married women may undergo an illegal abortion during the years between their thirteenth and fiftieth birthday."

Most of the illegal abortions were performed on married women, and about 85 percent were done by physicians, the Kinsey researchers noted. In the unmarried group, a large majority had become pregnant in their first or second sexual experience. Among the married women, two explanations for the abortions were offered: Those women who had been married a relatively short time wanted to delay having children, and those married longer believed that their families were large enough. Religious women had much lower abortion rates than women without religious commitments (Gebhard et al., 1958).

The thinking that underlies an abortion decision today, when the process is legal, is portrayed in a recent novel in which a graduate-student husband is unnerved when his wife, excited by the news, tells him that she is pregnant. She contemplates the prospect of an abortion:

> It was almost peaceful thinking about it. After all, they loved each other. It was because he loved her, and wanted the best for her that he was against having the baby now. The pregnancy was an accident; one didn't have to live with accidents anymore. There would be a time for having children—when they were older and more settled and could better afford it. It was important to plan for such a thing, not to walk into it blindly. (Bausch, 1992:16-17)

But these are only musings. The woman wants the child very much and, in the end, the couple agree to have it.

Psychological Consequences of Abortion

A fundamental point of debate concerns the consequences to a woman of bearing an unwanted child as measured against the consequences of undergoing an abortion. A thoroughgoing review by Nancy Adler and her colleagues (Adler et al., 1990; see also Dagg, 1991) of research on the subject concluded that for those who have abortions, the psychological distress is generally greatest before the abortion, and that the incidence of severe negative responses is "low." One study indicated that 76 percent of the women reported feeling relief and happiness, but the most common negative emotion, guilt, was reported by only 17 percent. One particularly comprehensive study compared 38 women, matched for ethnicity, age, the number of children they had, and marital and socioeconomic status, in terms of their experience with two forms of abortion and with birthing. Some of the women had undergone early suction abortions and some had saline abortions, and others carried their fetus to term birth. The authors concluded that the three groups were "startlingly similar" in their response to their experience.

Other findings about abortion include the following:

- The greater the difficulty of deciding to terminate a pregnancy, the more likely there will be negative responses after abortion.

- Women undergoing second-trimester abortions report more emotional distress than those undergoing first-trimester abortions.

- Women who perceive more support for the decision to abort are more satisfied with their decision.

- Having negative feelings toward one's partner, making the abortion decision alone, and experiencing opposition from the partner were associated with greater emotional distress.

- Women who maintained a strong relationship with their partner reported more regret one year after their abortion than did those whose relationship had deteriorated (Adler et al., 1990).

Physical Consequences of Abortion

The number of deaths that resulted from illegal abortions in the United States is sometimes estimated at between 5,000 and 10,000 annually (Kling, 1965). One writer, using unidentified source data, maintained that during 1968, 350,000 women were hospitalized in the United States because of botched illegal abortions and that 8,000 of them died (McGregor, 1969). However, Christopher Tietze of the Population Council has insisted that the death figures for women associated with illegal abortions that are usually reported are highly inflated, and that the actual total was closer to 500 such deaths each year, with a possible maximum of 1,000 (Tietze, 1972). The most reliable individual study was that by the Medical Examiner's Office in New York City, which reported that, prior to the legalization of early abortions, about 90 women died each year from the consequences of abortions performed outside hospital settings. This was the largest single cause of maternal death in the City (Mayor Endorses Abortion Appeal, 1970). In New York, abortion deaths struck minority group women much more than others. Illegal abortions accounted for nearly half of the pregnancy and childbirth fatalities among black women, 56 percent of those of Puerto Rican women, and only 25 percent of the fatalities of white women (Abortion and the Changing Law, 1970).

In terms of safety, Michael Policar, a gynecologist at the University of California, San Francisco, notes that abortion "has the lowest rate of deaths associated with it and also has the lowest rate of serious complications in comparison to any other operation which is widely performed in this country" (American Academy of Pediatrics, 1996:3878). The risks of abortion to adolescents versus those of live births is pronounced. The mortality rate is 11.1 per 100,000 for adolescent girls who deliver and drops to 1.2 per 100,000 for legal abortions for members of this age group (Greydanus and Railsback, 1985). The comparison, however, involves a number of methodological issues, most notably the fact that abortion is a single event, pregnancy a long-term condition.

There has been discussion in recent years of a possible relatively low linkage between abortion and breast cancer when a woman has an abortion before her first birth, but that relationship, if any, remains uncertain at the moment. In 1997, Danish researchers who reviewed the records of more than 1.5 million women reported no overall increased risk of breast cancer associated with abortion. This was true even if a woman had two or more abortions (Melbye, et al., 1997). Nonetheless, the Montana state legislature requires doctors to disclose information about a possible breast-cancer link to women seeking abortions (Blind et al., 1996).

Doctors and Abortion

The medical profession is generally regarded as among the more conservative forces in society. In one view, doctors enjoy high incomes, and people with high incomes tend to prefer that things remain as they are. In another view, doctors are committed by oath to the preservation of life and well-being, so understandably they would regard abortion as a violation of this professional obligation. In addition, their commitment to healing involves making decisions about what is right and proper for other people, with the use of such powers being defined as a matter of benevolence; that is, intended for someone else's good, even if that other person doesn't appreciate it.

In 1871, the American Medical Association offered its first pronouncement on abortion: "That it be the duty of every physician in the United States to resort to every honorable and legal means in his power to rid society of this practice" (Ethics of Abortion, 1957:93).

Nonetheless, a survey of 388 obstetricians conducted prior to the Supreme Court's decision in *Roe v. Wade* found that 10 percent admitted that they referred patients to abortionists, and that they estimated that 14 percent of their colleagues did the same. The majority of them made such referrals for four or five cases a year, though a few reported that they referred from 30 to 40 cases annually (Lader, 1966). Nonetheless, obstetricians generally remain wary of abortion. One doctor claims to know the reason why:

> Ob-Gyn's are mama's boys. They go into obstetrics because they identify with women and the whole reproductive process. Now ask them to do an abortion and it's against what they're psychologically attuned to. They're trained to deliver babies and put them at the mother's breast. The woman who doesn't want to go through the natural birth bit and the nursing—why, she's a tramp to them. (Scott, 1970:68)

There has been a decreasing willingness on the part of doctors to perform abortions. In 1982, there were 2,908 physicians doing abortions; that number had dropped to 2,380 by 1992, with older doctors making up a considerable portion of the total (Grimes, 1992; on the work of an abortion clinic in Oregon, see Korn, 1996). Younger residency-trained physicians are more likely than their older colleagues to have personal moral objections to performing abortions (Rosenblatt, Mattis, and Hart, 1995). Also, medical schools typically do not provide training in how to perform abortions, and 84 percent of the counties in the United States, with 30 percent of the country's women living in them, have no doctors at all who will perform an abortion (Joffe, 1995).

Abortion and the Unborn Child

Several highly emotional issues center around the nature and the future of the fetus that is destroyed in abortion. The destruction of the fetus ends its earthly prospects and returns the pregnant woman to her non-gravid state. A very large majority of women who undergo abortions are pleased that they have obtained what they desired, but some are saddened; others have second thoughts.

By far, the most prominent of those women with second thoughts has to be Norma McCorvey, the woman who was the anonymous plaintiff in *Roe v. Wade*. In 1995, McCorvey publicly said that she had changed her mind, and she was baptized by the leader of Operation Rescue, a militant anti-abortion group. Nonetheless, McCorvey remained convinced that early abortions should remain permissible; it was late abortions which had outraged her. When she consented to serve as the plaintiff in 1969 in the *Roe* case, McCorvey had to agree not to have an abortion; had she done so, there would have been no case. Plans had been made to put her child out for adoption, but a hospital nurse, unaware of that decision, handed her daughter to the mother. From that moment, McCorvey says, she felt tormented.

When McCorvey went public, she found herself often shunned by sophisticated pro-choicers: she was irreverent, hot-tempered, and uneducated: their leadership was elitist. "All Jane Roe did was sign a one-page affidavit," says the pro-life attorney who argued the *Roe* case. "She was pregnant and didn't want to be. That was her total involvement in the case." The attorney regrets picking McCorvey.

In 1991, McCorvey took a job in a Dallas abortion clinic and was sickened by witnessing second-trimester abortions. "It's a baby," she said. "It's got a face and a body." She found herself supported by the Operation Rescue people who picketed her clinic. For McCorvey, the bottom line remains: "I was worried about salvation. I can now go to sleep at night knowing that I'm not going to be responsible for a second-trimester abortion. I believe in the woman's right to choose. I'm like a lot of people. I'm in the mushy middle" (Waldman and Carroll, 1995:23).

It is often argued that forcing women to bear "unwanted" children would severely undermine the quality of life in store for those children. Other persons, though they may grant this as a statistical conclusion, insist that the most unpredictable kinds of outcomes may eventuate in the lottery of life for even the most unwanted children. There are also those who insist that the use of any outcome criteria is a presumptuous moral enterprise. Relatively few persons, they point out, no matter how objectively wretched their lives may appear, choose to end those lives themselves, although they always have this option. Pro-lifers argue that the person—or object—whose existence hinges on the abortion decision has no way of registering his—or its—view of the matter.

Studies of the consequences for a child of being born to unwanting parents indicate that to an extent greater than that for wanted children, their lives will be blighted. A Swedish study of children born to parents whose application for therapeutic abortions was rejected showed that as a group they fared worse than members of a comparison group, in terms of the range of measures of social adequacy and adjustment (Forssman and Thuwve, 1966), though the result may have been influenced by anger toward the state rejecting their abortion request, as well as hostility toward the child.

On the other hand, since abortion in the first trimester has been permitted by law, there hardly seems to be any notable decline in the amount of child abuse, sexual assault against children, and juvenile delinquency. It may be, of course, that these matters have now become a prominent concern and, therefore, more becomes known to the authorities about them. However, it is at least as likely that the existence of an abortive option has at best only a minimal relationship to what happens to a child.

Public Opinion on Abortion

Public opinion polls indicate that there is virtually no difference between men and women in terms of their support or opposition to legal abortion, with women only slightly less pro-choice than men. A majority of the abortion activists, however, are women (Walzer, 1994). Only in the over-65 age group are women notably less supportive of legal abortion than men. Men are significantly more in favor of legal abortion than women who are homemakers, but among men and women who work outside the home, there is no difference in viewpoint, despite the fact that women tend to be more politically conservative and have stronger religious commitments than men. But, of course, it is women who undergo pregnancy and birth, and they typically carry the larger share of responsibility for childrearing. Women's rights advocates believe that men opposing legal abortion feel strongly that it represents for them a move away from traditional family values and a challenge to the power that they have had over women. Part of that power has been rooted in a pattern that keeps women at home, responsible for rearing children. Abortion allows for more effective planned parenthood and family limitation, thereby freeing career women to more effectively plan a life for themselves in male-dominated businesses and professions where they can challenge men's power.

A similar percentage of white and black pregnancies end in abortion. But in all surveys, whites report more support of legal abortion than African Americans, though African American women are twice as likely to have abortions. The opposition within the black population largely reflects the views of women beyond the childbearing ages, who by a high percentage do not favor abortions (Lynxwiler and Gay, 1994). Three conditions are particularly associated with black anti-abortion views. First, blacks are more likely than whites to have been raised in rural areas of the south, where pro-life support is highest. Second, they are much more likely to oppose mercy killings, a strong predictor of abortion attitudes. Finally, they attend church more often and hold more orthodox religious views than whites as a group (Cook, Jelen, and Wilcox, 1992).

Abortion and Social Issues

Legal abortion, in one sense, runs contrary to the emergent public concern with the ecological view that has at its heart the premise that "natural" phenomena are good and that the effluvia of "civilization" are anything but civilized. Under such conditions, the assumption might be that tinkering with natural processes produces untoward consequences. In this regard, abortion might be defined as the interruption of a natural process, one that might bring about results detrimental to society. This is rarely the logic pursued, however. The major thrust of the ecological argument concerning abortion is that environmental degradation is itself a direct consequence of overpopulation, with too many people imposing destructive demands on their surroundings; and that legal abortion, to the extent that it would reduce the pressure of overpopulation, represents an ecologically attractive option.

There seems to be no dispute that access to legal abortion will cut into population growth, though the knowledge that abortion is possible may lead to a greater number of pregnancies, and that a significant number of the pregnant women will subsequently elect not to undergo an abortion. How many such cases occur as measured against the number of abortions remains a matter not readily determinable. But all countries that have instituted permissive abortion policies have shown a downward trend in live births.

The consequences of a lowered birth rate, however, are difficult to assess. An "excessive" population growth in India appears to be in considerable measure responsible for many of the dilemmas of that country, such as its high level of poverty and its high disease and death rate. In Japan, on the other hand, there is an absence of what is regarded as an adequate labor force; this has led to economic conditions which by some standards might seem undesirable, such as more demanding work routines and the postponement of retirement. Nonetheless, all told, readily available abortion appears to produce population disturbances that do not seem to be of such overwhelming importance that they would override other considerations in the pro-life versus pro-choice debate.

In the United States at the moment, the average family size is 3.2 children. For the population to be stabilized, that figure would have to drop to a 2.2 average. The consequences of a stable population are debatable: Some say that it allows for systematic planning and avoids cycles of expansion and contraction that are associated with fluctuating birth rates. Others maintain that it creates a certain flatness in a society, and that growth and advancement go hand in hand, just as do stability and stagnation. Neither view, however, has very substantial factual undergirding.

A prominent argument favoring legal abortion in the United States centers around the discrimination against poorer persons inherent in restrictive abortion policies. Affluent women can always locate places overseas that freely permit abortion.

In one sense, then, legal abortion becomes a form of back-up birth control for the poor. In this regard, it could be argued that it tends to reduce the birth rate among people least able to afford the financial and often psychological drain of additional children. This outcome, however, need not necessarily occur, and it is debatable whether present abortion policies affect birth rates to the extent that people most able to afford children have the greatest number of them. For one thing, the ability of certain people to better support offspring is often in part characteristic of the same traits that keep them from having large numbers of children. Besides, as better-educated women become more able to command sizeable salaries and higher work positions, they will inevitably reduce their birth rate and farm out much of their family's childrearing tasks to socially less advantaged women.

Furthermore, there is no strong evidence that the country would be better off with the production of a larger number of children from middle- and upper-class homes than it would be with a disproportionate number of lower-class children. It would be easy to point to welfare statistics and crime figures as they correlate with socioeconomic conditions, thus supporting the idea that the poor are too fecund. But social life is an extraordinary blend, and in some ways the diminution of membership in one socioeconomic class may produce quite unexpected consequences in the behavior and attitudes of those in other classes.

The argument is sometimes advanced that advocates of legal abortion are fundamentally racists, intent upon using this roundabout means to reduce the percentage of black people in society, thereby rendering blacks even more vulnerable than they are today. The premise underlying this argument might be considered accurate: legalized abortion does cut down the birth rate among poor blacks who tend to be relatively unable to afford birth control. But it seems unreasonable to maintain that black women should be kept from aborting unwanted pregnancies because of speculative ideas about the implication of such behavior for racial advancement.

History provides little evidence with which to determine the impact, if there has been any, of diverse kinds of abortion policies on the vitality of a nation over a long period of time. The early Greeks and Romans condemned abortion (Hertzler, 1956), and Middle Assyrian culture impaled women on stakes if they were found guilty of abortion (Pritchard, 1955). But the decline of these civilizations can hardly be tied to their abortion practices. Among preliterate societies, policies appear to run the gamut and show no particular relationship to tribal vitality or senescence. Some groups impose no penalties for abortion; others, such as the Truk Islanders, resort to mild scolding; still others, such as the Jakuns, exact the penalty of death for abortion (Devereaux, 1960).

Violence Against Abortion Clinics

The fiery passions aroused by anti-abortion sentiments have led to a number of murders. Paul Hill was sentenced to death after he killed Dr. David Gunn in March 1993 in front of an abortion clinic in Pensacola, Florida. Several months later, another doctor performing abortions was shot in Kansas, though not seriously wounded; the assailant, Rachelle Shannon, drew a 10-year prison term. In 1994, Dr. John Britton, who had taken over Gunn's job in Pensacola, was murdered along with his bodyguard.

The episode that probably aroused the greatest reaction involved John Salvi III, who entered the Brookline Planned Parenthood clinic in Massachusetts in 1994, shot the receptionist, and sprayed the room with gunfire. He then drove to the Preterm Health Service Clinic, killed the receptionist there (shooting her ten times at point-blank range), then wounded five other persons in a random firing spree. The following day, Salvi shot out the glass door of the Hillcrest Clinic in Virginia, where he was arrested. Salvi was sentenced to two terms of life imprisonment without parole. While in prison in late 1996, Salvi committed suicide by asphyxiating himself with a plastic garbage bag over his head.

Salvi, said to be deeply troubled, had placed a picture of a fetus on his pickup truck. His murderous acts greatly embarrassed the pro-life forces, and there were numerous calls to lower the level of angry rhetoric used in protests against abortion (Lemonick, 1995).

To de-escalate these outbursts of violence, President Clinton signed into law in May 1994 the Freedom of Access to Clinic Entrances (FACE) Act, which criminalizes the use of force, threats, or physical obstructions that injure, intimidate, or interfere with entrance to or exit from an abortion clinic (Campbell, 1996).

The FACE Act was strengthened when a Florida circuit judge, in the wake of the David Gunn murder, issued an injunction specifying that protesters could station themselves no closer than 36 feet from the entrance to an abortion clinic. Despite the belief of some that the rule infringed on constitutionally protected free speech rights, it was upheld in late 1994 by the U.S. Supreme Court in *Madsen v. Women's Health Center*, though the court declared that protesters could not be kept by law from holding up observable images, nor restricted from approaching nearer than 300 feet to staff residential quarters. The injunction had grown out of complaints from the Aware Women Center for Choice clinic in Melbourne, Florida, where protesters would yell at women entering the clinic: "Mommy, don't kill me. They're ripping my arm off." Such inflamed expressions are not confined to either side, as evidenced by the sign carried in a 1996 San Francisco rally by pro-choice proponents: "Get your rosaries out of my ovaries."

The new law and the Supreme Court decision, combined with a growing abhorrence of the violence directed at abortion clinics, may have contributed to a significant drop in the total amount of harassment during 1995. A survey of 310 clinics reported that blockades had all but disappeared and that there were fewer death threats. The number of clinics that suffered acts of vandalism had also dropped, from 35 percent in 1994 to 25 percent in 1995 (Navarro, 1995).

How do such acts as the Salvi murders configure into the debate over abortion and the law? Are they to be dismissed as simply the acts of disturbed individuals, or are they a significant symptom of the inflamed passions aroused in a debate that has gone beyond the pale of common sense and decency? Are the murders of abortionists, by one definition themselves murderers, nothing compared to the systematic extermination of human life on their part, as some would rationalize?

These are difficult questions to answer, but the observation of one pro-lifer seems to be in keeping with basic democratic values: "While there are two sides to the issue of abortion, there are no two sides to the issue of shooting people for their opinions" (Navarro, 1995:14).

Arguments Pro and Con

Among the reasons offered by pro-life proponents to support their position, in addition to those we presented earlier, is the argument that to allow legal abortions wedges deeper into more drastic reinterpretations of what it means to be "human." Permitting a fetus to be aborted legally, they insist, provides a precedent for the killing not only of unwanted babies (which are now defined as "nonhuman") but of infants themselves who could someday be declared to be "nonhuman" before they reach, for example, their first birthday or if they suffer from some serious physical or genetic defect. Such reasoning—called "slippery slope" arguments—represents what is usually a passionate but a fruitless kind of debate.

Illustrating this viewpoint, a critique of a pro-choice book commented that the argument that fetuses are not real people is undercut by the point that "fetuses become babies, not puppies." The critic goes on to say, "Soon enough there will be other harrowing questions, such as whether mentally impaired humans or simply unwanted humans are any more worthy of concern and respect than were the discarded fetal humans" (Wolfson, 1996:12). It is not mentioned, however, that during the many centuries when abortion remained untouched by the law, such issues never seriously surfaced.

Changes in social and legal definitions often set eddies in motion that spread outward, but to extrapolate later developments from these changes is a feckless enterprise. First, a change may represent the last movement of its sort along a continuum; second, a change may produce a counteraction, an antithesis, or a reversal of the direction; and third, any predicted consequences, if they come about, may not be anywhere near as dramatic as the predictor would expect.

For the pro-lifers, Marvin Olasky (1992:304), after a comprehensive review of what he sees as significant developments in America's experience with abortion, summarizes his position in these terms:

> Anti-abortion laws are crucial, not primarily because abortionists would be jailed—the history suggests that few would be—but because making abortion (or most abortions) illegal would make the practice of abortion a costly one for physicians. A cynical or existentialist doctor might well decide to double his income by performing abortions when there is no risk but for some verbal harassment. That same doctor may settle for delivering babies if the killing alternative might result in loss of license. On the demand side, the illegality at least deters many women from rushing into the practice.

Olasky (1992:405) believes, however, that anti-abortion laws will have little effect "as long as schools, television programs, and other educational outlets frequently equate premarital and extramarital intercourse with true romance." He further argues that no social stance will eliminate all abortion, but that the objective should be to reduce what he regards as an unconscionably high figure.

For the pro-choicers, in addition to their focus on the freedom of a woman to do as she pleases with her body, the argument often takes the form of a counterattack, as Tribe (1991:239) observes:

> Pro-choice advocates, for their part, tend to denounce the hypoc-
> risy of pro-lifers and stress their supposed insensitivity to life in
> other settings (military adventurism, gun control, the death pen-
> alty) and their supposed lack of concern for babies and toddlers
> in such contexts as infant nutrition, day care, and aid to families
> with dependent children.

Such counterattacks, of course, are part of a war of words and media sound bites that do not come close to cutting to the core of the real issues. If a fetus is a person, entitled to the kind of protection guaranteed to all humans, it matters not a whit what a person does or says about such matters as infant nutrition or gun control.

Nonsurgical Abortions

What are the possible implications of the widespread availability of nonsurgical abortions, such as those brought about by the ingestion of RU-486 (mifepristone), the French abortion pill that was nicknamed "the morning-after" pill and approved for use in the United States late in 1996? The RU-486 procedure involves several visits to the doctor and sometimes results in unpleasant side effects. The mifepristone regimen essentially induces a miscarriage by blocking human progesterone, which is vital to sustain pregnancy. Two days after a dosage of mifepristone, a woman is given miso-prostol, which induces uterine contractions. She will remain under the physician's care for about four hours to monitor possible side effects—nausea, cramping, and excessive bleeding (four of 2,100 women needed transfusions during the testing of the drug). For 95 percent of the women who took the drugs during the testing period, the embryo was expelled within 24 hours (Kolata, 1996, see also Lader, 1995).

When such drugs are marketed, the result will very likely be to defuse and perhaps even end the fierce conflict between pro-choice and pro-life groups; not because either side would have altered or lessened its position, but because the matter would have moved beyond the realm of any effective public policy, except for the unlikely prospect of boycotts against the pharmaceutical companies preventing them from selling the drugs. The Population Council, that will market RU-486 through an affiliate, intends to keep the name of the manufacturer secret to avoid retaliation. Legislatures might ban the drugs, but—as the situation with illegal narcotics has amply demonstrated—it would be impossible to keep them out of the hands of those who seek them. Besides, surveys indicate that as many as one third of the gynecologists who will not perform surgical abortions would be willing to produce chemical abortions if a satisfactory drug and suitable guidelines became available.

Conclusion

At its heart, the debate over whether abortion is a crime without a victim or whether it is a victim without a crime remains outside the realm of clear-cut resolution. As the U.S. Supreme Court declared in *Planned Parenthood of Southeastern Pennsylvania v. Casey* (1992:850): "Men and women of good conscience can disagree, and we suppose some always shall disagree, about the profound moral and spiritual implications of terminating a pregnancy, even in its earliest stage." For its part, the court believed that "our obligation is to define the liberty of all, not to mandate our own moral code." But it did not—because it could not—say how such a feat might be accomplished in regard to the abortion laws. Abortion is a moral issue without satisfactory legal response. Criminal law appears at times to be impotent in dealing with those whose moral evaluations of abortion are diametrically opposed to one another. Abortion is not a problem that can be solved by the law, not because the law cannot regulate the behavior of abortion, but because the law cannot provide succor to those whose evaluations are not represented in law.

References

"Abortion and the Changing Law." 1970. *Newsweek* (April 13):53-61.

Adler, Nancy E., Henry P. David, Brenda N. Major, Susan H. Roth, Nancy F. Russo, and Gail E. Wyatt. 1990. "Psychological Responses after Abortion." *Science* (April 6):41-44.

American Academy of Pediatrics v. Lundgren. 1996. *Los Angeles Daily Appellate Report* 96:3865-3894.

Asma, Stephen T. 1994. "Abortion and the Embarrassing Saint." *Humanist* 54 (May-June):30-33.

Barnes, Patricia G. 1995. "Minors Seeking Abortions Find No Court Resistance: Judges Approve 100 Percent of Petitions Sought by Teenagers." *National Law Journal* (March 13):A8.

Bates, Jerome E., and Edward S. Zawadzki. 1964. *Criminal Abortion: A Study in Medical Sociology.* Springfield, IL: Thomas.

Bausch, Richard. 1992. *Violence.* Boston: Houghton Mifflin.

Bellotti v. Baird. 1979. 443 U.S. 662.

Blanchard, Dallas A. 1994. *The Anti-Abortion Movement and the Rise of the Religious Right: From Polite to Fiery Protest.* New York: Twayne.

Blind, Joel, Vernon M. Chinchilli, Walter B. Severs, and Joan Sunny-Long. 1996. "Induced Abortion as an Independent Risk Factor for Breast Cancer: A Comprehensive Review and Meta-Analysis." *Journal of Epidemiology and Community Health,* 50: 481-496.

Bohlen, Celestine. 1995. "Pope Offers 'Gospel of Life' Vs. 'Culture of Death.' " *New York Times,* March 31:A1, A4-A5.

Bosanko, Deborah. 1995. "Abortion's Slow Decline." *American Demographics* 17:20-22.

Buddle, Michael. 1992. *The Two Churches: Catholicism and Capitalism in the World-System.* Durham, NC: Duke University Press.

Campbell, Regina R. 1996. "Facing the Facts: Does the Freedom of Access to Clinic Entrances Act Violate Freedom of Speech?" *University of Cincinnati Law Review,* 64:947-982.

Cook, Elizabeth A., Ted G. Jelen, and Clyde Wilcox. 1992. *Between Two Absolutes: Public Opinion and the Politics of Abortion.* Boulder, CO: Westview.

Dagg, Paul K. B. 1991. "The Psychological Sequelae of Therapeutic Abortion—Denied and Completed." *American Journal of Psychiatry* 148:578-585.

Devereaux, George. 1960. *A Study of Abortion in Primitive Societies.* London: Yoseloff, 1960.

Doe v. Bolton. 1973. 410 U.S. 179.

Dworkin, Ronald. 1993. *Life's Dominion: An Argument About Abortion, Euthanasia, and Individual Freedom.* New York: Knopf.

Edelson, Edward. 1965. "Abortion—an Endless Debate." *New York World-Telegram,* March 19:12.

"Ethics of Abortion." 1957. *Time* (July 15):93.

Faux, Marion. 1988. *Roe v. Wade: The Untold Story of the Landmark Supreme Court Case that Made Abortion Legal.* New York: Macmillan.

Fisher, Anthony. 1995. "What Abortion is Doing in Britain." *Human Life Review* 21:96-104.

Forrest, Jacqueline D., Christopher Tietze, and Ellen Sullivan. 1978. "Abortion in the United States, 1976-1977." *Family Planning Perspectives* 10:271-279.

Forssman, Hans, and Inga Thuwve. 1966. "One Hundred and Twenty Children Born After Application for Therapeutic Abortion Refused." *Acta Psychiatrica Scandinavica* 42:71-88.

Freeman, Lucy. 1962. *The Abortionist.* Garden City, NY: Doubleday.

Gebhard, Paul H., Wardell B. Pomeroy, Clyde E. Martin, and Cordelia V. Christenson. 1958. *Pregnancy, Birth and Abortion.* New York: Harper.

Greydanus, Donald E., and Linda D. Railsback. 1985. "Abortion in Adolescence." *Seminars in Adolescent Medicine* 1:213-222.

Grimes, David. 1992. "Clinicians Who Provide Abortions: The Thinning Ranks." *Obstetrics and Gynecology* 80:719-725.

Henshaw, Stanley K., and Jennifer Van Vort. 1994. "Abortion Services in the United States, 1991 and 1992." *Family Planning Perspectives* 24:100-106, 112.

Hertzler, Joyce O. 1956. *The Crisis in World Population.* Lincoln: University of Nebraska Press.

Howell, Nancy Lee. 1969. *The Search for an Abortionist.* Chicago: University of Chicago Press.

Imber, Jonathan B. 1986. *Abortion and the Private Practice of Medicine.* New Haven: Yale University Press.

Janklow v. Planned Parenthood, Sioux Falls Clinic. 1996. Cert. denied, 134 L.Ed.2d 679.

Joffe, Carole. 1995. *Doctors of Conscience: The Struggle to Provide Abortion Before and After* Roe v. Wade. Boston: Beacon Press.

John Paul II. 1995. *Evangelium Vitae.* Boston: Pauline Books and Media.

Kling, Samuel G. 1965. *Sexual Behavior and the Law.* New York: Bernard Geis Associates.

Kolata, Gina. 1996. "Pill for Abortion Clears Big Hurdle To Its Sale in U.S." *New York Times,* September 19:A1, B12.

Korn, Peter. 1996. *Lovejoy: A Year in the Life of an Abortion Clinic.* New York: Atlantic Monthly Press.

Lader, Lawrence. 1966. *Abortion.* Indianapolis: Bobbs Merrill.

Lader, Lawrence. 1995. *A Private Matter: RU 486 and the Abortion Crisis.* Amherst, NY: Prometheus.

Lemonick, Michael D. 1995. "An Armed Fanatic Raises the Stakes." *Time* (January 9):34-35.

Luker, Kristin. 1984. *Abortion and the Politics of Motherhood.* Berkeley: University of California Press.

Lynxwiler, John, and David Gay. 1994. "Reconsidering Race Differences in Abortion Attitudes." *Social Science Quarterly* 75:67-84.

Madsen v. Women's Health Care Center, Inc. 1994. 114 S. Ct. 2516.

Mathewes-Green, Frederica. 1995. "Embryonic Trend: How Do We Explain the Drop in Abortion?" *Policy Review* 73:55-58.

"Mayor Endorses Abortion Appeal." 1970. *New York Times,* November 4:3.

McGregor, James. 1969. "Clergymen Stir Debate by Helping Women End Unwanted Pregnancies." *Wall Street Journal,* June 23:1, 23.

Melbye, Mads, et al. 1997. "Induced Abortion and the Risk of Breast Cancer."*New England Journal of Medicine.* 336:81-85.

Mohr, James C. 1978. *Abortion in America: The Origins and Evolution of National Policy, 1800-1900.* New York: Oxford University Press.

Navarro, Mireya. 1995. "Abortion Clinics Report Drop in Harassing Incidents." *New York Times,* April 4:B4.

Nordheimer, Jan. 1971. "She's Fighting Conviction for Aborting Her Child." *New York Times,* December 4:14.

O'Hara, Thomas J. 1992. "The Abortion Control Act of 1989: The Pennsylvania Catholics." Pp. 87-104 in Timothy A. Byrnes and Mary C. Segers (eds.), *The Catholic Church and the Politics of Abortion: A View from the States.* Boulder, CO: Westview Press.

Olasky, Marvin. 1992. *Abortion Rites: A Social History of Abortion in America.* Wheaton, IL: Crossway Books.

Planned Parenthood, Sioux Falls Clinic v. Miller. 1996. 63:3d 1452 (8th Cir.).

Planned Parenthood of Southeastern Pennsylvania v. Casey. 1992. 505 U.S. 833.

Pritchard, James B., ed. 1955. *Ancient Near Eastern Texts Relating to the Old Testament.* 2nd ed. Princeton: Princeton University Press.

Purdum, Todd S. 1996. "President Vetoes Measure Banning Type of Abortion." *New York Times,* April 11:A1, A16.

Rex v. Bourne. 1938. 1 King's Bench 472; 3 All England Reports 615.

Roe v. Wade. 1973. 410 U.S. 113.

Rosenblatt, Roger A., Rick Mattis, and L. Gary Hart. 1995. "Abortions in Rural Idaho: Physicians' Attitudes and Practices." *American Journal of Public Health* 85:1423-1425.

Rossi, Alice S. 1967. "Public Views on Abortion." Pp. 26-53 in Alan Guttmacher, ed.*The Case for Legalized Abortion.* Berkeley, CA: Diablo Press.

Rothman, Barbara Katz. 1989. *Recreating Motherhood: Ideology and Technology in a Patriarchal Society.* New York: Norton.

Schroeder, H. J. 1941. *Canons and Decrees of the Council of Trent.* St. Louis: Herder.

Scott, Lael. 1970. "Legal Abortion, Ready or Not." *New York* (May 25):70-75.

Seis, Gerald F. 1996. "Abortion Debate: A Way to Move Back to Reality." *Wall Street Journal,* May 29:A20.

Simonds, Wendy. 1996. *Abortion at Work: Ideology and Practice in a Feminist Clinic.* New Brunswick, NJ: Rutgers University Press.

Taussig, Frederick J. 1936. *Abortion Spontaneous and Induced: Medical and Social Aspects.* St. Louis: Mosby.

Tietze, Christopher. 1972. *Birth Control and Abortion.* New York: MSS Information Press.

Tribe, Laurence H. 1991. *Abortion: Clash of Opposites.* New York: Norton.

Waldman, Steven, and Ginny Carroll. 1995. "Roe v. Roe." *Newsweek* (August 21) 126:22-24.

Walzer, Susan 1994. "The Role of Gender in Determining Abortion Attitudes." *Social Science Quarterly* 75:687-693.

Webster v. Reproductive Health Service. 1989. 492 U.S. 490.

Wells, Christina E. 1995. "Abortion Counseling as Vice Activity: The Free Speech Implications of *Rust v. Sullivan* and *Planned Parenthood v. Casey. Columbia Law Review* 95:1724-1764.

Wilson, James Q. 1994. "On Abortion." *Commentary* (January):97:21-29.

Wolfson, Adam. 1996. "Telling the Court What to Think." *Wall Street Journal,* May 24:12.

6

Conclusion

A sociological approach to law explores the social antecedents and consequences of law, as reflected both in statutes and court rulings. Such a conception seeks to understand the social influences that create law and the legal consequences for society of the use of the criminal sanction. This concern with causes and consequences is not the only approach to a social understanding of law (cf. McIntyre, 1994), but it demonstrates that law and society are inextricably intertwined, and that law is only one part of the equation. It is not invoked in a social vacuum. Instead, as some have argued, law is primarily a consequence of social needs and values rather than a shaper of those needs and values (Barnett, 1993).

In this final chapter, we will try to identify these social and legal relationships to further explore some of the issues generated in our discussion here and to draw conclusions about the role and purpose of law, especially under the circumstances of dissensus, that is, when there is significant disagreement.

Harm, Risk, and the Law

We began our examination of victimless crimes with the observation that the idea of harm is fundamental to an understanding of why certain behaviors are defined as criminal by the law. Criminal law is often regarded as protection against harm, whether that harm is directed against persons or property, although the law is far from foolproof and does not guarantee such protection. If there are differences of opinion about laws, they often revolve around the idea of harm—how much there is, who suffers from it, and the kinds of risks against which we can reasonably expect legal protection.

Life inevitably entails a potential risk of harm. Natural processes invariably produce the risk of bodily damage or deterioration over time. To drive a car is to risk involvement in a vehicular accident. Eating certain foods may pose the risk of such diseases as cancer. But none of us can hide somewhere in a protected corner, hoping to isolate ourselves from harm. Indeed, such behavior could itself be self-destructive and lead to mental illness, suicide, or some self-directed harm.

Harm and risk, therefore, are inevitable conditions of human existence. We are constantly weighing the risks of harm against the benefits of certain behaviors. We all know, for example, that there is a risk in air travel, but the time and convenience that flying affords us is often well worth the risk. Although the consequences of a plane crash are great, the probability is small; so many people fly. The essential question in regard to the behaviors we have discussed concerns the level of harm we are willing to tolerate in terms of other things which we value, most importantly our freedom to do what we please.

We must also recognize that there are two important qualities of criminal law that temper its effectiveness: the law's ability to express moral condemnation and its ability to solve problems. The essence of the criminal law is that it addresses human conduct that is so disapproved by the community that action must be taken, as opposed to civil law, which is concerned with conduct that becomes an issue only when a private citizen mobilizes the forces of law. It is the community's moral outrage that invokes—and ultimately supports—criminal law, not the personal outrage of a citizen. Although not all members of a community may feel or express such outrage, what differentiates criminal from civil law is precisely the fact that the morality violated by the crime is social, or sufficiently widespread that the community as a whole cannot ignore the conduct. In civil law, the wronged person is the only one affected, even though there may be social implications from that person's victimization.

It must also be recognized that merely outlawing problems on the basis of moral concern is not enough. Criminal law is generated and sustained by its ability to solve problems. Not all problems can be fruitfully addressed by the law, of course, and the community must be prudent in selecting for legal attention only those matters that are deemed appropriate. It is this determination that lies at the heart of social disagreements and disappointments over law. In general, large segments of the population expect law to solve many problems for which it may in fact be inappropriate or ill-suited to solve. From the examination of the four substantive areas considered here—abortion, prostitution, homosexuality, and drugs—there also seems to be considerable disagreement about whether these are problem areas suitable for a legal solution.

To argue that, for instance, drug use is ill-suited to a legal solution is not the same as arguing that drugs are not a problem. The use of drugs, such as marijuana, heroin, and cocaine, can lead to many problems, from crime to lost productivity to destroyed interpersonal relationships. Drugs, in fact, are related to some of the greatest human tragedies in American society today. The question here is whether the law can be the sole, or at best a principle, means by which these terrible problems can be alleviated. Many observers do not believe that the law can perform much of a role in controlling or reducing drug use, but others are firmly convinced that the law not only can but *must* be part of the solution (Bennett et al. 1996). The same could be said about the other behaviors we have considered in this volume.

Can the Law Create Problems?

Even in those areas where there is widespread agreement that the law must operate, we need to recognize that the use of law sometimes makes matters worse. The problems that can be created by law stem from it operating in areas where it does not enjoy a broad consensus regarding its role or limitations. Some observers have referred to these problems as the result of a "crisis of overcriminalization" (Kadish, 1967). When the law is used too extensively, when it is applied to areas where the chances of success are slim, and when it does not enjoy popular support, it is apt to fail. Sometimes, the context is the failure of the police to apprehend criminals, the failure of the courts to convict otherwise guilty defendants, or the prison system's inability to reform inmates. But legal failure can also arise when the law is used inappropriately, as well as when it is not invoked in those circumstances in which it should be.

Few doubt that there are many laws that have outlived their usefulness and should be eliminated from the criminal code. Many states and local jurisdictions have outdated laws that apply to life in an earlier time. It is against the law in Ames, Iowa, for example, to be drunk in public; it is also against the law, for some inexplicable reason, to *pretend* to be drunk in public (*Ames Daily Tribune*, June 20, 1996, p. 1). The historical origin of the law and the legislative intent behind it are obscure, though its obvious ludicrousness has not generated any action to repeal it. Prohibitions against such acts do not command much attention, largely because the behaviors reflected in outdated laws are not considered a problem these days.

Such statutes give the law an untidy veneer, but they are not important to public perceptions of either crime or law. More disturbing are those behaviors about which there is disagreement over their moral nature. For example, in the process of revising the California criminal law, a group of crimes were identified that apparently justified criminal convictions for such offenses as "failure by a school principal to use required textbooks, failure of a teacher to carry first-aid kits on field trips, gambling on the result of an election, giving private commercial performances by a state-supported band, and allowing waste of an artesian well by the landowner" (Kadish, 1967:157-158). Although an argument can be made that such acts ought to be regulated, the question is whether criminal law is the appropriate vehicle for that control.

More serious examples of the consequences of overcriminalization include the use of unethical or questionable enforcement techniques by the police. Because by definition some crimes do not have complainants, and because the police depend on informers or citizen reports to learn about most crime, enforcing some crimes necessitates more aggressive and police-initiated action. This proactive policing is difficult to carry out within the boundaries of constitutional safeguards that are deemed so important in a free society. As a result, the police are tempted to engage in a variety of unsavory practices. These include using "sting" operations, whereby police officers impersonate criminals, develop and maintain close relationships with criminals who can inform on other offenders, and employ illegal enforcement methods, such as unauthorized wiretaps and searches. In the recent trial of O. J. Simpson for double murder, for instance, Los Angeles detective Mark Fuhrman was heard on tape discussing how he ripped off the healing scabs from the injection sites of narcotic addicts' bodies in order to prove in court that he had nabbed them in the act of using drugs (Toobin, 1996:395). Such methods are either directly illegal or morally questionable, but the police are forced to skirt the moral boundary because of the nature of crimes. Who is going to report such crimes to the police? The prostitute? The prostitute's client? The illegal drug dealer? The illegal drug buyer? Laws governing crimes without victims place the police in a position of tenuous virtue.

Furthermore, the police are often stripped of the self-justifying rationale that the ends justify the means. One might be willing to excuse questionable police tactics against criminal syndicates, from whom the harm to society is both real and recognized; but the use of borderline methods against adults engaging in either a consensual homosexual (e.g., sodomy) or heterosexual (e.g., prostitution) relationship is quite another matter. These latter acts seem to generate victims without being crimes at all.

Because the law can both solve and create problems, it is essential to employ it wisely. Although the law is a necessary form of control for certain acts, in other instances it has been used to curry favor among some at the expense of others. This is especially true in regard to those crimes in which there is no agreement on the moral quality, or wrongfulness, of the act. The victimless crimes examined here illustrate the extent to which a lack of consensus interferes with the operation of the law.

We believe that the meaning of "victimless" crimes must be seen in the context in which there is no consensus regarding the wrongfulness of such acts nor any consequences from them being against any criminal law. In some instances, it is clear to us that the law does more harm than good; in other cases, the law may be necessary, even if it is ineffective in changing a behavior or act. In either case, the law's role is at best uneven and uncertain in the presence of the public's moral ambiguity.

Political attention to victimless crimes in the 1990s has produced some important, far-reaching legal changes. Although the law has constricted in some areas (e.g., prostitution), it has expanded in others (e.g., drugs). Not only are there more drug laws on the books, but the penalties for their violation have increased significantly. In addition, many jurisdictions, including the federal government, have instituted mandatory minimum prison sentences for those convicted of these crimes. As of 1996, the possession of the following amounts of drugs will each result in a mandatory five-year prison sentence without possibility of parole in the federal criminal justice system: LSD, 1 gram; marijuana, 100 plants or 100 kilos; crack cocaine, 5 grams; powder cocaine, 500 grams; heroin, 100 grams; methamphetamine, 10 grams; and PCP, 10 grams. These mandatory minimum sentences are disapproved of by 90 percent of federal judges and 75 percent of state judges (Donziger, 1996:27).

The problem is not merely one of equity, although the "one size fits all" approach to drug sentencing does violate the concept of justice to many people. The real problem is that already overcrowded American prisons are housing an increasing percentage of inmates convicted on drug charges, and that the great majority of these are in prison for drug possession.

Not all negative consequences of enforcing laws against victimless crime have only practical dimensions; there are moral qualities as well. How does a community balance the needs of consenting adults engaged in sexual relations with the community's need to follow moral guidelines? An act of prostitution may involve willing adults, but what is the quality of the community in which prostitution occurs? Such questions are difficult to answer even in the absence of any legal controversies, and it seems unreasonable to expect the law to adjudicate a response for all concerned. Other institutions, such as religion or the family, may be better venues in which to seek settlement.

What Should We Call Them?

One issue that we have not fully addressed yet involves terminology. Crimes associated with homosexuality, prostitution, drugs, and abortion do not have any widespread consensus regarding either the degree to which each poses a problem to the community, if it is even considered a problem, or the most appropriate solution. Because of this lack of consensus, the law has been used by default. A full understanding of these behaviors requires, however, that we know not only why Americans are so optimistic about the law to solve what may be nonlegal problems, but also what such crimes have in common. Why is there a lack of consensus about some crimes, but not about others? The first hurdle to overcome is the creation of a conceptual category that highlights the common features of these crimes, one that sets them apart from other crimes.

We have referred to these crimes as *crimes without victims,* but there are thematic problems with this term. One of the first systematic statements about crimes without victims was made by Sanford Kadish (1967), who called our attention to a particularly serious consequence of such crimes—the strain they create on the criminal justice system. Kadish used the term *the crisis of overcriminalization* to emphasize that there are crimes in which the law is inappropriate and "over-used." His argument identified a number of reasons to limit the use of law, in part because the law cannot prevent some crimes and at times can actually create more problems than it solves. Edwin Schur (1965) anticipated Kadish's concerns when he identified a group of offenses that he considered crimes without victims and that he believed should therefore be decriminalized, a theme that was amplified by Norval Morris and Gordon Hawkins (1970).

The expression *crimes without victims* draws our attention to the fact that first, crimes are supposed to have victims, and second, there is agreement on who is and who is not a victim of a crime. At times, however, it is difficult in practice to identify a discernible victim. Who exactly is the victim of the behavior of a person drunk in public? Who exactly is the victim of the sexual exchange between a prostitute and his or her client? Who exactly is the victim of a drug addict who injects heroin to satisfy a physical dependency? In many instances the notion of victimization does not present itself in quite the same way as it does with other crimes, such as robbery, theft, or murder. In each of the latter crimes, identifiable people are deprived of their property or lives against their will in unlawful and often dramatic ways. In crimes without victims, the notion of victimization is more nebulous, either because the only parties involved are willing participants or, in the example of abortion, because there is disagreement on whether the fetus is a person who therefore constitutes a victim of a crime.

One could claim, as many do, that these crimes do have tangible victims. Sometimes, the victim can be said to be a specific person, such as the robbery victim of a heroin addict who steals to support a drug habit or the victim of a drunk driver. In other instances, the notion of victimization is more general and amorphous. One could argue that the community and its moral climate, for example, are the victims of prostitution. Although the idea of a moral climate may suggest something immaterial and too abstract to be considered "real," contemplate the following question: How many communities, even so-called "bad" neighborhoods or high-crime areas, actually *encourage* prostitution?

There is no completely satisfactory single term or expression to denote crimes that do not enjoy a widespread consensus regarding their wrongfulness (Junker, 1972). Some prefer the expression "complaintless crime," but "complaintless crimes" could include the crime of bribing a public official, an offense not normally considered in this category. Others prefer the expression "public-order crime," and still others refer to these crimes as "morals offenses," a term that begs the question of whose morality and to what extent that morality is shared in a community. The expression *non-consensual crimes* may best typify these crimes, but it is not as catchy as *victimless crime*, a phrase that has generally been adopted in broad legal discussions. Yet another strategy is more conditional. Often, writers trying to convey their sense of neutrality—or perhaps uncertainty—will append words such as "so- called" before their use of the phrase "crimes without victims." Thus Schrage (1994:83) notes of gambling and prostitution that they are "so to speak, 'victimless crimes.' "

Regardless of the term, the quality these crimes share goes beyond the unwillingness of individuals to regard themselves as victims or complainants, although this quality leads to particular enforcement practices and moral debates. In our view, these crimes reflect behavior about which there is significant disagreement concerning wrongfulness and the appropriateness of legal response. Some people, for example, strongly believe that homosexuality is not only wrong but that it should be punished severely under criminal law. Others feel just as strongly that such behavior is neither wrong in a moral or pragmatic sense (because it does not harm others) and thus should not be considered a crime. Likewise, some people firmly believe that using illicit drugs is wrong and should also be punished severely; others completely disagree.

Other acts, such as abortion, provide a different moral picture. Some believe that abortion under all circumstances is morally wrong. Others believe that abortion is morally undesirable but that it should be permissible under certain conditions, such as for a pregnancy resulting from rape or incest. Still others believe that abortion should not be encouraged but that it is an inappropriate matter for legal action, because the affected woman and not the law should determine whether or not there will be an abortion. Clearly, this diversity of opinion reflects fundamental differences in how this conduct is conceptualized.

The different conceptions of crime are not always consistent with one another. A social conception might key on the normative qualities of an act; that is, whether that act should occur or not (Sellin, 1938). Normative conceptions obviously go beyond law and include many acts that are not now and never will be part of the concern of a legal system. Laughter is a normative behavior at a comedy show but not at a funeral. The prevention of dental cavities is something that most people believe is necessary, but the requirement to brush one's teeth is unlikely to be incorporated into the legal system. Even conduct that is commonly disapproved of in our society, such as having offensive breath, would obviously be deemed inappropriate for legal attention. As difficult a process as it is, one of the hardest tasks of lawmaking must surely involve the ability to define unpopular behavior as inappropriate for legal response.

The Wolfenden Report

Many of the issues surrounding victimless crimes, such as those examined in this volume, have been explored in public policy discussions. The Wolfenden Report, discussed earlier, was issued in England forty years ago with respect to the question of whether homosexuality should remain illegal. The report generated considerable public response not only in regard to homosexuality but to other victimless crimes, because the issues that surrounded homosexuality applied to other controversial behaviors, such as prostitution.

The general question that guided the Wolfenden Committee concerned the conditions under which criminal law should be used to control human behavior. In its analysis of the laws against homosexuality, the Wolfenden Report concluded that criminal law should not delve into the private lives of citizens except to preserve public order and to protect individuals from obviously dangerous and injurious action. The Committee believed that the law should also be used to protect people against exploitation and corruption, especially individuals who have some special vulnerability:

)erate attempt is to be made by society, acting through
the law, to equate the sphere of crime with that of
t remain a realm of private morality and immorality
~~iucn is, in brief and crude terms, not the law's business. To say
this is not to encourage private immorality. (p. 24)

The Wolfenden Report was widely read and discussed, and
many disagreed with its recommendations. Even among those who
agreed in general with the conclusions, the report generated considerable conflict over the proper role of criminal law. Part of the
problem was undoubtedly the status of the behavior at the time. Just
as it is harder, for example, to expel a student than to reject the same
person as an applicant, it is always harder to decriminalize conduct
than to make that same conduct subject to law. To many, homosexuality had been against the law and it was difficult and disconcerting
to think of changing that situation.

Lord Patrick Devlin claimed that criminal law, perhaps by definition, is little more than a collection of moral statements; as a result,
Devlin argued, it is not surprising that there is a strong moral component to law and in fact little to separate morality and law. The
legal philosopher H. L. A. Hart demurred and, following the view
of John Stuart Mill, argued the law should not limit individual freedoms in the name of morality. Hart, and the Wolfenden Committee,
argued that the use of law and criminal sanction always requires
compelling justification.

Devlin perceived the law in terms of not individual but political
morality: Legal norms are legal equivalents of social norms, statements of what "should" and "should not" occur; as such, they represent moral statements within a political jurisdiction. It is hardly
surprising that law should generate such controversy, since people
sometimes disagree on what should and should not occur. This is
not a problem with the law, merely one of its characteristics. Devlin
believed that the burden of proof regarding legal change (e.g., decriminalization) belongs to those who want to alter existing and
longstanding legal definitions and practices.

Hart and the Wolfenden Committee, on the other hand, viewed
law as a practical means of social control, one hopefully designed
to concentrate on acts about which there was substantial agreement
over their wrongfulness. As a pragmatic device meant to help insure
social order, the law has no business taking stands in moral debates,

unless the issue involves some discernible harm to others. Behavior that does not involve harm to others and poses no immediate danger to the social order is, as the Committee put it, "not the law's business."

Hart's position is not merely the result of abstract legal or philosophical reasoning. He and others cited a good deal of evidence that when the law is extended into areas where it does not belong, it can make matters worse. The law then becomes not extended, but overextended.

But Devlin was not opposed to the recommendation to decriminalize homosexuality in England. On the contrary, when the Wolfenden Committee in 1954 began considering possible reforms, the chair of the committee asked two judges to provide them evidence, one in favor of reform and the other against reform. Lord Devlin was the judge who testified in favor of reforming the laws against homosexuality. Devlin (1965:v) believed that these laws do more harm than good, except in those instances where it "can save youth from being led into it." In all other instances, he reasoned, the law is ineffective, although he thought that more study on the matter would be useful.

Are There Limits to Law?

To question the relevant boundaries of law is also to question the limits of criminal sanction. Criminal sanctions are powerful beyond their measure; they generate not only the direct sanction—fines, community supervision, incarceration—but social sanctions as well, often in the form of stigma and censure. Clearly, these are powerful considerations in a society that takes pride in freedom and openness. Such sanctions should not be used frivolously nor without regard to their full consequences.

But if there are to be limits to law, what are they? To ask what behavior should or should not be against the law and therefore subject to criminal sanction is to ask one of the most fundamental questions about law. A number of criteria have been proposed, including individual privacy, limiting law only to those acts that are generally regarded as immoral and for which there are no reasonable alternatives (Packer), to those which cause harm in others (Mill) and those which are potentially enforceable (Schur).

Immorality

In one of the most influential books on the role of criminal law, Herbert Packer (1968:264) proposed that "the criminal sanction should ordinarily be limited to conduct that is viewed, without significant social dissent, as immoral." Packer recognized that there are disagreements about morality, and that such disagreements can produce significant social conflicts, particularly in a diverse society such as the United States. Or as Packer put it (p. 289), "One man's deviance is another man's pluralism."

Many people regard as immoral that which threatens them either directly (e.g., robbery) or indirectly (e.g., making false claims about a product's safety). It is difficult to conceive of a criminal law that is divorced from moral judgments, as most people's conception of crime includes the notion that it is behavior that should not occur. The reason that it should not occur may vary from person to person, but a consensus exists that criminal behavior is that which should not be condoned.

Packer did not advocate making criminal all immoral acts. There are many instances of immorality that are undesirable but not of sufficient seriousness to prohibit by law. Breaking promises, forgetting a friend's birthday, and breaches of etiquette and manners are all immoral in the sense that they should not occur. But they are not by themselves good candidates for criminal law. Rather, other forms of social control are more appropriate for these acts of deviance. Those acts that generate strong, widespread condemnation are more likely to be candidates for criminalization.

No one has yet developed a mechanism to adequately measure morality or the extent of agreement in societies on moral principles. More than 70 percent of Americans find that homosexuality is immoral, but a clear majority also support equal rights for homosexuals and believe that people should not be discriminated against for being gay (Shapiro, 1994). Conflicting feelings can and do exist side by side, and perhaps the only reasonable solution is to encourage conversations about morality (Feldblum, 1996). Whether such conversations lead to changes in public attitudes and law with respect to homosexuality, of course, does not guarantee similar changes with other victimless crimes.

Privacy

Some observers think that the boundary line for what should and should not be outlawed can be found in the concept of individual privacy (Alderman and Kennedy, 1995). But what is and what is not private continues to be debated in the courts without any clear-cut resolution. The word "privacy" does not appear in the Constitution, although many people believe so strongly in it that they consider privacy from state intrusion a fundamental right rather than a privilege. The United States Supreme Court agreed and more than a century ago, Justice Louis Brandeis advocated the right of privacy, labeling it the "right to be let alone."

Individual privacy is more difficult to maintain in an age of computer records, video cameras, and the increasing awareness that the behavior of one person can sometimes affect many others. State and federal laws protect individuals against such invasions of privacy as unreasonable searches and seizures. There are also laws against unwanted intrusions into one's private life by the media; yet the press is protected by the First Amendment, which can be a powerful ally in privacy battles.

Although there is agreement that some acts (e.g., whether one should brush one's teeth) should remain beyond the boundary of law, there is no agreement on what criteria can be used to determine where the interests of the individual end and those of the state begin. As pointed out in Chapter One, wearing a helmet while riding a motorcycle can be seen either as a risk that affects only the rider or as a matter in which the state has an interest, insofar as it affects others by triggering higher insurance or medical premium rates.

Privacy interests often must be balanced. So although an individual should be able to expect privacy at the workplace, employers have a right to run a business and try to earn a profit. As employers face increasing competition and rising costs, such as those associated with employee benefits (e.g., health care), they come to expect more information about their employees and often obtain it through new technology. Some employers obtain data from psychological and drug testing and collect information about employees' lifestyles away from work. For example, two Phoenix police officers were fired when it was discovered that they had relationships with prostitutes (Alderman and Kennedy, 1995:307-308). The officers claimed that what they did off-hours was of no concern to the police department. But a court ruled that such behavior did affect their job performance, as well as the internal morale of the police department, and it upheld the firing.

Alternative Controls

Many believe that criminal law should be used sparingly when other alternatives are available; the law can play a unique role only when it stands alone. This view acknowledges that law is but one means of social control and not necessarily the most effective for any given act. Other institutions, such as the family, religion, community, and the military, all have their own systems of rule-making and rule-enforcement. Breaches of family rules or religious expectations are often met with appropriate sanctions, such as scolding a child or requiring special penance. Most acts that are considered serious are subject to multiple social and legal controls. For example, the deliberate taking of another's life is condemned by law but also by religion and family. What keeps most people from committing murder is not the force of law but the effect of these other controls.

Harm to Others

John Stuart Mill's 1859 essay, *On Liberty,* has provided for more than 100 years an important and durable limiting condition in regard to criminal law. . In that work, Mill argued that the only legitimate purpose for which state power can be exercised over citizens in a free society, against their will, is to prevent harm to others. Such a criterion recognizes that, whatever their moral quality, most crimes are dangerous. It is the physical, financial, and social costs of crime that criminal law should address. Mill did not believe that harm to the perpetrator was sufficient grounds to criminalize; nor did he think it ever proper to criminalize conduct solely because the mere thought of it offended others (see Richards, 1982:3).

Unfortunately, Mill failed to provide a concrete means by which to assess the extent or degree of harm (Feinberg, 1984), although some observers have defended Mill's principle (Sartorius, 1972). Harm from some acts can be both more immediate and more dangerous than that from others. Similarly, Mill fails to provide a means by which to draw a meaningful distinction between those acts that have some impact and those that have substantial harm. Consider an example: A stranger yelling obscenities in a public place, to some degree, will harm the sensibilities of those passing by who hear the obscene language, but that same stranger assaulting passers-by would present a more immediate and dangerous harm from which citizens have some legitimate expectation of protection. Although criminal law could be used to prohibit both acts, between obscene language and assault, assault is of more personal and social importance.

All acts probably have some consequences for others, either as "victims," witnesses, or innocent bystanders. Should criminal law regulate drinking of alcoholic beverages, because alcoholics could produce substantial and negative financial impact on their families? Similarly, a public drunk may bring substantial negative social stigma on his or her family. But how are we to decide whether these negative consequences are sufficiently serious to use criminal law to prohibit the manufacture, sale, and consumption of alcoholic beverages?

Are They Enforceable?

Some laws have a greater chance of controlling and preventing crime than others. When crimes are conceived as a risk of life, the law can only reduce the risk of some of those crimes. The law can do little about most drive-by shootings, random robberies, or residential burglaries. Although some gang members, robbers, and burglars will be apprehended and punished, they can return to crime later, or their place will be taken by others who will commit crimes. In a very practical sense, the law in a democratic society is limited to responding to most crimes after they have occurred. And although some criminals may be deterred from their offenses, not all are, and even those who may be deterred are not deterred forever. Most drivers will be deterred enough to slow down when they spot a police car in their rear-view mirror, but they may speed up once it is gone.

Many common crimes are related to conditions over which the police have virtually no control. Poverty, systems of social and economic inequality, subcultures that emphasize immediate gratification, and drugs are all strong correlates of crime, but the police cannot control or alter those conditions. Changes in crime rates are more strongly influenced by social, historical, and political forces than by adding laws, increasing penalties, or placing more police officers on the streets.

Although laws do not change the circumstances that bring about crime in the first place, it is probably better that we have such laws. Even though the police cannot control the conditions that give rise, for example, to most murders—arguments, alcohol, and the availability of firearms—it would certainly be a mistake to decriminalize violent crime, if only because the law conveys a very powerful message about the value of life and the degree of social abhorrence toward illegitimate violence.

What Problems Are Appropriate for Law?

One practical approach to the limits of law asks whether a given act constitutes a problem that the law can solve and if so, whether the law is effective in dealing with the problem. Problems can be divided into different categories, depending on the best solution to them. Broken arms are a problem to people who experience them, and the solution to this problem is properly sought in medicine rather than law; calculating one's income tax is not a medical but an accounting problem; and so on. The objective is to determine the nature of the problem and to apply the proper resource to solve the problem.

Criminal law has been asked, concurrently and at different times, to accomplish dissimilar and at times contradictory objectives: deterrence, rehabilitation, incapacitation, and retribution. (There are other traditional objectives and different ways to define them, but these four illustrate the problem for law.) Laws can be effective in extracting justice through punishment, but ineffective in changing the behavior of law-breakers.

A pragmatic approach also requires evidence of the effectiveness of law, and such evidence is often equivocal. How do we know whether and to what extent the law deters potential criminals? How do we know whether and to what extent the law rehabilitates actual criminals? The existence of crime, of course, does not mean that the law is ineffective, except if the standard by which one measures effectiveness is complete prevention (an obviously unreachable standard). By such a standard, all laws might be ineffective because murders, rapes, robberies, and other crimes continue to exist.

Conclusion

There are many acts that are presently criminal about which there is disagreement concerning their moral status. There may be no confusion about their legal status, but there is disagreement on the extent to which people think they are wrong, or whether the law is the proper source of social control. We have attempted to discuss four such crime categories to discern the nature of the dissensus and the dimensions of the behavior that lead to such disagreements.

To limit the role of law to crimes about which there is a moral consensus does not help us to generate that consensus. The debates surrounding victimless crimes are serious and frequent, primarily because there is much at stake, including the morality of particular groups and the ability of the law to serve as a resource for one group or another. We can only expect that various groups and individuals will continue to explore the use of the law to solve their problems, to further their personal or collective interests, and to attempt to reduce the incidence of undesirable behavior. In this process, we can expect at various times that the law will be used inappropriately and imperfectly. As much as we would like to limit the use of the law to mutually agreeable situations and conditions, this is unlikely to occur. And until it does, we will continue to have "victimless" crime.

References

Alderman, Ellen, and Caroline Kennedy. 1995. *The Right to Privacy.* New York: Knopf.

Ames Daily Tribune. 1996. "It's The Law." June 20, p. 1.

Barnett, Larry D. 1993. *Legal Construct, Social Concept.* New York: Aldine de Gruyter.

Bennett, William J., John J. DiIulio Jr., and John P. Walters. 1996. *Body Count: Moral Poverty . . . and How to Win America's War Against Crime and Drugs.* New York: Simon and Schuster.

Devlin, Patrick L. 1965. *The Enforcement of Morals.* New York: Oxford University Press.

Donziger, Steven R., ed. 1996. *The Real War on Crime: The Report of the National Criminal Justice Commission.* New York: HarperPerennial.

Feinberg, Joel. 1984. *The Moral Limits of the Criminal Law: Harm to Others.* New York: Oxford University Press.

Feldblum, Chai R. 1996. "Sexual Orientation, Morality, and the Law: Devlin Revisited." *University of Pittsburgh Law Review,* 57:237-336.

Hart, Herbert L. A. 1963. *Law, Liberty and Morality.* New Haven, CT: Yale University Press.

Junker, John. 1972. "Criminalization and Criminogensis." *UCLA Law Review,* 19:697-714.

Kadish, Sanford. 1967. "The Crisis of Overcriminalization." *The Annals,* 374:158-169.

McIntyre, Lisa. 1994. *Law in the Sociological Enterprise.* Boulder, CO: Westview.

Mill, John Stuart. 1859/1892. *On Liberty.* London: Longmans, Green.

Morris, Norval, and Gordon Hawkins. 1970. *The Honest Politician's Guide to Crime Control.* Chicago: University of Chicago Press.

Packer, Herbert A. 1968. *The Limits of the Criminal Sanction.* Stanford: Stanford University Press.

Richards, David A. J. 1982. *Sex, Drugs, Death, and the Law: An Essay on Human Rights and Overcriminalization.* Totowa, NJ: Rowman and Littlefield.

Sartorius, Rolf E. 1972. "The Enforcement of Morality." *Yale Law Journal,* 81:891-910.

Schrage, Laurie. 1994. *Moral Dillemmas of Feminism: Prostitution, Adultery, and Abortion.* New York: Routledge.

Schur, Edwin. 1965. *Crimes Without Victims.* Englewood Cliffs, NJ: Prentice-Hall.

Sellin, Thorsten. 1938. *Culture Conflict and Crime.* New York: Social Science Research Council.

Toobin, Jeffrey. 1996. *The Run of His Life: The People v. O. J. Simpson.* New York: Random House.

Wolfenden Report. 1963. *The Wolfenden Report: Report of the Committee on Homosexual Offences and Prostitution.* London: Her Majesty's Stationery Office.

Indexes

Author Index

Subject Index